LOVE WITHOUT FEAR

This is a book of the utmost practical value both to men and women. The reader—in the consulting-room, as it were, of a doctor who is also a psychologist—is told in plain, direct language why it is that nine out of ten married people never know the full joys which the sex-relationship should bring. A genuine technique of love is then taught, which all can master.

Dr. Eustace Chesser was born in Edinburgh and educated at George Watson's, Edinburgh, and the Royal Colleges. During most of his career he has been associated with sex education and marriage guidance, and has fought hard against intolerance and false attitudes. In a busy life as a lecturer and consulting psychologist, he has become one of our best known authors on sex, psychology and sociology. He is a member of the Royal Institution and a fellow of the Royal Society of Medicine.

D1270043

Dr. Eustace Chesser

LOVE WITHOUT FEAR

ARROW BOOKS

ARROW BOOKS LTD
3 Fitzroy Square, London W1

An Imprint of the Hutchinson Publishing Group

London Melbourne Sydney Auckland
Wellington Johannesburg Cape Town
and agencies throughout the world

First published by
Hutchinson & Co (Publishers) Ltd 1941
Arrow revised edition 1966
Second impression 1967
Third impression 1968
Fourth impression 1969
Fifth impression 1972
Sixth impression 1973
Seventh impression 1974

Made and printed in Great Britain
by The Anchor Press Ltd
Tiptree, Essex

ISBN 0 09 906660 2

Author's Preface to this new edition

When I first wrote this book I hoped that it would not only be read but used. The fact that it has sold well over three million copies and read by many more, makes me feel I achieved my purpose. Knowing a lot about sex is not enough, for it is only when we are able to put our knowledge into practice that it is of value. And to be able to do so assumes an ability to be relaxed, freed from repressive inhibitions and false attitudes inculcated by parents and Society. It is only then that we can enjoy the luxury of sexual technique, one which will help us to make the most of our marital union. Human communication involves both body and mind, but this is not easy when we have been brought up to believe that there is something shameful about our bodies.

I have avoided needless descriptions of the unsavoury, but at the same time have not hesitated to call a spade a spade. In the original edition first published in 1941 I dealt primarily with sexual technique, and the deviations from the so-called normal. So much progress, however, has been made in our knowledge of the psychology of deviant behaviour, and the part it plays in our sexual attitudes and actions, that I have had to treat this in much greater detail. Hence this revised edition—wherein I have not only brought the existing chapters up to date, but added several new ones. In particular, perhaps, 'Some Definitions', which in alphabetical order discusses words commonly used by psychiatrists and others, with regard to our sexuality.

We have moved a long way from the traditional and

puritanical climate of the past, when this book was first written, but we have still a long way to go. In this new, revised and enlarged edition I have attempted to help the reader to have a greater understanding of himself and his sexual make-up so that he will be better able to express and enjoy the life that is his.

This book will help you to these

1. A knowledge of the best ways in which to use your sexual powers.
2. Power to conserve them and to keep them within normal channels.
3. Ability not only to secure the maximum of enjoyment yourself, but equally—and as part of it—to give pleasure to your partner.
4. Freedom from fear in the sex life—fear which robs thousands of unions of joy.
5. Knowledge of contraceptive technique which will enable you to plan the spacing of children instead of leaving it to blind chance.
6. Sex satisfaction, which is the basis of a happy, well-ordered life generally.
7. Ability to help your children in their deepest needs instead of laying the foundations for their future marital misery.
8. Deeper sympathy and understanding of the problems of others.
9. Greater self-respect because of understanding of yourself.
10. Confidence, born of knowledge proved by your own personal application.

Contents

A number of line drawings appear
between pages 160 and 161

Introduction

Ye shall some day love beyond yourselves,
So first learn loving!

NIETZSCHE

Not one husband in twelve adequately knows the technique of love to enable him to impart and receive half the pleasure which should be derived from sexual union.

Not one in a hundred has learned, by study, practice, or experience, how to gain the maximum of pleasure.

The majority of wives *never* know the supreme joy which the sex act can yield to the ideally mated.

At least eighty in every hundred marriages must be written down as failures in the true sense, even though they may appear otherwise on the surface.

Economic considerations, mutual feelings of loyalty, and regard to appearance frequently hold together the most dismal unions and hide their real failures.

These are extreme statements. But they are amply supported by the available evidence. If they err at all they are understatements rather than exaggerations. And while all those whose work brings them into close relationship with the sex lives of modern men and women realise the sad—and, to the uninitiated, staggering—truth, the fact remains that nothing like an adequate effort is being made to remedy the situation.

It is often said that this is an age of frankness, in which

11

sex, among other things, is discussed very freely. But observation reveals that the discussion of sex is really very limited, and is often restricted to questionable jokes or vague innuendoes. It is true that discussion groups often face up boldly to the problems of sex and marriage, and this is all to the good. But individuals outside of such groups seldom discuss the real problems of sex in a serious, helpful manner. In any case, with a different type of upbringing and a more natural relationship between parents and children there would be little need to discuss sex. It is a natural process of growth, and should, ideally speaking, require no more discussion than, say, any other of our physiological functions, such, for example, as our digestive processes.

Our sexual expression vitally affects us all, directly or indirectly influences every phase of life.

For, although there is nothing unwholesome in the discussion of sex, we persist in acting for all the world as though there was.

Moreover, such help of a genuinely practical nature as is available is largely restricted to married people. In direct opposition to the old, sound adage: 'An ounce of prevention is worth a pound of cure', we admit that there is some ground for aiding married people whose unions prove unsatisfactory, yet withhold such assistance from the young. They are looking on life with eager eyes. They are, as a rule, anxious to learn all they can of love and its expression. They are far more receptive than the older folks. It is with them, the unmarried, that there exist the most hopeful chances of stopping the rot.

Unquestionably, a faulty outlook is responsible for our reluctance to fight marital misery before it has begun, to prevent instead of seeking, often too late, to cure. We fail to understand the plight of the unmarried mother, who is not only faced with social ostracism but with the difficulties of keeping her 'illegitimate' child. No morality having its roots in justice, as all true morality must, can be squared with such an attitude.

Young men and women, given the opportunity, are as eager to prepare for marriage as they are to equip themselves for their careers. It is at least as important for them to be able to acquire practical knowledge of the technique of love as it is to be grounded in the essentials of their calling. Yet hardly one in a thousand approaches marriage with even the minimum of knowledge which is desirable.

How should a young husband proceed on the wedding night when faced by a sexually inexperienced bride?

How can a woman co-operate in sexual congress so as to promote its full and happy completion?

How is it that millions—a growing number, too—are led along strange byways of sex, until they find themselves living in a world apart, unable to mate happily with normal beings, and regarded as outcasts?

What should be the attitude of the normal person to such people? Must they be regarded with scorn or is understanding the truer attitude?

These, and a hundred or more equally apt questions, ought to bring an immediate response from all adults, married or single.

Montaigne wrote, early in the sixteenth century:

'Who has rendered the act of generation, an act so natural, so necessary, and so just, a thing not to be spoken of without blushing and to be excluded from all serious and regular discourse? We boldly pronounce "kill", "rob", "betray", but the other we dare only to mutter between the teeth. Is it to say, the less we expend in words, we may pay so much more in thinking? For it is certain that the words least in use, most seldom written, and best kept in, are the best and most generally known; no age, no manners, are ignorant of them, no more than the word "bread"; they imprint themselves in everyone, without being expressed, without voice and without figure;

and the sex that most practises it, is bound to say least of it. 'Tis an act that we have placed in the franchise of silence, from which to take it is a crime, even to accuse and judge it; neither dare we reprehend it but by periphrasis and picture.'

To a very great extent this holds good today. The undressed act of love is known by millions not very long after they have passed their cradle days. But how many realise that there is a technique of love, as distinct from something which yields immediate gratification to physiological and biological need? And how many have mastered that technique?

Too many have the attitude of the young parson who, the morning after his marriage night, asked of his young wife whether she thought she was pregnant. On being told she did not know, he expressed the earnest hope she was, since he wished to be relieved from the experience of the previous night. Such feelings may seem incredible to many. Believe me, they are not unknown.

They reveal unmistakably the vital need which exists for a campaign of genuine sexual enlightenment.

Here, however, we must face the fact that 'sex technique', to use the term often employed in the past, is in itself too limited to meet the requirements of those who would enjoy to the full the blessings which love can bestow. It is essential that young people should be instructed in the physical basis of marriage before they reach marrying age. It is desirable that every husband should be fully informed on the best ways in which to impart pleasure to his wife, and equally that every wife should know the best ways of giving pleasure to her husband. Both partners find their own happiness increased in proportion as they contribute to each other's happiness. But marriage is much more than physical mating.

It is necessary to stress this fact. The older type of guide to sex technique did not completely ignore this aspect.

But it tended to concentrate attention almost entirely upon the physical relationship. And the plain truth is that the physical union, important as it is, forms but a part of the love relationship. Those who fail to recognise this usually suffer in consequence. There have been experimenters in what is miscalled 'free love', and they have mainly been people who have studied sex technique most thoroughly. They have had little to learn so far as erotic pleasure and the methods of imparting it are concerned. Yet, after passing from one 'affair' to another, as they so often do, they experience a sense of failure and frustration.

Naturally they are puzzled, for they have obeyed all the rules. Many—perhaps the majority—discover that so far from marriage being an old-fashioned, discredited institution, it is the visible and outward expression of certain fundamental human desires, not all of which are of a physical nature. In many cases this discovery is made too late to be of value.

Companionship, shared interests, the security which the home provides, the joys of family life—all these are important. In marriage, sex pervades them all, and is in turn affected by them all. Without these other vital parts of the full life, sex loses much of its significance. If we are to study sex technique wisely it is necessary, therefore, to consider it primarily in relation to marriage, and with the home as its background. We cannot take sex and regard it as something apart from life in general without leaving many important problems unconsidered. Nor must we make the mistake of thinking that sex is life itself. It is only a part of life, but so vital a part that it should not be ignored. The same is true of eating or breathing. But we do not regard eating or breathing as the end to be sought in living. Like sex, these are parts of our lives, but they are not the whole. In the pages which follow we shall, therefore, keep well in mind the relationship of sex to the total life.

Since this book was first published there has been heartening progress in sex education, both for children and adults. The Marriage Guidance movement has gone from strength to strength. In the schools, sex education has been increasingly fostered, and the Board of Education has given official encouragement to local authorities and teachers to further this work. In these days it seems incredible that not many years ago the executive committee of the National Union of Teachers passed a resolution that 'the giving of sex instruction is undesirable and against the interests of the child'. There has been a marked change of outlook among teachers generally, and teachers and parents are increasingly recognising their responsibility in this matter.

There has also been a great assessment of knowledge— particularly in so far as contraceptive technique is concerned—and there are many family-planning clinics in the country. Last, but not least, has been the direct and indirect approach to sex and its problems in radio and television programmes.

Even so, much remains to be done. As we shall see in our consideration of the love relationship, and of the steps which can be taken to eliminate fear from the marriage union. The influence of centuries will not be removed in a decade. But we can at least say at the outset, as we could not when the original edition was being written, that there are encouraging signs of a movement in the right direction.

1 : Love Embraces All

When two persons love each other, nothing is more imperative and delightful to them than *giving*: to give always and everything, one's thoughts, one's life, one's body, and all that one has: and to feel the gift and to risk everything in order to be able to give more, still more

GUY DE MAUPASSANT

It has been said that life should be regarded as a house with four storeys—physical, emotional, mental, and spiritual. The same may be said of marriage. It must, if it is to be counted wholly successful, reach to the fourth storey. Equally, if the partners cannot live happily in the first storey their life on the other three is unlikely to prove satisfying.

The physical is the one which has been most neglected. It is sometimes referred to as the 'lowest' part of the love relationship. That depends entirely upon the use made of it. The sound attitude is to regard it as one of the foundation stones of the whole structure. For if it is weak the rest will suffer.

But whilst it is true that the physical basis affects, for good or ill, the emotional, mental, and spiritual states, it is also true that these play a part in influencing the purely physical side. Sometimes their influence is profound.

We hear much about the power of mind over body, and nowhere is this more marked than in the sexual act. Such emotions as fear, jealousy, and hatred can interrupt sexual union. If I were asked to name the emotion which produces more sexual difficulties than any other I should say, without the slightest hesitation, FEAR, and the fear of fear.

Fear plays havoc with the sex life of tens of thousands of people. Fear of pregnancy can result in a woman becoming frigid. Fear of having yet another child to support may affect a man's potency. Fear of what one's partner may think can rob the sex act of all spontaneity for many who have been led to believe that there is something degrading or unpleasant in the relationship. It may even result in an inability to complete the act.

These feelings of fear may be experienced consciously or unconsciously. Often those who are consciously unaware that fear is interfering with the natural expression of their sexual instinct are really victims of it. This may be in the form of a feeling of inferiority, doubts arising from ignorance or a feeling of inadequacy. Fear in the sense of *anxiety* denies to thousands the joy of sexual satisfaction.

It also lies at the very roots of many sexual abnormalities, as we shall see later. Love must be unfettered from fear or it cannot fully function. That is why this book sets out to fight fear in the realm of sex, and confidence born of knowledge is the only weapon which can defeat it.

Anything which arouses disgust may yield similar results. It is remarkable how trifles can lead to interruption and failure. A word out of place. . . . A single action out of harmony. . . . A disturbing thought coming suddenly into the mind. . . . Such trifles as these often make coitus impossible.

But I shall deal with the emotional, psychological, and spiritual aspects of marriage only in so far as they influence the physical side in this and similar ways. Suffice here to make it clear that I recognise these other aspects, fully grant their importance, and realise how vital they are to happy, *lasting* union.

What must be stressed is this: there are thousands of

marriages where the psychological attitude of both partners is perfectly sound, where high ideals go hand in hand with an adult attitude to life, yet miserable failure results from ignorance.

Let us see just how technically ignorant many people are. An inexperienced girl whose life has been sheltered finds herself approaching marriage with little, if any, knowledge of what is involved. Even in these days such cases are not nearly as rare as many imagine. She may decide to ask a friend for enlightenment, but what kind of answer is she almost certain to receive?

It is safe to say that nine times out of ten the answer, if given, could be compressed into a single sentence—one simply defining the sex act. Nothing is said in regard to fore- or after-play and the general impression is conveyed that 'she will find out for herself', and this, of course, is exactly what she fears.

What of men? They usually boast that they know all that is to be known on the subject. But they know no more than the one thing—the one thing which animals as well as human beings can achieve. Urge them to cultivate an erotic technique and they feel that they are being tempted to 'lower' themselves.

Precisely the opposite is the case. To rise above the animals we must put thought, understanding, and skill into our love-making. Therein lies the difference, and it can be put into one word: technique. It is that which makes sexual union, as well as what leads up to it and what follows, something much higher than the animalistic. Thus we see that the technique of love on its physical side, so far from being degrading, is essentially an ennobling and uplifting factor.

The first storey of the house of marriage, the physical, has to bear the weight of the other three. How necessary, then, that it should be made as strong as possible. How?

By both partners frankly aspiring to become experienced lovers—physically and emotionally.

Not only is sex the very foundation of marriage, but for the majority it provides the motive-power which drives the machinery of life. The sexual impulse underlies all our activities. True, in some it is stronger than in others, but we must remember that no two individuals are alike and each will have his own particular need. Look at that youth brushing his hair carefully before entering a room. That girl devoting anxious thought to her dress for her first dance, the middle-aged woman visiting the beauty parlour—all are obeying, consciously and otherwise, the basic impulse of sex.

Inevitably, exceptions will spring to mind. That they exist cannot be denied. But many of these 'exceptions' are more apparent than real. And I am concerned less with exceptions than with the rule which they prove. Often the explanation is to be found in sublimation—the process by which the force of the sexual impulse finds expression through other channels.

Note what sometimes happens when love is spurned. There are well-recognised signs of disappointment, such as an unusual carelessness in dress, a 'don't care' attitude in business, a general weakening of resolve in the activities of life.

Few indeed have not observed, at some time or other, the sad spectacle of the once-smart woman, now slovenly, not caring a jot about her appearance. And who has failed to notice eager improvements in the personal appearance of those, whether young or not-so-young, to whom love is calling? The loss of interest in the one case, the growth of it in the other, often mark the absence or presence of love.

The emotion of love can grip our whole being. So long as it lasts, it demands the best we can give. It bestows upon us the blessing of exceptional zest for life, an enthusiasm which improves work and helps to make it pleasant.

Many firms ask prospective employees whether or not they are happily married because they know from experience that we must have a contented home life if we are to give of the best of our workaday life. Here again exceptions can be cited, but in many cases they are found in those who are not bound to tasks involving continuous concentration. For the overwhelming majority success in love is a tremendous help towards success in life.

Only the ignorant believe that the maximum pleasure can be derived by practising sexual intercourse in its simplest and crudest manner. The art of love lies in selfless giving, each intensifies the mutual feeling one has for the other, with resultant gratification for both.

It is this, too, which explains why preparatory love-play is so essential, and why it marks the successful lover.

Rule One for success in marriage and in life is this:
Learn How to Love and Make Love.

The attraction which leads people to mate in the first instance must be maintained. Failure to recognise this can end in disaster. For without attraction the flame of desire grows dimmer and dimmer until eventually it is extinguished. And that is not all—love can turn to hate.

Those who love most intensely are likely to loathe most heartily if their sexual relationship is unsatisfactory. Indeed, in such cases sexual repulsion and enmity seem to be proportionate to the strength of their former love. As soon as mutual attraction ceases and the old thrill is gone, monotony sets in. Then, what should bring ecstasy becomes nothing more than a routine, and, like all routine, deadly dull.

What is the result? A sense of grievance comes over both parties. The wife in particular feels it most keenly. Usually she has fewer opportunities of expressing herself through other channels and so we have the beginning of the end.

What you must bear in mind is that the scales are easily tipped between attraction and revulsion. That is why the man who would hold a woman's love must master *the technique of love-making*. Without this it is difficult for him to play his part well. With it he can take the lead in all that relates to sexual union and for the great majority that is as it should be.

He can educate his wife step by step in the art of joyous mating. He can lead her in an adventure along a road which is full of fresh and happy experiences. The considerate man, putting thought and skill into his love-making, creates a relationship with his wife far transcending the purely genital one.

I have said that the man should take the lead. Most women want him to. Intuition warns her of the type of man who is unlikely to play his part—and her intuition is sound. It is for this reason that many women are suspicious of the 'nervous' lover, since he is hardly likely to be the sexually dominant partner.

On the other hand, this type of man often advances very slowly, step by step, which is attractive to some women. Just as coquetry can strengthen a man's desire for conquest, so too can apparent male reluctance strengthen a woman's desire. Unfortunately, when it comes to action, the man may flatter to deceive.

After a slow process of becoming intimately acquainted he feels the girl yielding, but at this point, however, afraid of his bluff being called, he becomes nervous and loses interest. Unable to face up to all that is implied in the love relationship—he goes so far and no further. He seeks conquest but fears to take what he has captured.

True, he has enjoyed the chase, and each gain appeals to his vanity. Why? Because he is emotionally immature, and the world is his playground, women are his toys.

That is the nervous lover at his worst. But the extreme type thus briefly sketched is not so rare as you might suppose, in fact he is a well-known psychological type. While he refuses to accept the responsibilities of love and marriage, others who can roughly be grouped with him *do* marry. They make poor husbands.

They carry through their married life a constant fear of its results. They worry about what their wives may think of them, and of all sorts of imaginary dangers. Their fears may rob intercourse of all spontaneity. There are thousands of them—married, yet afraid of almost all that marriage involves. As husbands they are, more or less, failures.

How does this kind of fear arise? More often than not, the roots lie in early childhood experiences, which have given rise to feelings of inadequacy—inferiority or insecurity. These persist into adult life and can be brought to the surface very easily. Some slight physical defect, for example, or a general lack of good appearance can give rise to unnecessary and exaggerated anxiety. *Yet observation reveals beyond a shadow of doubt that 'looks' in men count for little where love is concerned*. What is rather wonderful is the fact that when we love a person blemishes or defects—which ordinarily sexually repel—can actually attract.

A woman may have a clear impression of the type of man she admires. Most women have. It may be, say, a tall, dark man, but as likely as not she will fall in love with one whose appearance is totally different. Men, too, may prefer blondes—but marry brunettes because they love them.

History provides examples of the most surprising contrasts in types falling in love. Indeed, so individual is the selection that it is utterly impossible to lay down rules as to which types are likely to appeal to other types, certainly so far as appearance is concerned. Without a doubt, however, there are some factors which count for

23

much, such as neatness, cleanliness of person and attire, and, above all, that subtle thing called personality.

What about women? Here is a truth which needs to be strongly emphasised, for thousands of women cannot bring themselves to believe it.

The plainest woman breathing can find a man somewhere who will marry and enjoy intercourse with her, but it is not only 'plain' women who feel that normal love is not for them. There are some, well endowed with looks, blessed with pleasing figures, and of high intelligence, who have a deep-rooted feeling that no man could possibly desire them. Such women are the feminine counterparts of the nervous male lover.

So here is *Rule Two*:

Realise that Love is as Much for You as it is for Other People.

If you repeat that rule and apply it to yourself you will simply be stating the truth. You will not be deceiving yourself in order to bolster up your courage. The confidence which that realisation should bring is essential to success in love.

Observation reveals that no hard-and-fast rules can possibly be laid down in the matter of sexual selection. But it is possible to mention one or two factors which unquestionably increase attractiveness.

Physical excellence is one. All efforts in the direction of fitness are sound from a purely sexual point of view. The man likes to find the feminine body beautiful, whilst the woman seeks a man who looks fully fitted to be both a good lover and a companion.

It is often said women prefer the well-built man of considerable stature. This, however, is hardly correct. It is truer to say that they look for fitness—all-round fitness —in a mate. The big man of the boxer type appeals to some, the lean, quick-moving type to others.

All kinds of men marry: sick men, lame men and fat

men go to the altar. But these are days when all the activities of life are conducted at a faster pace than formerly. Women realise, perhaps unconsciously, that the fat man—whose movements are slow—is unable to compete with the lean in quick movement of either mind or body and is therefore to a certain extent handicapped.

Whilst most men seek physical perfection in the woman they marry, the 'mannish' type of woman who reveals masculine qualities, either of mind or physique, seldom appeals. There are men of the masochistic type, to whom we shall refer later, who tend to mate with such women. That they do so is explained by their own particular make-up—the counterpart of which, in greater or less degree, is often present in the 'masculine' woman.

Clearly, it is important for a girl to realise that physical fitness is desirable. At the same time she must cling for all she is worth to the woman in herself. The normal man seeks a normal woman as his wife. The he-woman type, more conspicuous in recent years, is often popular with men as a companion on the tennis court or golf course but less as an object of sexual desire.

Rule Three, then, if you want to be successful in love, is this:

Don't Neglect Your Body.

'Marriages are made in Heaven!' according to an old saying. If this is true, then Heaven has much for which to answer. It is certain that the gambling method of selecting a partner in the dark, so far as sexual compatability is concerned, is responsible for many marital tragedies.

The question is often asked—should the young, contemplating marriage, seek medical advice? Yes, but something more than medical advice is needed, for usually the problem is one of human relationships, physical and emotional, and unless the doctor is also a psychiatrist he may be of limited help. Furthermore, he should not be the type who finds it difficult to discuss sexual matters freely

25

and easily. It is usually desirable for a joint visit to be made by the engaged couple, although there could well be reasons for an individual one. Even in marriage we are still entitled to hold sacrosanct those secrets that lie deep in the recesses of our heart. The examination should ensure that both are free from disease, and that there are no psychological or organic factors which would militate against successful marriage or having a family.

This is a matter in which it is infinitely better to be safe than sorry. *Rule Four*, then, is this:

Let a Medical Psychologist Examine You Both.

Here is another step towards making marriage less of a gamble than it need be. Spend a holiday together; the longer the better. We think we know those with whom we have worked side by side for many years. But do we? If the occasion arises for us to spend a whole day or a weekend with them in other circumstances we learn much of little-suspected facets of their characters, habits, and preferences. Such things are important.

So many factors can lead to marital disharmony. Idiosyncrasies of temperament, strongly held ideas which clash, religious differences, or even minor characteristics and mannerisms can, and do, influence the marriage relationship. Clearly it is well worth while for those who intend to marry to get to know as much as possible of each other, apart from the setting in which their love has blossomed. This is not to suggest that premarital intercourse is essential, although in some cases it might be helpful, but much can be learnt without this.

Many a couple who have known each other mainly as dance-partners, and whose dance style exactly harmonises, may well assume that they will find their partnership equally suitable in all other activities. This is not true. Many who marry have known each other almost entirely as business friends, with the office as a background. Others have 'hiked' together for miles, and feel that they are ideally suited to each other as partners for the long hike through life. This by no means follows.

Clearly the more opportunities we have of knowing and seeing each other in different surroundings and situations, the easier it is to make a reasonable judgement in our choice of partner for life. No, what is intended is simply to provide a means for the proposed partners to discover as effectively as they can precisely how well suited they really are. But let me again emphasise that I am not advocating a spell of loose and irresponsible living.

There are those who advocate premarital sexual experience as a desirable preliminary to a successful marriage. But, apart from other considerations, convention is still a powerful force, and one not to be lightly disregarded. Anything which tends to lower one's own feeling of self-respect must be ruled out. Anything which tends to lower the self-esteem of one's partner must be ruled out.

Nor can we readily afford to transgress society's codes and conventions. It would be less than honest however not to admit that there are many who feel that they cannot really make a choice of mate without prior sexual experience.

But for others the very idea of premarital intercourse is distasteful, and that alone, for them at any rate, rules it out.

Furthermore, strong religious or conventional scruples may render the idea of premarital intercourse objectionable, and anything which may go wrong later will, as a rule, be ascribed by the partners to the 'irregular' coitus.

Perhaps most people feel that there must inevitably be a large measure of faith, as distinct from knowledge, when two people marry. The benefits of a greater knowledge of each other are too obvious to need emphasis if marriage is to be successful, at least it would eliminate some possible surprises.

Many a man who, fully clothed, has seemed the embodiment of every male virtue looks very different with thin, hairy legs protruding beneath his shirt. Many a woman in whom the bright lights reveal nothing but charm looks very different on waking in the morning. These are some of the hazards of life which have to be faced, but this equally applies in many other aspects of our lives. We inevitably take a gamble in marriage—it might be better if we took a calculated risk.

It is, however, one thing to take a calculated risk in so far as sexual intercourse is concerned and quite another to marry in complete ignorance of our partner's total disposition and temperament.

There is, then, everything to be said in favour of our lovers seeing as much of each other as possible, and as often as possible.

Rule Five, at least as important as the others, must be:
If Possible, Get to Know Each Other Really Well.

Among those who seek guidance about their marital difficulties a large proportion are in trouble over the question of children. This applies to all sections of the community, the wealthy as well as the poor. It applies particularly, perhaps, to the professional classes whose incomes are rarely sufficient to provide 'middle-class' educational facilities for more than one or two children, and for whom the economic aspect of family life is vitally important.

In a later chapter I shall deal in some detail with the spacing of children, and follow it with a review and comparison of modern contraceptive methods and technique. Here, all I am concerned with is the vital importance of what might be termed a 'family policy' from the start —indeed, agreement on the whole question *before* marriage.

It is extremely desirable that the partners to a prospective marriage should discuss children. The object is to decide how many they shall have, and also how these shall be 'spaced'. Too many engaged couples fail to do so at present.

With the result that there are frequent quarrels between husbands who eagerly want children and wives who fear pregnancy or who wish to avoid the curtailment of freedom which children may bring. The constant discord between wives who yearn for children and husbands who fear the economic strain of supporting a family is not conducive to happy marriage.

Here it must be emphasised that for the majority one's real riches are found in the home. Those who put other considerations before a family may come to regret it. Today there are many who wish that, ten or fifteen years ago, they had put the pram before the car, the baby before a round of entertainments and pleasures.

Within a large family there is a feeling of security which is usually lacking in the small family. Many a couple determined at the start of their married life to have only one child experience a feeling of loss and emptiness when in later years their child has left home.

Needless to say, I am not advocating an irresponsible family policy, as though bringing children into the world entailed no responsibilities. But it is necessary to emphasise that family life is of vital importance, to the individual as well as to the community, and that the limitation of the number of children to one, or at most two, is not necessarily the best plan either for the children or parents.

Moreover, family allowances and other social provisions have in recent years lessened the economic burden of parenthood. The desire for children and the fear of the financial burden which they entail clash less than they once did.

Many marry because they feel they are 'madly' in love —and nothing could be more dangerous, since 'madly' is the operative word. Those in this state see each other through rose-tinted spectacles, which dim all faults and blemishes. It also means that they are less likely to recognise the dangers and obstacles which are inevitably encountered further along the road. Problems which are almost sure to arise in marriage should be considered before and not after the wedding ceremony—in other words, they should be boldly faced at the start. Chief amongst them is, undoubtedly, the question of children.

Rule Six, then, is this:

Be Clear as to the Number of Children Desired, and How They Shall be Spaced.

From the outset there will be a plan instead of the haphazard attitude which leaves the vital question of children to blind chance. There is nothing whatever to prevent an alteration of the plan whenever desired.

As has already been stated, we cannot afford to overlook the fact that no two individuals are alike. If a woman lacking in a maternal sense and with no genuine desire to have children embarks on this merely because she is made to feel it is the correct or proper thing to do, the consequences can be tragic both for her and the children. In these circumstances it would be much more honest, and certainly more healthy for all concerned—and that includes society—if such women did not bear children. Nor is there any reason for her to feel ashamed of her situation. She cannot be other than her own nature decrees; there can be no question of irresponsibility or selfishness.

Love embraces all. Every aspect of life is affected by it.

The House of Marriage has to be built stage by stage. Its orderly, happy construction demands a plan. Those who, before they enter the married state, take the steps urged here will have laid strong foundations upon which to build a structure both firm and enduring.

2 : The Stimulation of Love

In order to perform coitus according to Divine Law, complete knowledge and full mastery are needed of all things concerning man and woman.

OMAR HALEBY

What are the forces which stimulate desire? It is important to know. For love technique largely consists in utilising these wisely and well.

Buddha knew the answer. In a speech to monks he said:

'I do not know, young man, any other *form* which fetters the heart of man like a woman's form.

'I do not know, young man, any other *voice* which fetters the heart of man like a woman's voice.

'I do not know, young man, any other *odour* which fetters the heart of man like the odour of a woman.

'I do not know, young man, any other *taste* which fetters the heart of man like the taste of a woman.

'I do not know, young man, any other *touch* which fetters the heart of man like the touch of a woman.'

He was not speaking poetically when he said this, nor was he seeking to convey by exaggeration an impression of the strength of woman's allurement. No, he was telling the plain, unvarnished truth as he saw it. And he saw clearly.

For he went on to describe in detail the various sexual stimuli which man feels through the eye and ear, and through smell, touch, and taste, of all of which play their part in stimulating desire.

The sex impulse is aroused by various stimuli which affect our senses. Events outside of ourselves such as the approach of a thunderstorm is often sufficient to arouse desire long before thunder is heard or lightning is seen.

When the air is 'heavy' before a thunderstorm the feeling of restlessness that some experience is not unlike that resultant on extreme apprehension. This may be defined as anxiety, precipitated by something which has disturbed our way of living, or which darkens our outlook on life and the future. A domestic upheaval, for example, may produce this anxiety in marked form. In time of war, apprehension is widespread, and many feel that at any moment death may fall from the skies. And when they feel these things they can be aroused sexually.

An officer in the Royal Air Force described to a divorce court judge how he and the woman concerned found themselves 'emotionally aroused' at the time of the acute crisis which swept Europe in September 1938, and ended with the Munich Agreement. The judge commented upon this explanation of adultery, which probably struck him as being rather novel. But it is true that in time of crisis people are thus stirred. Similar confessions have come from both men and women.

It is often said that 'moral looseness' is one of the invariable accompaniments of war and rumours of war. Times of exceptional strain and anxiety produce in many the kind of restlessness we have noted. There is much more in it than a vague feeling of 'Today we live, tomorrow we die'. This unquestionably explains the loosening of morals, sexual in particular, which takes place in days of strain. But the desire to escape, even for a brief spell, from the anxieties of the times is at least equally responsible.

Our instincts, of which sex is one, are held in check only by restraint imposed, in the main, from without. The veneer is thin, and easily broken through. When men and women are removed from the familiar setting of home and family they find it much more difficult to maintain the strict observance of the code which has, in the majority of cases, been accepted without question while conditions remained normal.

Whenever there is a need for protection, people feel a *tendency* to fly to arms which will embrace them. Whether they yield to it or not is beside the point. When dire danger threatens, men often turn to a woman's arms as a child does to its mother's. Fear of the immediate future may have a similar effect. On the other hand, sudden terror may stay sexual feeling after it has been aroused. It may even interfere with intercourse to the extent of checking orgasm.

A little consideration in the way in which our senses play a part in stimulating desire shows that touch is easily the most important of them. All, of course, play their part, but in differing degree. I have known both men and women who have experienced profound sexual stimulation whenever they heard some particular piece of music.

Surprising though it may seem, cases are on record of girls who have had an orgasm while listening to great music beautifully rendered. These are extreme examples of sexual stimulation by means of sound.

Some acts which are generally recognised as sexually stimulating represent a combination of sensory appeals. The kiss provides a good example. In its simplest form this is nothing more than the contact of lips. Thus both the active and passive senses of touch are brought into play, the former being the sensations produced by touching something, and the latter by being touched.

But often there is an intaking of breath, however slight. This brings with it an element of taste and of smell. When, as is commonly the case, the tongue as well as the lips is brought into play, taste plays a more prominent part in the sensations experienced. Still more tactile impressions, either active, passive, or both, are also felt.

Kissing as we know it today is not the expression of any fundamental requirement of man. It has developed, slowly, to its present prominence in the realm of love. Animals do not kiss, nor do large numbers of human beings.

In some lands the lip-kiss is regarded as the height of immorality imported from Europe by colonists, or from the United States by films. The 'nose-kiss', which is common among certain Eastern races and the Eskimoes, involves the touching of the beloved's cheek with the nose. Simultaneous in-breathing results in the inhalation of the odour from the cheek. Here again is an act which yields sensations both tactile and olfactory.

The sense of touch in sexual stimulation will be dealt with in greater detail when describing love-play. But here we may note why this sense is the most important. It is not nearly so limited as the other senses in arousing sexual feelings.

We can see only with our eyes, hear only with our ears, taste only with our tongues, smell only with our noses. But we can experience the sensations arising from touch by contacts made by any parts of our bodies. This, indeed, is one of the reasons why touch plays so vital a part in sexual stimulation. It provides the basis of the love-play which represents the height of such stimulation.

The stimulation of the sensory nerves of the skin yield pleasurable sensations in the immediate vicinity. A touch, however light, upon a particularly sensitive area from a member of the opposite sex, especially if he or she is well liked, will often yield an immediate sensation in the genital organs. One may lightly touch a woman's back and cause her to experience a pleasurable feeling in her genitals. A woman's touch on a man's neck, or her kiss on his lips, may yield an erection.

Thus it is true to say that the whole skin area, rich as it is in sensory nerves and linked with the most sensitive parts, provides a single organ of pleasurable sensation. In *The Sexual Life of our Time* Iwan Bloch says:

'It has been well said that the first intentional touching of a part of the skin of a loved one is already a half-sexual union; and this view is confirmed by the fact that such intimate bodily contacts, even when they occur between parts far distant from the sexual organs, very speedily lead to states of marked excitement of these organs.'

While it is true that the whole body is a potential area of voluptuous sensation, certain zones are known to be much more susceptible to stimulation than others. These are called the erogenic or erogenous areas. They consist of those parts of the body where one is conscious of exceptional sensitiveness—where one is easily tickled, feels pain particularly acutely, and so on.

The primary areas are close to the openings of the body —the mouth, the genitals, the anus—while there are secondary erogenous areas where the buttocks join the thighs, inside the thighs, and the lobes of the ears. But it must be remembered that our reactions to these are individual. 'One man's meat is another man's poison.' With some the ear-lobes seem totally lacking in response to stimulation. In others the reverse is the case.

Even those zones which are generally regarded as being erogenous are not so to everyone. On the other hand, zones which lie outside of the erogenic areas may in fact prove to be highly sensitive to the slightest stimulation. Although for many people the buttocks play no part in tactile provocation, for others there will be a prompt response.

I have heard of boys—in one case a youngster of only six—who invariably had an erection when slapped on the buttocks. Incidentally, this shows how extremely thin is the dividing line between the normal and what is regarded as perverse. But more of this in another chapter.

Thus there is no hard and fast rule as to what can be

safely regarded as an erogenous zone in any one individual, experience alone reveals this.

After touch we must consider the sense of sight in love-stimulation. Various authorities, including Havelock Ellis, have concluded that for the majority the impressions received through the eye more largely influence the selection of a love-partner, or create the idea of an ideal mate, than those received through the other senses.

We are all familiar with the expression 'love at first sight'. A glance at a girl whose carriage, clear complexion, and attractive hair style combine to convey an impression of grace and beauty will often arouse desire. Similarly, a man's build, facial expression, and other visible attributes cause a girl's heart to beat faster, and make her long to be dated by him. These are the simplest examples of how visual impressions play their part.

Some men have only to see parts of the female form to feel strong desire. A well-turned leg, for example, invariably attracts attention; while the breasts seem to have a special significance in the stimulation of sexual feelings.

Strong erotic impressions are imparted by clothing. The female leg, naked, rarely attracts as much as the stockinged leg.

In their appeal clothes often combine the tactile and the visual. Take stockings again. Just as the neatly stockinged leg gains in comparison with the bare limb, so far as its visual appeal is concerned, so, too, it is generally regarded as being superior in tactile provocation. Most men would prefer to touch, or stroke, a nylon-stockinged leg rather than a naked one. Silk or nylon underclothing, too, combines for many the joint appeal of tactile and visual provocation, especially when worn by a person whose general appearance is attractive.

The appeal to the eye by no means rests on beauty as defined according to generally accepted standards. All sorts of factors enter other than 'beauty' as regarded by, say, a committee of judges entrusted with the task of selecting a local carnival queen. At a conference of gynaecologists several speakers, accepted as outstanding authorities, agreed that not more than five women in every thousand could claim to be really beautiful. Yet *every* woman has *something* of beauty for *some* men.

Facial perfection, if it ever exists; beauty of figure; clearness and smoothness of skin—these by no means exhaust the physical characteristics which appeal to the eyes of both sexes. I recall a woman who moved in artistic circles in London. She was so repulsive in personal appearance that she bore the nickname 'the Bug'. Yet there was a certain dynamic quality about her face which always claimed attention.

Men stared at her wherever she went—first repelled, then fascinated. Her movements were strikingly graceful. Her hands were slender and attractive. The very repulsiveness of the first impression caused one to stare. But to look at her for long meant that, invariably, one gradually saw the immense attraction which she possessed.

The appeal to the eye is not limited to beauty in its everyday sense. Bodily movement, the way a person crosses a room, sits, stands, moves the hands—all these play a part. For some, the 'little things' of appearance are tremendously important. I have known of cases in which people have fallen in love with one part of a person.

There was a woman who admired long, shapely hands, and found herself seeking them for years. She recalled that she had admired her father's hands. Often early memories or impressions which cannot be recalled account for people being attracted to an unbelievable degree by such trifles as the turning up of a corner of the mouth in smiling, a mannerism of movement, or an occasional fleeting expression. All these are among the visual impressions which stimulate desire.

Recognition of the importance of this in love-provocation has accounted for many changes of fashion. Thus the woman who dresses to 'suit her colour' is following sound instinct. In his *Confessions* Rousseau has described how the lovely courtesan Giulietta gained by clothing her body so as to heighten its appeal. 'Her cuffs and collar had silken threads running through them,' he said, 'and were adorned with pictures of roses. These made a beautiful contrast with her fine skin.'

Such women know the value of these aids to allurement. Indeed, most modern women do. But far too many wives look upon marriage as an end in itself, and fail to realise the importance of keeping love alive in this and other ways. Men, too, having suceeeeded in their conquest, are likely to grow negligent of many of the things which heighten love-provocation through the eye. Both lose much in consequence.

The winning of love is but the first stage of a long adventure. Its maintenance calls for more thought and skill than its gaining. And all the means of stimulating desire must be enlisted in the task.

What is normally forbidden inevitably tends to attract attention. If you doubt that, just think of the way in which people strive to read a banned book, see a play which has been passed after a first ban, or feel constantly inclined to pursue a course of conduct which is expressly forbidden. Many patients confess that if an article of diet is forbidden by their doctor they immediately feel a craving for that one item far stronger than they would have believed possible. It is precisely the same with the human figure.

The completely nude form does not provoke nearly so strongly as the partly clad or artfully concealed body. I have heard men who visited an indoor nudist establishment say that they were quite unmoved by the sight of a mixed company completely unclothed. But when they saw the girls dressing or undressing they experienced sexual feeling.

It is not without interest that in some brothels the girls are not allowed to be naked when first seen by their clients. Lengthy experience has taught the brothel-keepers a great deal about the stimulation of desire by way of the eye.

In the early days of the Salvation Army, when hymns were sung to popular music-hall tunes, someone protested to General Booth that this seemed irreverent. 'Why should the devil have all the best tunes?' he replied.

Why should wives be satisfied with anything less than the best desire-stimulating technique? As an example, the actual marking of the body, as in tattooing, may be mentioned. Many suppose that, today, tattooing is almost entirely limited to soldiers and seafaring men. This is not wholly true. I have seen some astonishing cases among the wealthy classes.

One woman had various obscene figures tattooed on her back. Her thighs and hips had been treated in such a manner that she appeared to be wearing stockings and panties. This, she informed me, was to please her husband, who had repeatedly urged her to be tattooed in this manner.

This highlights the influence of visual impression in provoking desire. The field is almost limitless. Even eyes themselves call to eyes in that type of glance which is sometimes described as 'making eyes'.

Mention has already been made of the power of music to move some people sexually to a marked degree. 'The food of love', Shakespeare called it in *Twelfth Night*. That is true not only of fine melody such as we find in classical works. It applies also in such forms as jazz, which place their emphasis primarily upon rhythm and which spring largely from the sex-rhythmic creations of the Negroes.

Enthusiastic lovers of jazz, both modern and traditional, confess to feeling sexual exaltation when listening to the works of, say, Duke Ellington and other masters of this type of music. To see a crowd swaying rhythmically to the drumbeats, tapping their feet on the floor, and displaying in their faces signs similar to those which mark orgasm in the sex act confirms this to the full.

There is a saying among jazz-players that one can excel in this branch of music only when 'high'. By that they mean when under the influence of marijuana, a drug made from Indian hemp which has appeared to an increasing extent in this country in recent years. It is particularly favoured by coloured dance-band musicians. This drug is known in the East as 'the bringer of seductive visions'. It is said that one of its characteristic effects is the arousal of ungovernable desire.

Some dance musicians state that it enables them to cram more into a bar than is normally possible. Thus it aids those 'breaks' of individual playing which hot-rhythm lovers admire so much. Certainly it affects one's sense of space, which may account for the claims made on its behalf by some musicians. At least a score of jazz ballads sing its praises, though it is not always recognised, for in such songs Indian hemp is referred to as 'tea', 'weed', or by some other expression used by addicts.

What could reveal more plainly the essentially sexual basis of this form of music? In different form, and perhaps to a different degree, all music, as all dancing, springs from the sexual impulse. So it must be regarded among the stimuli of desire.

But, apart from music, there are other forms of passive stimulation which come to us by way of the ear. Jokes about people falling in love with the voice of a crooner or pop-singer are by no means so wide of the mark as they may seem. The voice, singing or speaking, in either sex, can be a most powerful sex-stimulant.

Taste may appear to have little connection with the arousal of love. Yet all authorities are agreed that it cannot be excluded from any complete list of sexual stimuli. Often it is so closely linked with smell that it is difficult to determine the degree to which an impression arises from one or the other. The sensations of both are often intermingled.

Poets have talked of 'tasting' the lips of their mistresses. In such kisses as those given by the tongue—which must emphatically be included among the caresses of perfectly normal lovers, whether bestowed upon the lips or body of the love-mate—taste must come into play.

So far as odour is concerned, if we are to believe some of the alarmist advertising which serves to sell certain soaps and deodorants at the present time, it can only destroy all chances of love for those from whom the odour origininates. But the very 'B.O.' which repels some may strongly attract others. Indeed, a whole chapter might be devoted to the influence which personal odours have had upon love thoughout the centuries.

We all have our own special smell, although we may not be conscious of it. Dogs know their masters or mistresses by it. And in so individual a thing as love, personal odour plays a considerable part. Strange as it may seem, there are some people, men and women alike, whose perspiration odour is extremely agreeable to their partner.

One author, Van de Velde, mentions two youths at a dance, one of whom remarked of a girl: 'I don't like her as a dancing partner. She is a nice girl, but she has such a disagreeable smell.' To which the friend replied: 'I don't understand that at all. It is just the smell that I like.'

Attempts have been made from time to time to list personal odours as agreeable or disagreeable, but that is impossible, for what appeals to one may repel another. Even perfumes used to attract love have totally different effects upon different people. But it can be stated confidently that odours which at first may prove offensive can become agreeable when they are associated with one who is

41

loved. Those which arise from uncleanliness, however, are almost invariably distasteful.

An understanding of the forces which stimulate desire can furthur love-technique. Our physical senses are the paths which lead to desire. We must know them if we are to tread a way which will bring us to that love which, as Stendhal has well said, 'means taking pleasure in seeing, touching, perceiving with every sense, and in the closest possible contact, someone whom we find lovely, and who loves us'.

Whatever has been said in this chapter, we must recognise that the stimulation of sexual love as a part of a total relationship is both healthy and desirable; as an exercise in itself, however, it is limited.

3: Secrets of Sex Appeal

The late Calvin Coolidge once remarked: 'If I want 'em, I want 'em; if I don't, I don't!' True, he was speaking of apples. But he might have said precisely the same of women. And so might all men.

What accounts for the marked attraction which some persons possess to the opposite sex generally? Ability to answer that question demands understanding of that oft-used but little-understood term, 'sex-appeal'.

This may help us to understand why a Tony Curtis or a Frank Sinatra has millions of feminine admirers. It may explain why the officers of the regiment occupy the stalls, the N.C.O.s the pit, and the privates the gallery to watch the caperings of a French lady who is singing a song in a language most of them do not understand.

But what is commonly called sex appeal will not explain why James, who is plain and rather stupid, and Pamela, who is beautiful and brilliant, are madly in love with each other. That would entail solving what for centuries has been called 'the mystery of love'.

Sex appeal is linked with what has been described as 'the abstract conception of love'. The mutual infatuation of James and Pamela illustrates 'personal differentiation and fixation'. The love of each is fixed upon the other.

Most people believe that all attempts to explain love are utterly futile. Yet those who have read carefully what has been said regarding its stimulation will have a greater

43

understanding of how it arises. They will appreciate how the 'abstract conception of love' is built upon innumerable impressions which reach us by way of eye, ear, nose, and the other senses.

It is often said that sex appeal is something like personality—'impossible to define, but readily recognised when met'. Yet if we consider personality we find that it includes certain qualities which are particularly marked in those whom we credit with a strong personality. Such factors as keen eyes, a pleasant speaking voice, charm of manner, grace of movement, spring immediately to mind.

If we make a closer study of these factors we find that certain qualities such as mental penetration, a wide range of ideas, and a fluent gift of expression contribute greatly towards this highly prized endowment.

As with personality, so with sex appeal. Some of the factors which count, though in different degree so far as their appeal to different individuals goes, can be tabulated. We have dealt with some of those in the previous chapter. The sum total will determine the particular individual's sex appeal, just as the qualities of appearance and mental power mentioned above constitute personality.

There are personalities which are far from pleasing, as we all know. But generally we credit people with 'personality' when it is present in a striking and pleasing degree. Everyone has *some* sex appeal, but usually we employ the term in reference to those in whom it is strongly marked.

Clearly there is a very close connection between what are commonly called 'personality' and 'sex appeal'. But the physical element undoubtedly plays a much greater part in sex attraction than in 'personality'. Unconsciously, if not consciously, it constitutes the greater part of the appeal, particularly in women.

Some women admire intellectual ability above all else. For them, mental power pulls more strongly than handsome features, excellence of physique, or charm of manner. It is much rarer to find men attracted by intellectual power in women. As a rule, they are more susceptible to the physical allurements and charming ways of women than to any outstanding mental ability.

Cases of exceedingly plain men who have won the undying devotion of beautiful women could be cited by the score. Often the explanation lies in the woman's intense admiration, which attains to the height of love, for the man's brilliance in creative work. The orator, artist, writer, may be brutal in his treatment of women, coarse in private life, grossly selfish. All these vices, combined with physical repulsiveness, may be overlooked by a woman who loves him *for his work*.

This love of a man for what he achieves must not be confused with a mere regard for the material results of such work. No, in spite of all that the cynics may say, admiration of the work itself, and love of the man capable of it, provides the explanation.

Iwan Bloch, in *The Sexual Life of our Time*, says: 'It is a distinctive fact that, throughout the history of civilisation, men have always had a clearer understanding of "masculine beauty" than women. Women have preferred *power, intelligence, energy of will, and marked individuality*'

Caroline Schlegel, writing to Luise Gotter about Mirabeau, said: 'Hideous he may be but Sophie loved him; *for what women love in man is certainly not beauty.*'

That women often do love repulsive men to distraction especially when they are geniuses is undeniable. But such men would hardly be classed as among those possessing 'sex appeal', were the term more commonly applied to the male sex. Yet for some, as we have seen, the strongly developed individuality *is* a desire-inspiring factor.

Whatever rules are laid down regarding sex appeal, a hundred cases can be cited which seems to disprove them. For, as we shall see later, there are many deviations from normal which cut right across the usual lines of sexual approach. Even so, we know that some persons possess to a strong degree the power to stimulate desire in those of the opposite sex. They may not be conscious of this power, and never knowingly exercise it. Nevertheless, they possess sex appeal.

Those love-stimulating impressions already dealt with may play a part, and contribute towards a complete endowment of the power to arouse desire. And, since the stimulation of desire comes through all the senses, *everything* matters. Thus the individual can develop his or her sex appeal.

Every step towards all-round development—physical, mental, cultural and spiritual—is a strengthening of sex appeal. But on no account must the basic physical element be crushed by emphasis on the other elements.

We have seen, for example, that men, in the main, are attracted by physical charm in women, and may be repelled by intellectual ability, particularly when it takes precedence over physical appeal. Who has not met the 'blue-stocking' type of woman whose profound studies leave her little time for anything else? In consequence she appears to be outside the stream of life. Here, however, appearances are sometimes deceiving. Many woman of this type, outwardly lacking in sex appeal, nevertheless possesses extraordinary power of attraction when known intimately.

She takes off her blue stockings when she goes to bed. She is an ardent lover whose warmth and zeal are felt as soon as close contact is effected. The barrier which the intellectual side of her life sets up then serves by contrast to heighten the pleasure of intimacy with her. All she knows, all she has read, reinforce her power to love and arouse love. That is why such women are often outstandingly successful in their love lives.

Who has not heard adverse comments on the marriage of a typical 'blue stocking' to a handsome, alert man whose interests seem totally at variance with hers? So far as appearances go, such unions seem utterly hopeless in every way. Yet they are often extremely happy. All of which goes to prove that sex appeal does not lie entirely on the surface.

With personality, as we have remarked, there are qualities which are immediately obvious and so are seen by all, yet more important are the deeper qualities which are revealed only on closer acquaintance. The same is true of sex appeal. It has a surface aspect which is general; a deeper one which is individual.

Attempts have been made from time to time to standardise, measure, and apportion the approximate values of the various elements in sex appeal. They were doomed to failure.

Hollywood once held a solemn congress to decide who should possess the proud title of 'America's Sex Appeal Girl No. 1'. The young women in the film industry were passed under review in order to select the one whose measurements were 'perfect', and whose general conformity to the film colony's idea of the 'perfect type' would entitle her to this honour. Alas, for all her perfect measurements, her conformity to fixed standards, she could hardly claim to possess so strong an appeal to men as, say, an Ingrid Bergman or a Greta Garbo, whose measurements would have ruled them completely out from the start.

We can easily list some of the *general* factors in sex appeal. We know that men generally prefer 'nice' legs, clear, smooth complexions, attractive hair, and so on, while women like an impression of strength or of efficiency in men. But what of the values which lie deeper? It is completely impossible to assess them. Their appeal is not general. It is intensely individual. This is a point which is overlooked when competitions of the kind just mentioned are held.

Clearly, the balanced development of all the elements

tends to heighten sex appeal. Physical culture, elocution, cleanliness of dress and person, and all that helps to build physical, mental, and cultural power, in harmony, is helpful for all who would be successful in the realm of love.

They can bring us as near to perfection as our natural powers permit, so far as the 'processes which crystallise round the sexual approach' are concerned. That we benefit in consequence, not only in love, but in life generally, is undeniable. But the maximum of sex appeal which is possible according to one's general endowment does not necessarily yield personal love.

One may be well liked, regarded as an entirely desirable lover, even singled out by the multitude as an exponent of 'sex appeal'—yet miss the joy of love in spite of all this.

Women, more than men, are attracted by a voice. Possibly the male voice has a wider range in speech, and is capable of conveying stronger and deeper impressions than the female voice. There are, of course, cases in which men are profoundly moved by hearing a female voice. But unless it is linked with other impressions, either present or remembered, the female voice alone rarely arouses desire.

The expression 'Falling in love with a voice' is hardly an exaggeration. Love at first *sound* is possible, just as love at first sight is, although the former undoubtedly is rarer. And we must bear in mind that when we speak of love at first sight we mean that all the impressions gained at a first contact have aroused attraction.

In his delightful talks over the radio, under the title of 'It Occurs to Me', since published in book form, Lord Elton had some interesting things to say about the voice. He pointed out that every individual's voice is subtly his own: *that it is different from everyone else's.*

'There are some people,' he added, 'so sensitive to voices that their likes and dislikes are founded more on the sound of the voice than on what it says. Yes, and let me tell you that no one has the least idea what his voice sounds like. You may think your own voice is the sound you know best in the world. But you have never heard it—not as other people hear it! If you doubt that, listen to a gramophone record of your own voice.'

When Lord Elton first heard his own voice, as others hear it, he could not believe it was his. Officials at Broadcasting House played over a record of part of one of his wireless talks. 'I thought they were playing a practical joke of me,' he said. 'I didn't recognise a single syllable as my own.'

That the voice is one of the strongest factors in sex appeal is not surprising, for it is the principal instrument of self-expression. That it is often the main desire-stimulating factor in the approach stage of love is due to a feeling that 'here is a voice with which I could well live'. Or 'I should like to be comforted by it, inspired to action by it, obey it'—whatever one's temperament demands. But, over and above that, the extremely individual character of the voice accounts for its importance.

We can distinguish the factors which produce general or surface sex appeal since in the main they appeal to all, though in varying degree. But those which lead from the approach stage to individual selection cannot be chartered. Sometimes, in fact, they are non-existent. For people who love attribute all sorts of qualities and virtues to the objects of their affection. Where love reigns, that 'beauty is in the eye of the beholder' is the very truth. The eyes of love often see what others do not—*cannot*—see.

We know that a combination of sexually stimulating impressions will bestow sex appeal upon those of either sex from whom they emanate. But why, whilst they lead to admiration in the many, they awake love in the few, perhaps in only one person, was a mystery for a long time. It is no longer.

The average man does not love women in the mass; neither does the normal woman desire 'men'. No, the male seeks a mate of the opposite sex who will arouse within him a desire which is all-embracing. The average female hopes to love and be loved by *one man*. This is, of course, something very different from the purely sexual instinct being expressed, as it were, in the raw. In other words, a man may wish to have sexual intercourse as a limited transaction with more than one women. This is what we mean when we speak of man being polyerotic. Some women too are polyerotic, but they appear to be a minority. Whether this is so because of an innate difference between the sexes, or whether it is due to environmental factors, it is difficult to say, I suspect the latter.

When physical preparation for love has taken place men and women are ready to love and be loved. They seek deliberately for a mate. And even when they are not consciously engaged in the quest, so deep-rooted is their desire for a mate that their actions are largely governed by the seeking impulse. Thus young men and women—and often the not-so-young—who are 'unattached' place themselves in situations favourable to making suitable contacts.

They go to dances, or on cruises, attend social functions, and meet the opposite sex as frequently as possible. In other words, they place themselves in positions where they can exercise sex appeal and test that of others. They may not reason it out thus. They may not consciously realise why they seek the society of the opposite sex. But fundamentally they are responding to this underlying urge to find a mate.

We all know that contacts thus made often result in what is called 'falling in love'. But why? What accounts for this mutual attraction, sometimes between people who seem to the outside world hopelessly unsuited to each other?

To answer such a question we must know something of the past life of the person concerned.

Take the case of a girl who, when she felt the first stirrings towards the opposite sex, noted with extreme pleasure the serene, shining eyes of her music master—by no means an unusual thing. His eyes were to her the most striking feature he possessed. A kind man, all his kindliness seemed to shine out through them. A learned man, all wisdom seemed reflected in his eyes.

Whenever he was giving her lessons she would feel his eyes upon her as though warming her. When she could do so she would look into them and experience a feeling of elation. Years after, the music master a dim memory, she still had a vague liking for eyes of one particular kind —his.

She may even have forgotten what the man was like. But deep in her unconscious mind, where memory is unfailing, the impression remains. Although she could not recollect those particular eyes, as soon as she saw eyes like them something within her seemed to say: 'I think I could love that man for ever'.

Actually the young man possessing eyes which reminded her of a pleasurable early experience may not have been at all like the music master. All that was necessary was a sufficient resemblance to arouse the unconscious impulse linked with a forgotten association of pleasurable sensation, and so start a process which can rapidly move from liking to love.

No impression which reaches us through the senses is ever completely lost. It is stored, as it were, in the unconscious mind. Thus, one may forget the details of the house in which one lived as a child, yet, on seeing a picture of it, say at once: 'I'm sure I've seen this place before, and that house in particular seems very familiar.' The picture has provided the stimulus to recall the old memory, though one's powers of recollection could not do so unaided.

The earliest impressions linked with love have a tremendous influence over our lives. They lead men and women to 'fall in love'. Sometimes, too, they lead people along strange ways off the normal route, as we shall see later.

When A falls in love at first sight with B, a deep-rooted, unconscious liking for some quite trivial feature, mannerism, or quality may provide the explanation. The trifles which account for selection, often in a flash, may take the form of an article of dress, a tone of voice, a very full moustache or a closely clipped one, a personal odour or a perfume—anything which can stimulate the calling-out from the past of the 'love-ideal' which has been forming vaguely in the mind for years, and which had its beginnings in some early experience.

Whether B falls in love with A or not, the chances of his doing so are increased by the love which A has for him. The very fact that one is loved by another tends to stimulate love for that person. Thus, while A loves B intensely, B may love in an almost reciprocal manner. Or he may not love A at all. Or he may find the process of individual selection speeded up by some quality in her, so that he, too, loves at first sight. When two people are simultaneously stimulated by impressions which yield immediate selection in this manner we have one of those mutual infatuations which are of terrific intensity while they last. Note: *while they last*.

The great danger of infatuation lies in the manner in which the lovers build up complete structures of virtue in each other out of some tiny feature, peculiarity, mannerism, or the like—edifices which are totally non-existent outside of their own imaginations.

Friends may laugh, and point out to an infatuated man that the girl of his dreams is—well, something entirely of his dreams, day and night, and non-existent in fact. He will scorn their laughter. Relatives may point out all sorts of obvious reasons why the girl should not marry the man. The girl simply cannot understand their well-meant criticisms. To her the object of her love possesses nothing but virtues.

But gradually the mutual passion spends itself because of its very intensity. Then, with a cooling of the fires, each begins to see faults in the other. They are apt to be intensely annoyed when they do so. They feel almost as if they have been cheated. This irritation often destroys their chances of happiness together. For, as the infatuation wanes, so, gradually, does the truth emerge, and shocks those who have seen nothing but perfection in each other.

Is the state of infatuation which is often called 'being in love' a sound basis for sexual union? Is it a safe guide for marriage? Both questions have been discussed. That this state is highly dangerous is undeniable. Indeed it is not far removed from a form of insanity. Such common expressions as 'I am crazy about her', or 'I am madly in love with him', are not entirely figurative.

But the form of insanity, or intoxication, to which it is akin is *temporary*. That is why the marriage of a couple in the throes of infatuation is a risky gamble. For so long as the infatuation lasts the critical powers are in abeyance. They return, keener than ever, immediately infatuation ceases. Then the lovers, clear-eyed and with judgement restored, are surprised to see each other as they really are.

Dr. W. Beran Wolfe says: 'Falling in love is truly more closely allied to madness than to love, for it is compounded chiefly of selfishness, possessiveness, illusion and delusion. People who "fall in love" seldom fall in love with flesh-and-blood men and women; they fall in love with single traits or qualities which superficially recall some subconscious symbol or totem.'

There you have the truth in a nutshell.

When disillusionment comes, with the passing of infatuation, those concerned rarely consider their position calmly and understandingly. They vent their resentment on each other. They not only have grudges but try to punish each other in various ways.

Those who seek happiness in love, and a lasting union, must realise that while the emotions should guide, reason and common sense must have the final word.

For, as Dr. Alfred Adler has said: 'Romance alone is not sufficient. Of romance and reason, the latter is more important.' The engaged and newly married would do well to read those words aloud every day.

Romance Alone is Not Sufficient.

An immense amount of marital misery is due to the almost general belief that romance is everything. Yet, truth to tell, many marriages fail not because the partners have never really loved each other but rather because they have been blinded by love to incompatibilities which are perfectly obvious to others.

What is the remedy? Simply to give reason and common sense a chance. The rational marriage stands the best chance of success. It is one in which both partners have put deliberate thought into their selection, and discussed all aspects of their union.

Clearly such a marriage has a far greater chance of success than one undertaken under the influence of a blinding infatuation which is so often spoken of as love— and, worse still, for all the world as though it were the only genuine kind of love, which is utterly absurd.

Usually, people who are the victims of infatuation literally cannot take advice. But here is the best advice which can be given, whether those who need it most take it or not.

Be a little suspicious of the love which comes suddenly, seems all-consuming and carries you away.

A *little* suspicious. It may prove short-lived. On the other hand, it may pass into the more rational form of love. This is the more likely if an honest attempt is made by both parties to apply informed judgement, along the lines already indicated, as to their suitability to each other.

To quote Dr. W Beran Wolfe again:

'Love is the highest form of human co-operation. It implies the willingness to see your partner as he or she really is, to love despite faults, to demand nothing and to be ready to give all.'

Yes, see your partner as he or she really is. And help your partner to see the real You. That way lies safety and happiness. For the love which lasts is between two human beings—not dream creations.

LOVE'S TEN COMMANDMENTS

1. Bring to the altar of love a healthy body and a knowledge of its powers and their employment.

2. Keep your mind out of splints. False modesty and a belief in the superiority of one sex, are examples of mental splints which ruin the love life.

3. Be appreciative. Failure to give approval when it is due means that soon it won't be due.

4. Happy love relations are like good business bargains in that both parties must gain.

5. Be self-respecting. To hold a love-partner's respect you must hold your own.

6. Never hurt the self-esteem of the one you love.

7. Avoid rigid routine. Love has happy surprises for those who experiment.

8. Be bold in your sexual relationship. It is still true that 'perfect love casteth out fear'.

9. Make use of the technique of love so that you can enjoy the sex act to the full. Slaves of love, like all other slaves, sooner or later desire their freedom.

10. Give love its due—that and no more—and it will be the greatest thing in your life.

4: The Technique of Love-play

It is the task of the man to summon his whole power of self-command, to employ all his skill, to take all the care in his power, that the woman may be, as one says, 'ready'. The man who thinks only of his own gratification, and who leaves his partner ungratified, is a brutal being, or, if not brutal, he is simply ignorant of the harm he is doing.

GEORGE HIRTH

Love-play is not an invention of vicious or degenerate people, but a physiological necessity, and we must no more hesitate to discuss it than we do other manifestations of sexual life.

Encyclopaedia of Sexual Knowledge

Nearly every human being of adult years has indulged in some form of love-play. Yet there is widespread ignorance of the subject. It reveals itself not only in faulty technique but in fear that certain caresses which are perfectly normal may be perverse. Consequently many a healthy inclination is smothered.

In this chapter I shall deal *only* with sexual practices which are entirely normal. Individual likes and dislikes regarding various forms of love-play must inevitably affect the precise procedure adopted in specific cases. What pleases one may annoy, even disgust, another. Only experiment, a constant discovering of how each may give pleasure to the other, can enable lovers to achieve the height of mutual joy through their joint efforts.

Here, love-play in the *broad* sense is our concern. It includes everything that leads up to that stage of sexual communion which is usually called coitus, or congress, and which begins with the insertion of the phallus (*erect* penis) into the vagina, and ends with ejaculation and its withdrawal. Thus it includes all the preparatory conversation, embraces, kisses, and so on which lead up to actual congress—in short, the preliminaries which prepare the parties for the supreme act of love.

Some authorities prefer to divide these preliminaries into two: Prelude and Love-play. But in actual practice it is impossible to indicate any particular point as the end of the one and the start of the other. For all practical purposes they are one. Words of love whispered in the ear may stimulate desire just as much as actual touches on the most sensitive parts of the body. Let us begin with conversation.

Looks and words can produce definite physical reactions. Quite apart from the more rapid heart-beat which both parties may experience when talking of love to each other, they may feel definite local sensations which reveal unmistakably the part which conversation, glances, and the like, can play by way of *preparation*, even though they have not so much as touched hands.

During this conversational prelude, distillation or lubrication—the result of mucous secretions from the genital glands—provides the physical sign of the desire for closer contact. This shows itself in both sexes. Often, too, without any physical contact, but solely because of the stimulant effect of words of love, both may be genitally ready.

Those who are most experienced in erotic technique never rush ahead during these early stages, unless, of course, they have acquired by experience a close knowledge of their partner's attitude. In that case there may be little need to practise the art of stimulating desire. The man who has led his wife, step by step, through many adventures in the field of love, may make a gesture, touch her hair, nod, or by some other trifling sign not only suggest intercourse but fully rouse her for it. Until, however, there has been a good deal of actual intimacy—and not in every case even then—the slower approach is necessary.

The woman knows instinctively how much coquetry can aid her—the adoption of a certain defensive attitude, a giving followed by withdrawal, an advance, then a quick retreat. No words set down on paper can counsel just how far she should retreat without running the risk of finding that her man is no longer in pursuit. Women know such things intuitively. It is useless to seek to advise in detail just how they should employ one of the oldest weapons in Eve's armoury. They know without being told.

But it is necessary to point out the value of this weapon, since some 'modern' women despise it. They regard men as creatures whose desire needs no arousing. They expect them to 'cut out sentimentality', to quote an oft-used expression. The result of this attitude is likely to be that the man concerned comes to regard such a woman as being cold and distant. His own ardour may be damped accordingly. Not without adequate reason has Eve, throughout the centuries, used coquetry to win love. Both parties to the love act can help materially by playing their full part from the start.

'If a man wants me, that's sufficient; there is no need for me to arouse him,' is the kind of remark which is often made by some modern young women and thought of by others. Of course, there is some truth in it. Theoretically, the fact that a man desires a woman may be enough. He can proceed to complete intercourse without any stimulation such as love-play affords. But the woman who acts on that theory usually regrets it. Love's fires need fanning. Women as well as men must help in a sphere which demands co-operation if the highest mutual pleasure is to result.

Apart from those exceptional women referred to elsewhere, who want to be seized, compelled, mastered in spite of their own resistance, the great majority *want* to be led step by step through the various stages of sexual intercourse. Tender words, compliments, loving expressions, always provided they are discriminatingly employed, with no suggestion of parrot-like routine about them, mean much to us all. And they play a valuable part in arousing desire, gently and gradually, just as various tactile and other stimulatory impressions quicken the pace of preparation, of 'making ready', when the more intimate forms of love-play begin.

It must not be assumed that mere words are sufficient. Closely attuned to each other as the partners are, emotionally, each will be quick to detect a false note, any enforced endearment which lacks sincerity. Each must feel that the deepest emotional being of the other is being genuinely expressed. Women particularly are extremely quick to detect insincerities, just as a bad setting to a love relationship will often influence them much more than it will the man.

As soon as *touch* comes into play, whether active or passive, love-play in its closer form takes over. The first kiss marks the most obvious step from the prelude to the love-play stage. During the former, touches, which may have deeply aroused one or both of the parties, as in the holding of hands, may have strengthened desire. But the kiss, especially if both partners give themselves up to it, marks the passing of the more distant relationship. It is in a sense the real beginning of physical intercourse. From the first kiss, touch is likely to play a much more important part than any other sense.

Bloch has written: 'It is a true saying that a woman who permits a man to kiss her will ultimately grant him complete possession'. That is a rather sweeping assertion in these days when kisses cover so wide a range, from the friendly kiss and the one which merely says: 'Thank you for a pleasant evening', to the erotic kiss in which not only the lips but the tongues of the lovers come into play. It may have been true, at one time, that—to quote Bloch again—'by the majority of sensitive women the kiss is valued just as highly as the last favour', i.e. complete possession. But it certainly is not so today. Many a woman will offer her lips to a man with whom the very idea of complete sexual union would be absolutely out of the question.

But it is safe to say that a woman who yields to, and participates fully in, a deeply erotic kiss is well on the way to yielding herself completely. For the erotic kiss, as distinct from the lip caresses which are often given and accepted much in the same way as handshakes, is one of the most powerful stimuli of desire. Moreover, as an Arabian poet has said:

> 'The most intimate embrace
> Leaves the heart cold and unsatisfied—
> If the rapture of the kiss is wanting.'

Those who become expert in the art of love may kiss a hundred times and every kiss is different. And the kisses which give the greatest pleasure to one's love-mate may be of a kind which with any other partner would create feelings of nausea.

A man who, in intimate contact with any woman save the one he loves, would restrict his kisses to the type which consists of the pressing together of the lips, may, with the one he loves, pass his tongue along her lips; penetrate deeply into her mouth; enclose her mouth with his so that his teeth press round her lips and impart a loving hurt which she finds pleasurable, but which, coming from any other, would be both distasteful and totally un-acceptable.

There may be gentle meeting of tongues, with the lips pressing against each other. Or an in-and-out movement by both partners may result in the constant touching and withdrawing of these sensitive organs. Then the kisses may range over a wider area—to those parts of the body which seem made to be kissed, like a woman's breasts and gradually to others.

With kissing, as with all love-play, experiment is necessary in order to discover where pleasure may best be given. One of the joys of love-life lies in this finding of the best method and manner of stimulating desire. It may take some time to ascertain precisely which parts of the body are most sensitive to the touches of love—i.e. the erogenous zones—and which forms of stimulation are welcomed there. The kiss may start with the lips, then the tongues may come into play (the tongue kiss), the partners then kissing each other's necks, and proceeding downwards until, reaching the thighs, both are not only giving intense pleasure, but are experiencing it through active and passive tactile sensations.

Some who have never heard or read of the numerous kinds of kiss which are perfectly normal and right between those who love, are guided by instinct to employ them. Others, after long years of married life, discover them and find new joy by further experimenting. But with kissing, as with all forms of love-play, individual characteristics count for much, and this has to be borne in mind. But as a rule lovers can learn, step by step, to enjoy such erotic kisses as the tongue kiss, and the body kiss, always provided that if one partner is not pleasurably aroused by such caresses at the start, the other proceeds slowly.

In the kiss in its commonest form, where lips are pressed to lips, the main sensations are tactile, and smell and taste are involved to a slight degree. But with the tongue kiss, especially when it takes the form of exploring all regions of the partner's mouth, taste inevitably plays a greater part than in the lip kiss, though here again the lovers may be totally unconscious of the fact. Erotic kisses between lovers, unlike the conventional kiss, are not dry, but moist, and this may pass from one mouth to the other.

The term 'Maraichinage' has been applied to a form of kissing in which lovers 'mutually explore and caress the insides of each other's mouths as profoundly as possible, sometimes for hours'. Young unmarried people used to enjoy this love-play in public in the Pays de Mont district of Brittany. The local mayor, who was a doctor, warmly advocated the practice as 'a real antidote to depopulation'. In this country such lengthy bouts of tongue-kissing are unusual, certainly in public places. Even so, lovers who spend long periods together in the fields and woods, or in the home, frequently employ 'Maraichinage', though they may never have heard the term.

Kissing by suction, too, is another form in which taste plays a part. Whether actively employed or passively felt, this kind of kiss can yield much pleasure, and is frequently used as a variation of the different kinds of kiss.

To some, these caresses may seem strange, even distasteful. Yet they are all invaluable aids to effective love-play, which has for its object both the giving and receiving of pleasure, and also the preparation of both parties for the act of union which follows and completes it.

The degree of stimulation which is attained by both partners from mouth-to-mouth kisses is usually heightened if the love-play proceeds downwards towards the genital regions. The neck provides a pathway, for it is highly sensitive, especially to the tongue kiss. Most women like to have their breasts kissed. They may say no word, but move their breasts invitingly towards the lover's mouth. The tongue kiss around the breasts and applied to the nipples is usually found to be most stimulating by both partners.

Particularly in the earlier days of love adventure the man is likely to play the lead, as, indeed, most women expect him to do. If he proceeds from mouth to neck, and from neck to breasts, his love-mate's response will usually assure him that he is succeeding. Ovid, in *The Art of Love,* says: 'He who has stolen a kiss and knows not how to steal the rest deserves to forfeit his advantage.' Certainly he who has been permitted the range of caresses here indicated should be able to prepare his love-mate adequately for all that is to follow.

If the emphasis is put mainly upon the man it is because so many women are rarely, or never, brought to an adequate stage of preparedness and expectancy before coitus is attempted, that insistence upon the man's duty to perfect his love-play technique is a bounden duty. He usually reaches the summit of desire much more quickly than the woman. She must be helped, so that she can catch up with him. By suitable love-play he may even give her a start.

Let there be no fear that the woman may be hurried too far ahead of her husband, for he can follow and join her. But if he arrives first he may ejaculate and leave the woman unsatisfied without having experienced orgasm. *That is what happens in the majority of cases.*

Some people of both sexes are exceedingly sensitive to tactile impressions at the point where the neck joins the shoulder. The whole of the back is often an erogenous zone, particularly the lumbar region of the spine. The hips may also prove highly sensitive. Here it must be remarked that some persons who are quite unmoved by kissing of the back are responsive to gentle touches applied to this region, especially with the tips of the fingers.

Kissing and stroking, skilfully combined, may follow many different courses. It is desirable that they should do so, since nothing kills love more than dull routine, and this is particularly true of intimate contacts. To follow one order of procedure rigidly—as many do—robs love-play of the element of search and discovery which is so precious, and which makes physical intercourse a constant adventure. It should always yield fresh surprises, always unfold new ways of giving and receiving pleasure.

We have indicated some of the erotogenic zones—the most general. Only experiment can show where the most sensitive parts of one's mate lie, and which of them respond best to various forms of love-play. Even the eyes are erotogenic in some people. The kissing of the beloved's eyes may yield pleasurable sensations. In some female patients, according to Dr. Emil Bock, quoted by Bloch in *The Sexual Life of Our Time*, a gentle inunction of certain ointments into the eye 'gives rise to changes of countenance showing that a sexual orgasm is occurring'.

But while exploration is essential to discover the most sensitive areas, and variety essential to avoid monotony, great tact must be used. Individual differences are such that what brings pleasure to one brings a shudder of disgust to another. The man must be particularly careful when dealing with a bride of little experience. Women, too, must not overstep the mark which divides the pleasurable from the repellent. Specific instances cannot be given, since reactions differ in different individuals, particularly where the contacts involving the genital areas are concerned.

Since these are the ultimate objective, love-play which tends to provide impressions moving ever nearer to the genital zone is most likely to succeed in its purpose of ensuring rising passion. The actual touching of the genitals must be approached with care. There are some (of both sexes) who enjoy a firm touch, others, a gentle one.

A man's testicles are exceedingly sensitive and great care must be exercised. The woman who would impart as much pleasure as she can should begin by touching them *lightly and with the tips of the fingers*.

There is a certain risk in this type of stimulation, and it should only be used when a woman knows her partner well and so is perfectly assured that an overture of this kind will not be repelled. Many a man, ready himself to take the lead in love, is shocked by what he regards as the 'forwardness' of a woman who attempts genital stimulation. However, the natural intuitive sense of most women should be sufficient to enable them to judge correctly.

Both sexes are often greatly aroused when the genital parts are touched at the same time as other erotogenic areas. Thus, a woman who feels the man she loves touching her genitals, or the inside of the thighs, and at the same time is having her breasts fondled or kissed finds her pleasure much intensified.

Generally speaking, actual local stimulation is much more necessary to women if they are to experience orgasm. Unless the man is tired, or lacking in virility, it will not usually be necessary for the woman to apply penile stimulation, save perhaps as an added sensation which will help to ensure variety. But it is generally *essential* that the man should apply vaginal stimulation, at any rate until the woman has become erotically experienced.

For the overwhelming majority of women the most sensitive part in the early stages of sexual embrace—the love-play period—is the clitoris. Many do not realise this, far less act upon it, with the result that *most*—not merely many —wives are rarely fully prepared for actual congress. Thousands *never* experience genuine, full, culmination in the whole course of their married lives.

Naturally, with an inexperienced bride, special care is necessary, when, other forms of love-play having aroused a measure of feeling, the husband turns his attention to more local stimulation. Here we may quote Van de Velde:

'In any erotic play executed with delicate reverence and consideration—and, above all, when the lovers have not become quite accustomed and attuned to each other—a considerable amount of time should be given to kisses and manual caresses, before the genitals are touched. After gentle strokings and claspings of the accessory organs, the hand should lightly and timidly brush the abdomen, the mon-pubis, the inner side of the thighs, alight swiftly on the sexual organs and pass at once to the other thigh. Only by a cautious and circuitous route should it approach the holy place of sex and tenderly seek admittance.'

He goes on to point out that if the seeking and stroking hand is the husband's the wife's thighs will separate slightly at his touch, so that her genital organs become more accessible. The excitement caused by the previous caresses will probably have caused a certain degree of lubrication and increased blood supply.

When this stage has been reached the man can easily touch the clitoris, which, already excited by the love-play, though not hitherto directly touched, is congested and enlarged. The slightest touch yields marked excitement and intensifies desire to an incalculable degree.

This form of stimulation, together with words of love, kisses, and other love-play, may be extended to the whole genital area. But more often than not the titillation of the clitoris affords the woman the greatest excitement. Then, with the height of passion and emotion very nearly reached, is the moment for the man to insert his phallus into the vagina and, with forward and backward movements, coitus replaces the preparatory love-play.

We have seen how the tongue kiss can be employed, to meet tongue, to caress the partner's mouth or body. It is often used as a means of genital stimulation, the advantage of this kiss is that it provides natural lubrication. And this is most helpful in those cases where the genital mucous secretion is inadequate.

Surprising though it may seem to some, this form of stimulation is widely practised. There is no reason why it should not be, provided it is not distasteful to either partner.

Lack of adequate lubrication renders friction of the

clitoris and vagina painful, both during love-play and—still more—during actual coitus. Artificial preparations are often used in substitution for the natural lubricant when this is obviously delayed or insufficient. The object, of course, is to avoid irritation or hurt, by making the parts smooth.

Many of the preparations used for this purpose have proved far from satisfactory, and actually tend to promote the very irritation they are designed to prevent. Some are not easily removed, even by fairly vigorous washing, and so may remain until they become rancid. Vaseline, which is often recommended for this purpose, does not become rancid, but it is not soluble in water, and is therefore not easily washed off. Preparations which can be dissolved by the application of water are much to be preferred.

Anything which serves to interrupt intercourse is to be avoided. This applies to many contraceptive techniques; it is important that their application should be done as unobtrusively and naturally as possible. That is why lubrication of the genital parts is best performed by means of a caress which is productive of pleasure to both parties.

It cannot be too strongly stressed that any caress calculated to overcome frigidity and fear in a hitherto inexperienced woman must be applied with the greatest gentleness. The one thing to be avoided at all costs, when dealing with an inexperienced bride, is doing or saying anything which is likely to repel her in any shape or form.

The husband has to be exceedingly cautious in first love-play. He must guard against anything which will frighten or disgust. This is especially necessary where more intimate forms of love-play are involved. When dealing with a genuinely inexperienced bride 'Hasten slowly' is a sound rule to follow.

I say *genuinely* inexperienced, for I am not thinking of the woman who, although she may not have experienced actual coitus, has nevertheless indulged in deep petting or has read much on the subject of sex, and so knows that direct stimulation is both desirable and natural. Many an inexperienced woman approaches coitus itself with fear, but knowing that it opens up paths to a fuller life, proceeds with it. In precisely the same way women regard as desirable such perfectly normal love-play as we have discussed in this chapter, provided that they accept the fact that there is nothing either harmful or unwholesome about such practices.

If every woman had read a good sex book prior to marriage, then much marital misery might have been avoided. Men are more likely to seek such guidance than women. They feel—rightly—that they have to play the part of the initiator and guide. But since women are far more the victims of inhibitions produced by faulty teaching and a hypocritical attitude towards sex, they, even more than men, need guidance.

A bride who is ignorant of sexual technique must be guided slowly into it, with intimate caresses, and these should come naturally and *at the right moment*.

The right moment is when her initial timidity has been overcome and she is ready to co-operate rather than remain passive. She will, at an early stage, show plainly by her attitude and movements that she desires such forms of stimulation. This can convey, more plainly than words, what a woman desires.

Direct stimulation by means of the kiss is not, of course, limited to that form in which the man plays the active role. The woman may stimulate her partner in precisely the same manner. Here again, her instinctive reserve and intuition will generally be a guide as to when such a caress will help, and not seem lacking in delicacy. Again, too, the degree of experience of both partners will play a part.

Up to the present we have been concerned mainly with active love-play—forms of stimulation in which one of the partners has played an active role, or in which both have shared actively. Generally overlooked, but important, since many practise it, is the passive *contact of bodies*. This may lead to coitus and generally there will be an intermediate stage in which some of the forms of love-play already described will be employed. But in itself it involves nothing beyond the contact of bodies. It consists of the partners resting together in any position in which their bodies touch.

Thus one partner may read, while the other may simply snuggle in quietly, or both may read or rest. Some lovers will remain thus for hours, doing nothing, yet their senses will be aroused by bodily contact, an experience which they find pleasurable. *Passive* love-play, by the touching of bodies, makes them pleasurably conscious that they may be called to closer communion. And the moment will come when one of them makes the first move of active love-play—perhaps a kiss, or a stroking of the love-mate's body, or simply the whispered words of love which bring to life the desire which, in the passive-contact stage, has been only faintly felt.

The dividing line between the normal and the abnormal is exceedingly thin. It has been said, and with much more truth than one likes to believe, that any woman could make a pervert of any normal man within six months, provided that she went about the task with earnestness and art. For all perversions spring from the same impulse as love itself. The basic sexual impulse is there, but deviations of aim or object cause many people to miss the way of normal love, and so to follow strange paths. It is not easy, nor is it likely to prove of practical help, to catalogue various sexual practices and to mark some as normal, others as abnormal. Far better to follow the form which I adopt here, of indicating the methods of normal love technique, than to examine some of the byways of sex, with indications as to how people are led along them.

The great essential is to realise that normal love leads to genuine satisfaction. Deviated practices, originating in the lives of unhappy victims of abnormalities of various kinds, are sometimes imitated by those who think that wisdom comes from experience, and that pleasure is best ensured by 'trying anything once'. Supreme unwisdom comes from this tasting of every sexual 'joy', and the price which has to be paid is often high. Moreover, whilst sympathy is the right attitude to adopt towards those who are truly abnormal through no fault of their own the 'amateur perverts' are in a different category. They bring upon themselves, and often upon others, miseries which can easily be avoided.

Normal sexual intercourse is not easy to define, since in a sense it could be said that anything that was enjoyed and accepted by both partners was normal, certainly for them. It could, however, be regarded by society as abnormal. However, perhaps as good a definition as any would be intercourse which took place without the need of any artificial stimulants, or any act of cruelty, and which culminated with ejaculation into the female vagina in the case of the man, and orgasm on the part of the woman. I think, however, that whether or not the woman achieves orgasm is secondary to whether or not she enjoyed the act and feels fulfilled. The same could apply to a man.

As we know, many women never experience orgasm but none the less derive the greatest pleasure from love-play and intercourse. Furthermore, whilst orgasm for the male is readily defined it is not so in the case of the female. Some women are unable to tell you whether or not they have ever experienced orgasm, for the simple reason that its intensity seems to vary considerably. Moreover, a woman may experience physiological orgasm without an awareness of the fact.

There are some who believe that anything which leads

up to emission of the male semen into the vagina is normal. But this is not entirely true, for many sadists practise cruelty, yet finally enjoy coitus with the person they have ill-treated.

For those who are normal the best way in which to guard against becoming addicted to perverted practices is to develop a normal erotic technique. It bestows a pleasure which cannot be approached by any abnormal technique, and instead of resulting in an aftermath of remorse and morbidity it leaves a glow of health and happiness. Normality, too, is the best safeguard against the loss of virility. The words, spoken in jest by a young girl, are profoundly true: *'It's not the man in your life, but the life in your man that matters.'*

Thousands of married people are afraid of love-play they feel that there is something degrading in any contacts beyond 'chaste' kisses, by which they mean kisses with little or no passion in them, and the sexual act itself. They do not realise the vital importance of love-play not only for pleasure but for physiological reasons. *It is no less important than coitus itself. It is the key to happy and successful congress.*

The development of a sound technique in this sphere will enable the lovers to adopt a pleasing variety of stimuli, so that neither can feel certain of what is to follow. Too many make a routine of what should be a highly-skilled undertaking. The husband, as initiator, must be bold, and imaginative.

He must not make the mistake, which is all too common, of expecting his wife to be a virgin and sexually experienced at one and the same time. This absurd attitude springs from the insistence of some men upon a loose code for themselves and a strict one for their wives, the so-called 'double standard'. A husband cannot have it both ways. If he demands of the woman he marries that she be a virgin, then he must accept the fact that she will be

71

sexually inexperienced. This involves recognition of the
need for a good deal of patience and restraint in his approach. He must not be surprised if, at the outset, his
wife shows signs of repression and inhibition.

'To grasp quickly the subtleties of pleasure,' as Balzac
has said, 'to develop them, to give them a new style and
an original expression—therein lies a husband's genius.
Between two beings who are not in love this genius is
lasciviousness; but caresses over which love presides are
never lascivious.' The range of normal sexual intercourse
is wide enough to permit this. But the technique must be
mastered and applied.

5: How to Manage the Sex Act

A well-known American psychologist—John B. Watson —says that sex is 'admittedly the thing which causes the most shipwrecks in the happiness of men and women'. Most people would agree. Yet, in spite of all our modern education, 'frank' books, and lectures, most couples who enter the married state are 'matrimonial illiterates'.

They do not know the first thing about sexual relations. Yet they would scoff at the very idea that they need to know how to manage the sex act. But believe me an enormous amount of marital misery would disappear if only the married were fully informed on what has been called 'the supreme act of love'.

Most people think that they know all that there is to be known on this subject. But psychiatrists are constantly adding to our knowledge. Why, then, should the layman so often adopt a superior attitude?

The first point to bear in mind is this: love-play does not cease with coitus. It should be continued, ideally, during the actual sexual union. There are some positions for sexual congress which do not permit love-play to any great extent. But these are exceptional. Generally, caresses can be continued throughout the culminating act, and it is desirable that they should be maintained right through it, *and after*.

There is nothing more surprising—it comes as a shock to many women—than the manner in which their lover, once orgasm has been attained, seems to lose all interest.

They turn away and compose themselves for sleep. No wonder the woman feels slighted.

Sexual congress begins with the insertion of the penis into the vagina, but there should be no breaking-off of other relations then. On the contrary, the caresses should continue, so far as the position adopted for actual coitus permits.

It is necessary to stress this. Since many husbands, having learned of the importance of adequately preparing their wives for the act of union, tend to treat love-play and coitus as two completely separate phases. They pause after the former to decide on the best position for the latter, thus breaking continuity.

The object of love-play is twofold: to yield pleasure in itself and to prepare the parties, particularly the woman, for the final act. Clearly, then, any unnecessary pause or 'break' at this stage is unsatisfactory. Ideally, there should be a continuous intercourse with tension rising, naturally and inevitably, until the two bodies merge into one, and complete physical union reflects the emotional and spiritual union felt.

It is as though the tension has reached such a point that it *must* be relieved—indeed, that is how it should be—and the sexual act is the natural means of relieving this tension.

References to the man as the active partner in coitus, and to the woman as the passive party, have led many to suppose that women invariably remain passive during congress or, if they do not, that they must be creatures of exceptional sexuality. This is quite erroneous. For, in point of fact, the woman's reproductive organs are far from inactive even when she appears to be adopting a passive role.

Too many wives deliberately assume a purely passive role. They regard it as indelicate to show any signs of pleasure or to take an active part. This more often than not is the result of a faulty attitude of mind, usually due

74

to the influence of early upbringing or to ignorance of sex. There are men, too, who are surprised, possibly shocked, if their wives respond in a normal manner to their embraces.

The physiological effects which take place during erotic stimulation are much the same whether the woman be active or passive. The man generally becomes conscious of the changes which have taken place in the woman, and is stimulated by them. There is congestion of the woman's reproductive organs, whilst the clitoris becomes tense. At the same time the external genitals are moistened by the secretions of the mucous membrane of the vagina.

There are rhythmical contractions of the vagina which increase as the pace of union quickens, as it usually does. This is particularly marked during orgasm, the increased rate being followed by an increased flow of secretion.

Many women, once able to relax and abandon themselves in the sexual act, move their bodies in response to those of their mates. Thus they make of congress an act in which both partners mutually and *actively* co-operate. Reciprocity is an essential for ideal union.

That this is so is easily understood when it is realised that the excitement needed to secure the maximum pleasure in the sex act is obtained through a succession of movements yielding friction. These are of a stroking or thrusting nature, as the erect penis is brought into contact with the soft folds and pads of the walls of the vagina. In this manner there is stimulation of the nerves of the penis, especially the glans, which is relieved by the reflex discharge on ejaculation.

The pleasurable sensations are not by any means limited to the genital organ. The strong sensory impressions are conducted by the higher nerve system to all parts of the body. And release, when it comes, yields not merely local but complete gratification.

Most men prefer their partner to be prepared for the

final act. He may attain orgasm while the woman remains comparatively passive, but usually he likes his partner to adopt a more active role. The selfish man who does not bother about whether his wife is 'ready' for the final act or not, like so many selfish creatures, is just a fool. His selfishness loses him much joy. On the other hand, it must not be thought that mutual culmination is necessary— very far from it.

The strong physical stimulation aroused in the man as soon as his member is brought into contact with the woman's genitalia is immeasurably increased if she, on her side, is strongly aroused. Then, and only then, will she experience the congestion in her organs which adds so much to her own pleasure in congress, and also to that of her mate. It is only when the woman's organs are congested, and she, as well as the man, is in a state of 'erection', that the soft warmth of her vagina and vulva will clasp the penis, and add a gentle pressure, so increasing the voluptuousness of the act.

Having said all this, we must not overlook the fact that technique is not the be-all and end-all of the sex act. The real criterion is whether both parties are happy and satisfied in their union. No two individuals being alike, what makes one contented can make another discontented. It is necessary that married people should have some knowledge of the advantages and disadvantages of the principal positions for intercourse. Here I shall not endeavour to indicate *all* possible positions. Some 'love manuals', both Oriental and Continental, have listed over a hundred. My concern is simply to impart sufficient information to enable husbands and wives to know the effect of different attitudes, so that they can overcome any difficulties due to physical peculiarities and ensure variation in procedure so as to avoid monotony.

Many regard any departure from what has come to be considered the normal position for intercourse as somewhat indecent, if not positively obscene. There could be no greater mistake. In fact, *any* position can be used if there are no physiological or psychological reasons for avoiding it. In this, as in love-play, experiment is not only permissible but desirable.

Broadly speaking, positions for coitus may be divided into two main groups: those in which the partners are face to face, and those in which the woman's back is turned to the man. But these groupings have numerous divisions into which we need not enter in detail. Suffice it to say that the face-to-face category includes attitudes in which the woman lies on her back; in which both partners lie on their sides; and in which the man lies on his back. The second group (that in which the woman's back is turned to the man) includes all variations of this position.

1. *Usual Position.* Here the woman lies on her back, with legs apart and knees slightly raised, the man's body covering hers. There is a notable significance in this attitude, which reflects both the woman's desire to yield completely to the man she loves and his desire to possess her fully. It has the advantage of permitting the full range of love-play, the partners' bodies making contact as much as in any position, whilst kisses can be exchanged. Of course, the man partially supports himself on his elbows in order to lighten the weight of his body. The act completed, both can roll on to their sides—so that there is no loss of contact—and in each other's arms they can relax.

This position is suitable if the woman reaches her climax easily, as penetration is not particularly deep.

2. *Flexed Position.* As in usual position but the woman flexes her knees until they reach almost to her breasts and to the man's shoulders. It has the effect of shortening the vagina and constricting certain muscles, so that her clitoris is raised upwards, thus receiving stronger stimulation. Penetration is deep. If, however, the woman's uterus is particularly sensitive, coitus may prove painful, nor should

the inexperienced be in too great a haste to adopt this method. In this position it is difficult for the woman to contract her vaginal muscles, which makes penetration difficult if not impossible. It is useful, therefore, in those women who suffer from what is called vaginismus—i.e. muscular tightening and closing of the vagina. This condition is usually due to deep unconscious fear of intercourse. *It is a position to be avoided when the woman is pregnant; or soon after confinement.*

3. *Usual Extended Position.* The usual position is first assumed. Penetration having been affected, the woman then closes her legs, so that they lie between the man's legs.

This position is suitable for first intercourse, when, as we shall see in the following chapter, deep penetration is to be avoided. It can be employed whenever health considerations—such as pregnancy or congestion of the uterus or vagina—make deep penetration undesirable.

Advantages are that while deep penetration is avoided, the woman is given great pleasure by the excitation of the clitoris and of the labia majora. This position is useful, too, for men who do not get a full erection. The closed thighs help the penis to remain in the vagina, in spite of its lack of rigidity.

4. *Astride Position (face to face).* The man lies on his back for all astride positions, in a face-to-face attitude, so that *the woman definitely assumes the active role.*

Penetration is effected as the woman lowers herself until she is sitting on top of the man. She then raises and lowers her body rhythmically until culmination is attained. Many find this method exceptionally pleasurable.

For the woman it provides all the stimulation given by the other positions already described, together with the maximum stimulation of the mouth of the womb. Penetration is at its deepest and conception is less likely.

Such a position is most suitable when the man is tired

or lacking in sexual vigour, since the woman plays the active and he the passive role; indeed, he need make no movement.

A penis not fully erect is more likely to remain in position when this method is adopted, since it cannot readily slip out of the vagina. Among the disadvantages are the limited opportunities for love-play and lack of full contact between the bodies. However, in this position they have a full view of each other's bodies.

The position is unsuitable when the woman is not highly sexed and her partner is vigorous. Nor should this attitude be adopted during the earliest acts of intercourse, during pregnancy, or when the woman's vagina is short. It is a good position for the obese.

5. *Astride Attitude* (*from behind*). This is similar to the previous position, except that the woman's back is towards her partner. It can be varied by the woman's resting on her hands and knees, in which case penetration is slight. It is particularly suitable during pregnancy, after confinement, or, indeed, whenever the woman wants to control the degree of penetration, which she can do quite easily. It is also an ideal position when the male partner is obese.

6. *The Seated Position* (*from behind*) is similar, except that the woman sits astride the man with her back to him.

7. *Side Positions*. The partners lie on their sides, either in the face-to-face position or with the woman's back towards the man. These positions are favoured because of the manner in which they permit the sequence of love-play, coitus, after-play, and composure for sleep without a break in the continuity.

Ovid has said: 'Of love's thousand ways, a simple way and with least labour, this is: to lie on the right side, and half supine withal.'

Many believe that coitus is quite, or almost, impossible when the partners lie side by side. All that is necessary is that the woman should draw up the right leg if she is lying on her left side, the left leg if lying on her right side. When this procedure is followed intercourse in the side-by-side positions is simple enough.

It should be noted that in pregnancy, or whenever deep penetration is not desirable, the side-by-side position with the woman's back to the man is recommended. Deep penetration is difficult in that position.

From the brief remarks I have made regarding the various positions it will be gathered that not only individual preferences but health and other considerations can be taken into account by varying the attitudes adopted for coitus. For these reasons the tendency of so many people to adopt one, or perhaps two, attitudes, and to keep rigidly to them, is undesirable. Naturally, all possible variations are both normal and desirable.

It is through ignorance and a hypocritical attitude to sex that so many feel that experiment in this sphere is wrongful or degrading, and which is responsible for so much marital misery. The sooner we rid ourselves of these ideas the better. A full relationship should bring together body and mind at all levels and in all positions. It is for this reason that some of the positions have been described. At least it should help to break down the barriers erected by a sense of shyness, guilt or shame.

Our attitude of mind is of vital importance. We shall see, later, how it often lies at the root of frigidity in women, and impotence or weakness in men. Only those who regard sexual relations as perfectly normal and healthy can experience the true joys of the love act. It is necessary here to stress the mental and psychological aspect, for although the greater part of this chapter deals with purely physical matters, the most thorough understanding of them will not conduce to happy married relations if the right mental attitude is lacking.

In almost every activity of life success comes to those who consciously and deliberately *will* to achieve. Despite the great part which emotion and physical sensation play in the sex act, the willing to attain the desired end is of vital importance. In coitus partners should concentrate their full attention upon one thing: *the attainment of mutual pleasure and satisfaction.*

Business worries, domestic cares—these have been known to produce physical reactions which have made complete intercourse impossible. During intercourse a partner's thoughts may stray. From that moment the act can be robbed of its spontaneity and enjoyment. It is essential that the act of loving should reach heights which transcend technique consciousness. And this can only come about when we are able to be fully relaxed and at one with our partner and ourselves. There is nothing worse in the sex act than one part of ourselves thinking about the effects of what we are doing, yet another, watching this, and still another part of us doing the doing. As a technical performance we may be successful—but we will not be spiritually moved or lose our awareness of self as we are transcended into a different world.

It should hardly be necessary to state that absolute cleanliness of mind and body should be observed by both partners. It is surprising how often the elementary procedure of keeping one's genitals clean is ignored.

When intercourse has taken place during the night and it is hoped to repeat it in the morning, the parties might be well advised to take a bath before attempting the second union. Although of course this can be a matter of mutual taste.

The frequency of sexual relations is a subject upon which no ink has been spared through the centuries. All sorts of rules have been made, limits imposed, and so on. But so much depends upon the individuals concerned that it is utterly impossible to say, with assurance, where reasonable indulgence ends and excess begins. It is all a matter of adjustment. People have to find out for themselves what best meets the needs of their mates and themselves, in regard to both method and frequency. One thing is certain—sexual intercourse should only be indulged in when there is a natural desire to express mutual love. That's all that matters. For some this may be once a day, for others once a week or a month—in some it could be three times a day, others three times a year! But just so long as it is in response to a natural desire—not artificially produced—whatever the frequency, it is perfectly normal. Nor is there any law that love-making should take place only in the evening—or only in bed, whatever is mutually enjoyed is the yardstick by which we should measure the quantity, quality and place of our love. The point is, there is nothing abnormal in the number of times we make love, what can be abnormal are the reasons for it.

It is not of great help to learn that Luther urged 'twice a week'; that Mohammed advocated an interval of eight days between sexual acts; that Socrates thought ten days should elapse before coitus should be repeated. Different people, and even the same people at different periods in their lives, will have to provide different answers to the question: 'How often?'

But while personal needs must provide the answer, it is necessary to stress one point. On no account should lovers reach satiety. There should always be the feeling that there is something in reserve. 'Be moderate in all things' is sound advice in sexual relationships, as in other spheres. *Never make yourself tired of love.*

But although I have thought it desirable to pause to deal with one or two points arising out of our description of sexual congress and the various forms it may take, I have not finished with intercourse. For the culmination should not mark the end of intercourse—rather it represents the summit, and there is a certain way of going down the other side of the mountain. This final stage of intercourse is sometimes called the postlude, and it takes the form of after-play.

The man who, orgasm achieved, turns over to go to sleep, may deeply wound his partner's feelings. 'All he cares for is physical satisfaction—like an animal,' the woman may say, or, at any rate, think. That is an impression which must be guarded against. A kiss, a tender embrace, loving words—all these will help a wife to feel that she is genuinely loved and not wanted for her body alone. Quite understandably, a woman who desires orgasm but is left—colloquially speaking—'high and dry', resents this disregard of her needs.

Apart from this, a woman's sensations die down much less quickly than do the man's, which makes it all the more imperative for him to indulge in some form of after-play. If his wife wishes to attain orgasm he can bring this about through manual stimulation of her clitoris or vagina —or both. Indeed, many women find this is the only way they can achieve orgasm. Some prefer to be genitally kissed—and if a husband finds this acceptable there is no reason against it. There is nothing abnormal in these kinds of loving, other than that which the mind makes it so.

Let us be honest and admit that many men experience the desire to sleep as soon as orgasm has been attained. A woman seldom feels the same way, and so she feels hurt when, culmination reached, she is ignored.

When a couple have separate beds, and after congress is completed, it can be cruel for a man to hurry away from his wife. Of course, if the lovers go to sleep in each other's arms the fact that the man may fall asleep before his wife does not matter nearly so much. Her maternal feeling will go out to the man sleeping like a child on her breast.

It is when the physical act has been completed that true lovers rise together to the heights of spiritual communion. Their bodies, which so lately were joined, are now apart. But there is a union of the spirit which is strengthened by the afterglow of the physical union.

Let no thoughtlessness or selfishness spoil that.

6 : First Intercourse

Do not begin your marriage with a rape!

BALZAC

Marriages can largely be made or marred on the honeymoon. This is especially true of those cases where the bride
has had no previous sexual intercourse.

The old saying that 'the course of a wedding is determined by the wedding-night' is partly true for two reasons.
First, the significance of the occasion from the physical
standpoint; second, the tremendous emotional significance
of the occasion for the woman. To a lesser degree, something of the same significance applies to the man. Right
throughout life, women tend to place importance upon
'occasions', such as birthdays, anniversaries, etc. Dates
which marked changes in their lives, trifling though they
may be, nevertheless seem significant to them. These are
recalled throughout the years, celebrated in various ways
and treated with a seriousness which few men can appreciate. Thus a wife is likely to be much more troubled by
a husband's omission to remember her birthday than he
would be were the position reversed, and she the forgetful
one.

The great majority of wives look upon the honeymoon,
and particularly the wedding-night, as the greatest occasion of their lives. Whatever impressions are made then,
stay *right through life*. That is why it is hopelessly wrong

for the husband to regard the wedding-night solely, or even primarily, as an occasion for his own sexual gratification. If he regards it thus, not only will his own pleasure be marred but he will wound his wife emotionally and so their married life may be adversely affected.

Too many men feel that as long as they secure physical gratification their wives must also be equally satisfied—an impression which we have already seen is erroneous. But this is particularly likely to be the attitude of the uninstructed husband who may attribute lack of pleasurable excitement in his bride to sexual coldness, and even regard it as a sign of lack of affection.

The clumsy, brutal claiming of 'marital rights' frequently gives rise to inability on the wife's part to enjoy sexual union. Many such a wife thinks she must be 'under-sexed' or 'frigid', when in truth she is suffering from the effects of what to her was an alarming experience on the bridal night.

Nothing is unimportant on the wedding-night. In many respects, precisely how the husband should act must be left largely to his own judgement, because circumstances vary so much. Hard-and-fast rules cannot be laid down which apply equally in every case. Much depends upon whether the bride is totally inexperienced and, if not, upon the amount of experience which she has had. It is essential that the husband should be kind, considerate, and willing to wait, if necessary, before attempting complete consummation.

Of course, cases do occur in which the woman is much more experienced than the man. What follows, however, applies primarily to the much more frequent marriage of a man with some experience to a woman with little or no such experience.

It must be borne in mind that the average woman feels an instinctive urge to resist complete sexual union. This resistance is not entirely due to a fear of possible pain from the rupturing of the hymen, though that may play a part.

Much deeper is an instinctive recoil from full congress. This arises in part from the prospect of losing something which has been carefully protected. There is also often a deep-rooted feeling of embarrassment which may arise from early upbringing and social convention. And it is important—too important to be ignored.

The sense of shame is often so strong that it is felt in connection with intimacies outside of the actual sexual act. For instance, a bride who has gladly kissed and been kissed, who has willingly and happily consented to being touched by the hand, so that most of her body has been explored by her lover, may feel terrified at the very idea of appearing naked before him. True, she may look forward to doing so—in time. But the thought of a sudden revelation, so that there is nothing left for her to hide, fills her with fear.

In the same manner she may not welcome—as some others might—the sight of her nude husband. If he, as an example of what is sometimes called 'sexual athleticism', should feel a desire to display himself as quickly as possible, he would do well to restrain himself. For it is a fact that to a virgin the penis in erection appears *huge*, and often conveys an impression which leads to a combination of fear and distaste. The sudden shock thus produced may yield from that moment a dislike of all sexuality, which will render intercourse difficult, if not impossible.

Instances could be cited of brides who have fled from the bedroom when, on their wedding-night, the husbands, eager to impress them with their sexual endowment, have displayed themselves. The husband therefore should proceed slowly, realising that his task is to initiate his bride step by step into all phases of the sex relationship. If the honeymoon is to be the beginning of the married state, then much of the inevitable experimenting would be better carried out *in advance*.

Generally, too much is crowded into a limited period—perhaps into a mere matter of a few days. Worse, attempts are often made to force the pace so that marriage is consummated fully in one brief night. Unless there has been experiment and close intimacies, prior to marriage, this is nearly always attempting too much. For each partner to reveal all to the other; for each to be explored fully by the other; for defloration to be effected—is full of danger when the wife has had little sexual experience.

That literally nothing is unimportant on the wedding-night may be gathered from the effect which is sometimes produced by a chance remark, or even by a facial expression. The husband who uncovers himself too soon before a young bride may see in her eyes a look of terror, or, at least, of distaste. Or she may remark that she cannot bear to see 'that thing'. Some men are so wounded in their self-esteem by such trifles that they go through life feeling that there is something repugnant about themselves.

A patient told his doctor that for years his only sexual experience had been with prostitutes. With them he felt safe from too critical comment or dislike, since he paid them for 'putting up with me'! He had practised a form of mutual cuddling with his wife, which was usually sufficient to produce orgasm for him, but never since the wedding-night had he appeared naked in his wife's presence, nor had he again attempted intercourse with her. This was a case in which both husband and wife had been affected in different ways by a false step on the wedding-night. Similar instances could be multiplied.

In the *Encyclopaedia of Sexual Knowledge,* edited by Drs. A. Costler, A. Willy, and others, a somewhat similar case is recorded, although here the difficulty arose when a young man of twenty visited a prostitute. She laughed at his small member, and the same thing happened the second time he associated with a prostitute. So deeply wounded was his vanity that he not only went without any sexual relations for years, but actually decided that he would never marry.

Eventually he fell in love with a girl, but he felt that he could not possibly propose to her because of his disability. But one night, after taking her to a theatre and then seeing her home, he felt so lonely that he visited a cabaret where a prostitute found him easy prey. Once in her room, he again felt shame at his inadequacy. He made for the door, intending to leave. She stopped him, questioned him, learned of his obsession. Not only did she assure him that his organ was no smaller than most men's, but added: 'Why, I know many who would like to have one like it!'

Not entirely assured, the young man sought other expert advice—from another prostitute! She confirmed the previous verdict with the result that from then on the young man's obsession left him. He decided to marry, eventually becoming the father of two children.

These are, of course, extreme examples, none the less they illustrate how easily a chance remark can affect one's whole outlook. Few women seem to realise just how sensitive the average man is about his genital organs and sexual prowess. Despite an assumed self-assurance, the slightest wound to his pride can be disastrous in its effects. With women, as with men, obsessions are particularly likely to arise from any small incident, such as a disparaging remark, smile, or gesture on the wedding-night, when emotions are exceptionally sensitive. Many women, for example, are extremely self-conscious about their breasts. Others develop a fixed idea that they are unattractive when in fact they are quite attractive. Indeed, the great dislike of undressing before their husbands which some women show is often due to this.

All that has been said regarding love-play applies to the wedding-night with special force. When love-making is tender, and the husband's erotic technique good, the result will be a gradual growth of confidence, and with it will come a steady lessening of reluctance to give, or show, all, until this is replaced by the *desire* to do so.

Many a bride is hurt by the brusque attitude of her husband on the wedding-night. Often she is left to undress, perhaps urged to do so quickly, when in fact she should be initiated slowly. It may be better for the husband to wait until she is undressed before entering the bedroom, unless she suggests otherwise.

Clothes nowadays are so skilfully built around one's personality and body that they often tend to display to the world a very much more impressive figure than the naked man or woman.

The man wonders whether he is unmanly, or, being hairy, fears that his wife will liken him, mentally, to an ape. Whilst the broad-shouldered male who owes much to his tailor may be fearful of his slender physique, thin legs, narrow chest. The bride may have similar fears about her breasts, thighs, skin, and so on.

With the man, extreme sensitiveness is likely in regard to his sexual organ, for many men feel that all vitality, all manliness, all power to give sexual pleasure, is contained in their penis. Thus, as in the cases we have mentioned, the possession of a small member may give rise to a feeling of inferiority. Actually, some women prefer a small penis, just as some men prefer a large vagina.

Almost every demerit in build or appearance which one can think of may appeal to some. Since, however, the revelation usually comes only with marriage, little can be done about it, and we see once more how helpful preliminary petting can be.

But since most men desire a large organ and feel a sense of inadequacy if nature has not so endowed them, it is as well to point out that good technique in love-making, including that of the sexual act, is not dependant on the size of the penis. It is a fact that many men with large members are clumsy and inefficient lovers. A penis which is smaller than average can penetrate far enough to give and receive full pleasure.

This book is for men and women of *today*, and we need not pause to discuss the various explanations put forward to explain the sense of shame, felt by the young bride, or describe how it has been developed and influenced by clothing, customs, and other factors throughout the centuries. Suffice that it is usually there, and accordingly must be taken into account.

That clothes serve largely as a mask, hiding the 'secret' parts, explains it, to some extent; the woman undressed feels that her very soul is laid bare. This, however, is largely a matter of individual taste. Consider the manner in which a woman will appear at public functions in a very *décolleté* gown, where she may be seen by hundreds of eyes, yet, as soon as she is alone with a man, she will feel obliged to draw a wrap over her naked shoulders. In the same way strict conventional upbringing tends to impose barriers of restraint where none are needed, as during the early days of marriage. But it is just as well in the early days for a husband to respect such barriers.

Girls who from an early age have been taught that it is a sin to expose an inch of 'intimate garment' will not hesitate to disport themselves at the swimming pool in a 'bikini'. They will turn their heads so as not to see nudity should they encounter it. They find it hard to undress for the first time in the presence of a member of the opposite sex. It is a false shame, which should not exist in marriage. *But it none the less does.*

There is, of course, a less artificial sense of shame which puts a check on excess. This, however, is closely linked with self-respect, and is felt when self-respect is outraged. We cannot ignore the presence of this sense of shame, if we do we may rape a woman's very spirit—and this is a more grievous offence than to rape her body.

In a pamphlet issued by the British Society for the Study of Sex Psychology F. W. Stella Browne wrote: 'No woman has been given her full share of the beauty and the joy of life who has not been *very gradually* and *skilfully* initiated into the sexual relation. A really satisfactory lover must have insight and intuition as well as virility and passion; he must respect his mate's individuality and be able to exercise an iron self-control. His own enjoyment will be all the keener in the end.'

Many a husband feels that on his wedding-night he must prove his virility to the full, and that he owes this both to himself and to his wife. Thus he may inflict mental anguish upon her by exposing himself, by baring her body, and then causing her physical pain by thrusting his way through to sexual union.

In the *Encyclopaedia of Sexual Knowledge* the following very excellent advice to a young husband is given: 'On your wedding night *seduce* your wife by all means; but do it with delicacy and consideration, keeping in mind that the least false step will make in her heart wounds that will never heal.' And again: 'The marriage lines do not give the man *carte blanche* to do as he chooses; if the bride's modesty and instinctive resistance raise obstacles that are too great for him to seduce her, consummation of the marriage is better postponed for a night, several nights, or even for weeks, until she has accustomed herself to physical contact and learned *to desire actual penetration.*'

It must not be supposed from this that the man is advised to remain inactive until his wife makes a request for intercourse. He must seek to arouse her desire, and in so doing help to overcome any timidity or resistance. The average woman likes to feel herself conquered. The masterly touch of her lover is invariably pleasing. But brutal brushing aside of all resistance, ruthless disregard of pain inflicted, whether mental or physical, is quite another matter.

How necessary it is to proceed slowly in the education of a bride in erotic technique is shown by the fact that some authorities hold that complete sensibility in coitus is impossible for *any* woman until she has had some considerable experience. In these early days inability to enjoy sexual congress to anything like the full is normal. Women have to *learn* how to enjoy voluptuous pleasure. Their husbands can help them.

What has been said of love-play covers all that is necessary of technique needed by the young husband to bring his bride to a state of excitement where penetration is desired. But it must be emphasised that in the case of a little-experienced, virginal bride, love-play should be limited to kisses, tender stroking of the erogenous zones, whispered endearments, and so on.

It is safe to say that in a number of cases the inexperienced bride will not be pleasurably moved by attempts to stimulate her by way of the clitoris, indeed, it may have the opposite effect.

The body kiss, sometimes indicated as an invaluable help in bringing an inexperienced bride to the highly stimulated state where penetration is sought, should be ruled out for much the same reason. On the other hand, if she is 'virgin in body only'—that is, one who has had much experience short of actual defloration, full use can be made of this aid—if mutually desired.

Clearly, since we have counselled caution regarding exposure of the husband's or bride's body, we must urge still greater caution regarding the most intimate of all kinds of kiss. But the bridal night emphatically is not the right time, unless both parties are well aware of its usefulness and accordingly expect to employ it at an early stage.

Of course, when the parties have already practised deep petting much greater freedom is possible, and it will be expected and eagerly sought by both. Young husbands often inquire about the best method of effecting defloration. In the usual position, which is most likely to be adopted by a newly married couple, with the wife lying on her back, the husband will introduce the penis from the front and slightly above, pressing against the membrane until, after tensely stretching, it gives—or is split. As a rule the woman feels a little discomfort when this occurs, but it does not last long. Often there is a slight loss of blood, due to the tearing of the membrane.

Sometimes, however, the flow may be considerable. When this occurs the bride should close her legs, and lie still on her back. Seldom is anything more required.

There may be difficulty in effecting defloration. If, at the first attempt, the membrane is not ruptured, the effort should not be repeated. The next night, or much later, will suffice. Neither should the man feel that he is called upon to make exceptional efforts to ensure rupturing the hymen. That may produce fear and nervous strain in the bride, and so set up such acute fears that future pleasure in intercourse will be gravely prejudiced. A not-too-vigorous thrust forward on the man's part is needed—one which can be checked immediately if the bride obviously suffers pain, or if the resistance of the membrane is too great.

It should be noted, too, that a wife can assist defloration if, when her husband thrusts forward, she makes a marked response. Instead of remaining inactive, or drawing back slightly, she should make a slight counter-pressure towards her husband. This will facilitate the rupturing of the hymen.

The average woman wants to be 'possessed'. She expects her husband to 'take' her. Extreme nervousness on the man's part, undue hesitation, anything which robs the act of spontaneity, may lower her estimate of her lover. In exceptional cases women desire something approximating to a rape, they are of the masochistic type.

Extreme cases of this nature confess that, ideally, they would choose to be forcibly possessed—struggling hard all the time to resist the man and finally being overcome. Such a woman pictures, in her imagination, scenes in which the man she loves seizes her, and, in spite of all entreaties, possesses her. But mostly a woman demands, in her lover, a combination of masterfulness and kindliness, of confidence and consideration.

Two points need to be kept in mind should postponement of defloration prove necessary. First, constant unsuccessful attempts must be avoided; three, or at the most four, should be regarded as the maximum. Second, the issue should not be avoided, for prolonged postponement unquestionably is harmful. A doctor can always effect defloration surgically and this is a trifling operation which takes only a few minutes. When manual defloration has been tried but has proved difficult the membrane can be dilated to the requisite extent by means of vaginal dilators.

We have referred to the rape of a bride's spirit which can take place on the bridal night. Clearly a brutal first penetration can be described as physical rape. Gentle continuous pressure rather than force will usually prove sufficient.

Undoubtedly many husbands feel that they part with something precious, some right which is properly theirs, if they do not themselves effect defloration. Nevertheless, a growing number favour surgical defloration.

Whenever possible it is better still for the bride to *prepare herself* for defloration, as she may easily do. The method which I advocate is that for two or three weeks before the wedding a prospective bride should herself dilate her hymen, preferably when bathing, since warm water encourages relaxation and makes it easier. Dilation can be effected by gradually inserting first one, then two, and possibly three fingers into the vagina. Alternatively, the husband could manually dilate—starting with the gentle insertion of one finger, and then gradually attempting two. This should be done as a form of love-play and not carried further than the woman permits.

Defloration, whether surgical or otherwise, should only be attempted in the case of those who are afraid of the 'first night'. Others, of course, feel excessively embarrassed at the thought of the possible soiling of the bed-linen.

The kind of upbringing which tends to make girls, and men, to a lesser extent, feel that all sexual intercourse is in some way wicked, results in many inhibitions which are likely to reveal themselves most plainly on the bridal night. As a means of breaking these down, and as a sedative, a little alcohol can be very useful.

Love-play should be employed to the fullest extent, subject only to the limitations regarding hand stimulation of the bride's genital parts. Sweet words and endearments, together with intense admiration, which more than anything can kill shyness and awkwardness, must be expressed. The woman, not less than the man, should be active in love-play, ardently responding to every lead of the man, and herself taking the lead if she feels the urge to do so.

The kissing of her lover's body as well as his lips; the soft touching of the sensitive skin; the tactile stimulation of the spine—love-play such as this should be within the power of any bride who may not yet be prepared for all the stimulating technique which she will employ later. The man, guided by the degree of experience his bride possesses, but still more by her response to his caresses, will make use of all the technique he knows to arouse her desire for penetration.

In first intercourse no more than partial penetration should be sought. To ensure that deep penetration does not result from desire proving too strong and leading to loss of control, a position should be adopted in which the husband's legs are *outside* those of the woman. Thus, should he become over-excited, deep penetration would be impossible. This precaution is very necessary. Notwithstanding intentions to the contrary, a husband may easily be 'carried away' by the stimulation of congress, and so penetrate too deeply—regretting, immediately after, that he has done so.

What is sometimes termed 'labial love' may also be employed at first intercourse to provide pleasurable sensations to both parties, but without deep penetration. Here, all that is involved is the caressing, with the penis, of the woman's labia, both the outer and inner lips. Where such local genital stimulus goes hand in hand with expressions of love, there is a rapid rise of emotion linked with physical pleasure, leading towards further shared adventures, and anticipation of what lies ahead.

Satiety must on no account be reached on the bridal night. As we have seen, the woman has to be *taught*, gradually, how to enjoy love on its physical side. For the husband to attempt too much, even with the best of motives, is a mistake. It will be sufficient if his bride is aroused, wanting more, eagerly anticipating the further embraces of succeeding nights; indeed, it is best that this should be the case. Most women do not derive anything like the maximum enjoyment at first intercourse. Many are left with a feeling of disappointment, without, as a rule, having reached climax, and sometimes feeling a little cheated in consequence.

We have spoken of first intercourse on the wedding-night and it has been taken for granted that this is not only expected but is a 'must'. It seems to me a great pity that we should attempt to commune with our genital organs before having learned to commune with each other on total bodily levels. Prior to marriage we are brought up to believe that we can be in relationship with a member of the opposite sex with our minds and to a very little extent with our bodies. As a result of this type of upbringing, it is small wonder that just as 'fools rush in where angels fear to tread' so they genitally attempt to rush in. We feel that marriage gives us a licence for this behaviour—it is almost as if having been engaged for years we are over-anxious to express our new-found freedom. Many would find it much more rewarding and enrichening to confine themselves to total bodily relationships without thought of intercourse until such time as they felt physically at ease and relaxed with the other. This may take days, weeks, or months but the dividends are out of all propor-tion to the capital (patience) invested.

Of course, for some this would be an impossibility. I feel, however, that whenever possible this approach should be attempted.

7: Prolonged Intercourse

> If there are varieties (as of melody) between one erotic occasion
> and another, a man can always enjoy happiness with one and the
> same woman.
>
> BALZAC

Can intercourse be prolonged? Is there a method whereby
the tantalisingly brief spell of pleasurable sensations may
be lengthened? Many people, who have no desire whatever to experiment outside the area of the strictly normal,
ask these questions. They ask, too, how variety can be
introduced into their sexual experience.

Already the reader is familiar with a wide range of love-
play, and of positions for actual coitus, so that there is no
need to limit the embrace to brief love-play consisting of
a few kisses, followed by immediate congress.

In spite of experience of married life and of sexual intercourse, we have a vague feeling still lingering within us that
although physical communion is right between married
couples, it is something to be got over as quickly as possible. What produces this attitude? This: the failure of
married people completely to emancipate themselves from
the feeling that one should not enter too enthusiastically
into sexual relations.

That is why they accept intercourse as something inevitably of extremely brief duration. They often remark
that the pleasure of love, on its physical side, is overrated,

since coitus is 'over so quickly'. For them it *is* of brief duration.

They have become accustomed to making it so. But others, who prolong intercourse, have discovered that, provided they are prepared to forgo the most intense sensations which follow a more rapid approach and a culmination which is literally irresistible, they can, by exercising considerable self-control, prolong the act.

With every step forward something has to be left behind. And those who would prolong intercourse can do so only by substituting for the more intense sensations milder ones spread over a longer period.

In this connection it is interesting to note the effect of circumcision upon a man. This does not affect his sexual vigour in any way. But it unquestionably results in the tactile sensibility of the glans penis being less than in those who have not been circumcised. This usually results in the circumcised man taking longer to reach a climax. Indeed, it has been stated that one of the reasons for circumcision among certain primitive peoples was that it prolonged coitus.

The question has often been posed—does the man whose exposed glans takes longer to reach the summit of stimulation suffer in consequence from diminished sexual enjoyment? That he may not experience the same intensity of stimulation at any moment is probable. But that he gains from the prolongation of the act, even though his sensations may be less intense throughout, seems certain. Clearly, too, his partner gains. He is more able to bring her to the state of preparedness for the culmination. By adding to her stimulation he adds to his own pleasure. However, this is obviously a question on which one cannot generalise from the particular. Each must find his own way of obtaining maximum satisfaction not only for himself but for his partner.

Most authorities agree that it is perfectly normal and

understandable for people to desire to prolong the sexual act. Eastern races have devoted much attention to this. An Oriental who can prolong intercourse over a lengthy period is proud of his achievement. Why? Not merely because of any added pleasure he may directly derive but because he feels he has given greater enjoyment to the woman. In this respect the attitude of Eastern men is generally far ahead of that of men of the white races.

The use of a condom (rubber preventative) as a contraceptive device can prolong intercourse for some. Hot baths, too, which stimulate some people sexually, appear to have precisely the opposite effect on others. They seem to cool ardour, and so are regarded as an aid to the prolongation of intercourse.

Will-power can be exercised by many men as a means of withholding orgasm. Passion is reduced at will when it threatens to gain the upper hand. Extreme cases have been cited of men who, in order to turn their minds away from the sexual act, interrupt the proceedings in order to smoke, or even eat or drink. Such artificial means of distracting attention rob the act of its essential spontaneity, besides being likely to offend the woman's sense of the fitness of things.

But without going to such extremes it is possible to increase the time spent in actual intercourse by means of *coitus reservatus*. This is a form of coital play which, with practice, can be maintained for lengthy periods. It can be accompanied by orgasm in the woman. The man, too, can keep within the definition of normal congress. He can attain culmination using the method as a means of prolonged *coitus* rather than as a substitute for it.

Coitus reservatus (or Karezza) deserves serious consideration. This method of prolonging intercourse has been so widely condemned that it is worth examining in some detail, particularly as clinical evidence exists covering thirty years of the life of a community which widely practised it. This evidence certainly does not lend support to the solemn warnings which have been expressed against the method.

Dr. Robert Latou Dickinson, the eminent American gynaecologist, in his book *The Control of Contraception*, after discussing the Oneida community which practised coitus reservatus, says: 'The method has its place for a small number of couples desirous of a studied elaboration of gratification, and may some day develop a wider appeal as a refinement of method, but at present it is the cause of scoffing to the many, and of threat of apoplexy to one authority.'

Dr. Alice Stockham, in her book *Karezza*, described and advocates a method of intercourse which had as its aim the increase of 'spiritual delight' by means of manifestations of tenderness and love, without physical or mental fatigue. 'The caresses lead up to connection, and the sexes unite quietly and closely. Once the necessary control has been acquired, the two beings are fused and reach sublime spiritual joy. This union can be accompanied by slow, controlled motions, so that voluptuous thrills do not overbalance the desire for soft sensations. *If there is no wish to procreate*, the stormy violence of the orgasm will thus be avoided.'

Those who practised Karezza until they had become expert maintained that if love were mutual the intercourse could be prolonged for an hour or more, yielding complete satisfaction without emission or orgasm. 'After an hour the bodies relax, spiritual delight is increased, and new horizons are revealed with the renewal of strength.'

Dr. Marie Stopes said that there are 'marriages in which the husband is so undersexed that he cannot have ordinary union, save at very infrequent intervals, without a serious effect on his health. If such a man is married to a woman who has inherited a strong and frequent desire, both will suffer. It is just possible that for such people the method of Karezza might bring the health and peace they need; conserving the man's vital energy from the loss of which he suffers, and giving the woman the sense of union and physical nerve-soothing she requires.'

It must be remembered too that the woman can experience orgasm unless she chooses not to do so. Indeed, the majority of those who practise Karezza do so in order that the woman may be brought slowly, by soft sensations, to her culmination. The mutual avoidance of orgasm is employed only *as a method of preventing conception.*

This avoidance of orgasm is not essential to the method. It is the birth-control application of it, intended for use when the parties desire to avoid conception. There is no reason at all why it should not culminate in orgasm for both parties, and that it often does so is clear, since the community in America which practises the method has multiplied.

Dr. Dickinson's brief definition of Karezza (which is sometimes called Zugassant) is as follows: 'Prolonged intercourse, accompanied by maximum and varied excitement, with orgasm for the woman if desired; with no seminal emission—or rare external emission—but with the substitution of a gradual subsidence of feeling for the man. Much of the criticism, therefore, applies not to Karezza itself but to one form of it—that in which the woman forgoes orgasm.'

'The Oneida community began as a social and religious community, coitus reservatus being taught and practised by its members in days when plural marriage was permitted. During a period of thirty years, for which evidence is available, the community developed until it had three hundred members. The older members taught the young how to practise coitus reservatus as a standard method of birth-control. This form of intercourse was frequent and prolonged. On the average, it occurred every second night, when it was *continued for two or three hours*. With what result?

'Competent medical and gynaecological examination, at the end of the experiment, revealed no apparent harm among this selected group of people living under favourable circumstances. As further evidence, the fifty-eight children, who were conceived by parents deliberately selected, *present a level of health and intellect unparalleled in any group in eugenic literature.*'

Clinical evidence, covering a thirty years' period, and of so striking a character as this, seems to put the critics of Karezza on the defensive. One cannot help feeling that they have imperfectly understood the practice. Certainly little ground exists for objection to Dr. Marie Stopes's very guarded advocacy of it.

Most of the critics appear to take the view that coital play, prolonged in the manner indicated, leads to impotence. Here again one would like to know what evidence they can produce in support of the contention. The fact that the community which practises Karezza has grown, and now constitutes 'a rather ideal social group of two thousand people', after reversion to strict monogamy, does not support the claim that Karezza is unfavourable to continued virility.

It may appear that the practice is 'beyond the reach of average people'. But average people are so ill-informed on sexual matters, and follow so narrow a groove in their love-relationships, that they do not know what they can attain once they have improved their knowledge of love-technique. Given the will, they should not find this method beyond their reach. The refinements of love, its higher technique, demand skill born of knowledge, patience, and practice.

Dr. Alice Stockham's definition of what she advocates is as follows: 'During a lengthy period of perfect control, the whole being of each is merged into the other, and an exquisite exultation is experienced. This may be accompanied by a quiet motion, entirely under the subordination of the will, so that the thrill of passion may not go beyond a pleasurable exchange. With abundant time, and mutual reciprocity, the interchange becomes satisfactory and complete, without emission or crises.' She goes on to say that when in the course of an hour the physical tension subsides, the spiritual exultation increases.

Undoubtedly she attaches considerable importance to what she terms 'spiritual exultation'. That expression alone is sufficient to convince some that the practice must be beyond the power of the average married couple. Yet when we investigate the facts we often find that it is precisely these 'average' people who succeed in attaining to a satisfactory love-relationship. Those whose married lives are happy accept their happiness; indeed, they rather tend to take it for granted, assuming that people whose sex life is unsatisfactory are exceptions and not the rule.

In point of fact, prolonged coital play is by no means beyond the powers of the average married couple. I have found that where both partners recognise that marriage at its best involves a constant effort towards greater mutual adjustment they tend to develop in their love-relationship a merging of the physical and the spiritual, and so often that conscious effort causes them to practise Karezza.

In the past there has been an over-concentration on the physical aspects of sex at the expense of the mental and spiritual. It is not helpful to describe in great detail the technique and implications of the physical act of congress, and then to go on and assure the reader that, ideally, marriage includes union on the emotional and spiritual levels as well. The reader is left with the impression that there are three totally different unions to be effected, whereas in truth there is but one—a bodily and spiritual merging of two people. This total union, which represents marriage at its best, cannot be divided into separate compartments, one labelled sex, another intellectual interests, another spiritual ties, and so on.

A deeply felt spiritual union must inevitably affect the physical act. Naturally this may not be fully apparent in the early days of marriage, when experimentation inevitably occupies the foremost place. It is true that—except in a minority of cases—the lovers are not then deliberately experimenting in order to ascertain how best each may promote the other's welfare and happiness. But that is what they are in fact doing. It takes time for them to discover precisely how best to adapt their physical intimacies to their requirements. But if, as the years pass, they feel a fervent desire to make sexual union something more than a violent, passionate episode, but an expression of the admiration and love which each feels for the other, there is an inevitable tendency to prolong the act.

At best the physical embrace must express the emotional urge which is felt. During the early days of marriage, when the 'first fine rapture of love' is strongly felt, the tendency is naturally towards the more passionate, ardent embraces. As the years pass, however, if the first feelings of love were soundly based, and were not mere infatuation, the relationship assumes a less violently passionate nature. A quiet, comfortable reliance upon each other; the feeling of security which this gives; less passion, perhaps, but more understanding; fewer moments of excitement spent on the hill-tops, but more in a valley the level of which is higher than formerly. Is it surprising that, with the change from the more violent feelings to the quieter forms of love there comes the need for a softer and less fiery physical union?

Many, including the elderly, find this method ideally suited to their needs, and at the same time exactly expresses their mutual feelings.

I would like to quote the words of Dr. Wilfrid Lay. In

his book *A Plea for Monogamy* he describes the ability to exercise the measure of control which Karezza involves as 'the most potent factor possible in producing that superiority of virility over feminine power which proves the greatest fusing medium between the two partners'. He goes on to say that the accomplishment of the necessary control to withhold ejaculation in this way 'during which the husband can observe the greatest possible effect that man can have upon woman', gives to the husband 'a sense of exaltation that could not be paralleled—a feeling of power that produces in him a keenness and penetrating sense of satisfaction that he has never felt before.' 'After an experience of this kind he is fully alive, as he never was before, to the possibilities of erotic ecstasy emanating from the preliminaries and every several and separate phase of the love episode as responded to by his wife.'

Self-control, within marriage, yields possibilities which have been too little explored. It is true that the deliberate control necessary to prolong intercourse does not come easily to all. The authorities appear to be agreed on its beneficial effect upon the woman; the doubts which have been expressed relate to its effect upon the man. But I have found that a considerable number of husbands—particularly those who have been married for some years—accept Dr. Lay's conclusion that once the ability to práctise Karezza has been acquired, 'the former hurried, mechanical sexuality appears as a dry leaf compared with the full-blown rose of his present triumph'. 'He recognises that he has stepped from one level of existence to a higher plane of life; that he is human in a new and enlarged sense.'

Elsewhere we have seen that a woman's sexuality appears to be much more closely linked with her general emotional make-up than is a man's. That is why it is more difficult for her to regard sex as something separate from the rest of her life. The emotional side of a woman's nature is often little touched by physical union. She may gladly accept her husband's embraces and respond, happy in the knowledge that she is thus able to co-operate in affording him relief from tension. Many a wife goes on in this way for years. Her deepest nature is not touched by the sex act.

The gentle, prolonged intercourse of Karezza, on the other hand, tends to appeal to woman's emotional attitude. The very fact that the husband is deliberately holding himself in check, and is finding his own happiness in seeking, above all else, to ensure hers, is a powerful factor in drawing forth a response from his wife's deepest nature. A part of her being, a vital part which hitherto has remained untouched, is brought into being and expressed in the sex union. She cannot 'love' with her body only. Love to a woman is her whole existence, something inseparable from her other thoughts, activities, and life-goal. Only when her deepest nature is thus touched and expressed in the sex act can full and genuine union result. And when this is achieved the wife's deepest emotional and spiritual being is so intensely stirred that a sense of spiritual exultation is experienced.

Here we approach the highest attainable joys which marriage can yield. Some exponents of the enlightened Christian view of marriage insist that, at best, the sex episode should be of a sacramental nature. They maintain that the coming together in the physical embrace should be the outward and visible sign of the love which each partner feels for the other—the act which symbolises their devotion. Does any form of physical union better express this than Karezza?

That it takes time, patience, and a great deal of mutual effort directed towards happy adjustment is an argument for prolonged intercourse, not against it. It would be an advantage if young couples would take the sound advice given by the Rev. David R. Mace in his admirable book,

Does Sex Morality Matter?—that they should regard, say, the first five years of marriage as a sort of 'novitiate', during which they would think of their relationship as a process of gradual adaptation to each other.

'The period would, of course, be much shorter than this for some couples, and it might be even longer for others. But if the end of mutual adjustment is faithfully fulfilled, it will lead sooner or later to that rich, deep, mellow unity of mind and purpose, which grows out of the creative union of two personalities at all the levels of being, physical, mental and spiritual. This, and nothing less than this, is the divine purpose for men and women in marriage.'

It is worth stressing that when love is too easily gratified it tends to lose its charm and power. Freud has shown that this is true of both individuals and nations. 'It is easy to prove', he says, 'that the psychical value of the need for love sinks as soon as its satisfaction is made easy. An obstruction is needed to drive the libido upward, and where the natural obstructions to satisfaction do not apply, men have at all times conventionally inserted them, in order to be able to enjoy love. . . . In times when the satisfaction of love found no difficulties, as occasionally during the fall of ancient civilisations, love became worthless and life empty, and there was necessary a strong reactionary influence to restore the emotional values.'

Karezza creates an obstacle to quick and easy satisfaction. Both hold the basic instinct of sex in check for the purpose of mutual enrichment. That is a point worth noticing, for generally the assumption is that only the husband is called upon to exercise control. Consider this statement, made by a man aged fifty-one, who had been married for twenty-six years:

'Our sex life was, I should say, of the "up-and-down" kind for the first ten years or so. I suppose we felt a bit awkward about it. Anyway, we never took long over intercourse, and I must admit that the sex act was of a purely physical nature. Mark you, there was nothing gross or repugnant about it. Yet to speak of spiritual joys associated with it would be laughable.

'When I discovered that sex technique included careful preparation of the wife by means of love-play I tried very hard to improve matters. It came as a shock to me when I learned, after being married for fifteen years, that my wife had never once experienced orgasm. I wanted her to see a doctor, but she refused. She felt shy about it. Then I found that while my sex powers were becoming, so far as I could judge, rather less strong, I tended to withhold ejaculation for much longer periods than formerly. It seemed to me that there was no break in the love-play. Before it would have been true to say that our mating was in two parts, even when I was trying to apply the technique I had learned from books. There was the love-play, and there was the culmination. But as I gained power to withhold my ejaculation longer, I found that—slowly, but surely—the love-play merged into the full act. It became one continuous process.

'At first, my wife tended to be the more active partner in some respects. I found myself increasingly relying upon her slight movements. Of course, I can see now that we were still finding our way towards the full adjustment which we have achieved. For years, now, we have been able to enjoy a union which is infinitely more satisfying than anything we knew before. Whereas at one time the act lasted for perhaps two or three minutes, it now lasts for half an hour or more. If one shows a desire for rather more friction or contact, the other can easily respond. Thus we don't follow any set routine. There is a constant reciprocal love-play which cannot be broken up into stages, and sometimes my wife experiences orgasm twice in the course of a single embrace.'

I have quoted that statement because the man concerned was able to express himself clearly. Others who have had much the same experience have described results which reveal conclusively that (a) prolonged intercourse proves practicable for many people, but only after considerable experience and with a genuine desire to achieve mutual adaptation; (b) that the wife as well as the husband has to discover, by experience, the way to exercise the control needed; and (c) that, far from proving prejudical to either partner's welfare, this mature form of sexual intercourse yields joys which were unattainable in the more violent embraces of the earlier years of married life.

To lovers of the contemplative type, whose spiritual union is strong, and whose physical intimacies seem but a small part of the greater whole, the method must inevitably appeal. It meets the need, so often felt, particularly by people of refinement and intellectual superiority, for lengthy communion on a soft note, in preference to the more violent and speedy congress. For them it is the obvious method, once they understand it. And it is safe to say that a very large number of people, who have never heard the word 'Karezza', and have no idea that the practice forms the standard love-technique of a community in America, have discovered it for themselves as a result of loving experiments.

Ideally, it should be employed as coital-play leading up to orgasm. It then represents *controlled* congress. This controlled intercourse opens the way to variations *at will*. Therein lies its appeal.

It should be added what is possible for one will not necessarily be so for another. Suffice it to say that we express our sexual potential to the fullness of our particular capacities in the manner which suits both our partner, and ourselves.

8 : Causes of Sexual Failure

> I do not ask that the man of advanced age should play with his sexual powers, but that he should possess the consciousness of power to use them—that I demand.
>
> GEORGE HIRTH

Why is it impossible for some—men and women alike—to effect sexual union? Why do others, although neither impotent or sterile, experience various degrees of sexual weakness and so are unable to gain or give anything like the maximum pleasure in intercourse?

These questions are constantly being asked. One man once inquired: 'Am I impotent because I'm fat, or fat because I'm impotent?' He sensed a connection between obesity and sexual failure. And once he was restored to normal weight his sexual potency returned.

When illness accounts for sexual failure or weakness, the cure of the disease is usually the answer, but it is safe to say that in the majority of cases sexual failure springs from psychological, not physical, causes.

'Erection', in both men and women, is induced in two ways. It may be induced centrally—from the brain, when stimulating ideas or impressions have been received. Or it may arise from direct local stimulation. Failure to secure normal erection may likewise be due to mental impressions. Or it may spring from physical causes.

But before proceeding further let us be clear about terms. *Impotence* is inability to effect copulation. It means incapacity to attain an erection. Women who never enjoy —though they may perform—the sexual act are said to be *frigid*. Inability to procreate is the condition known as *sterility*, whether in men or women.

Most people do not realise that a man can be sterile. He can be, although he may still be able to enjoy intercourse. If no children result from a marriage, and the parties are known to desire a family, it is invariably assumed that *the wife* is sterile. For if a man is obviously sexually vigorous the whole world thinks he must be able to procreate.

It is totally wrong to assume that because a woman bears a large family she must be a good lover. She may be sexually cold yet be perfectly capable of having children. And a sterile woman, one who is completely incapable of becoming a mother, may be passionate, with a genius for love. She is the feminine counterpart of the 'virile' victim of male sterility.

Apart from impotence which is more or less permanent, temporary failure may occur. Many a man has feared that he has lost his sexual power when on some particular occasion he has failed to secure a normal erection. Trifles can cause this—absurd ones.

'Probably not one man in a thousand can emerge victoriously from the public congress', writes Vanette. He refers to a curious ceremony sometimes staged in the Middle Ages. Men accused of casting spells designed to render others impotent were compelled by the legal authorities to prove their own power—in public. If they failed they were adjudged guilty. The consciousness that hundreds of eyes were on them invariably resulted in temporary loss of their powers. As Vanette adds: 'Our natural parts are not always obedient to our will . . . they may be frozen when our hearts are burning.'

'Conscience doth make cowards of us all'—often at the most inconvenient times. Many a man indulging in an illicit love-affair has been astonished to find himself utterly incapable of taking what he has captured. The sense of guilt often stills ability to act. Passion remains, but the power to apply it goes.

The man who experiences a disaster such as this may brood over it. He may convince himself that he lacks virility. Depend upon it, he will find ample evidence to support his belief. As soon as a man satisfies himself that his sexual power is gone—gone it is. And if the psychological barrier can be broken down, potency returns.

Self-suggestion, which can work wonders in restoring powers that appear to have gone for good, can play havoc after a pronounced shock associated with the genitalia, in either sex. Painful defloration may result in a psychological trauma sufficient for a woman to associate it with intercourse for the rest of her life. And the man who once has failed to secure normal erection, just at the moment when he deemed it particularly desirable, may well persuade himself that henceforth he is impotent. *As long as he thinks so, he is.*

Custom, too, can play its part in promoting temporary impotence. Men who have grown accustomed to intercourse only at night, and whose hours of labour have been altered so that they sleep during the day, sometimes find that they cannot secure an erection outside of the accustomed hours. In his book *Impotence*, published in 1800. J. S. T. Frenzel describes the case of a man who for years had had intercourse only immediately on going to bed. He proved completely impotent when this habit was interrupted. He could attempt the act only in the early morning. But then his power failed him. Gradually, under treatment, his old potency returned. It was the break from habit which had caused the trouble.

Anything which is abhorrent—a word out of place, a gesture which disgusts, or anything which produces fear, such as illicit intercourse with the possibility of discovery ►—may yield temporary inability to complete the act. And this temporary failure may become lasting *through its effect on the mind*.

Many a youth fails to secure erection when attempting coitus for the first time. I have met men who have been impotent for years, and inquiry has revealed that their first attempts at congress failed. They often turned to masturbation for relief, certain that ordinary union was beyond their powers. In an extremely high proportion of such cases further inquiry has revealed that fear and nervousness were present during the first attempts.

Fear of being seen when performing the sex act in a field or some other place where people might pass; fear of contracting venereal disease—these and many other feelings frequently account for temporary loss of power. Autosuggestion does the rest. A very large proportion of men who never secure a normal erection can be cured simply by removing the mental barrier. Physically there is seldom anything wrong with them. The trouble springs from an attitude of mind. Early failure, hurtful to pride, has made its mark.

Nervous impotence, arising from such causes as these, is easily the most common. Malformations of the genitals do sometimes account for impotence, but such cases are extremely rare. In one Continental army a brigade of six thousand men produced only three such cases. These were, of course, all men fit for military service. It is probable that the proportion of such cases to total male population would be higher. But it is abundantly clear that only a very small proportion of impotent men suffer thus from purely physical causes. Acquired defects, psychological in origin, disable the overwhelming majority.

Obesity is generally accompanied by diminished sexual power in both sexes. This is hardly surprising. For the obese are slower in their movements and mental reactions than those of normal weight. Diminution of sexual capacity is therefore to be expected. Excess of fatty tissue goes side by side with a dulled sexual capacity, a fact which is being increasingly recognised.

Undernourishment, on the other hand, has precisely the same effect on the sexual powers. 'Even if he escapes impotence', says one author, 'an underfed man is always a poor lover.' Women do not doubt this. They generally regard it as their duty to try to persuade their husbands to eat as much as possible. They imagine that the more one eats, the fitter one must be.

The fat are seldom fit. They suffer loss of shapeliness—which does not help them as lovers. They find many of the most used positions for coitus difficult or impossible. And their ability to achieve full erection invariably lessens.

But it is not only excess of nourishment which leads to complete or partial impotence. Any other excess tends to have a similar result. Alcohol in moderation often serves to assist intercourse by breaking down inhibitions. But in excess it leads to impotence. No wonder Shakespeare said: 'It provokes the desire, but it takes away the performance.' The heavy drinker, like the over-eater, is likely to pay a heavy price for his excesses, of which a part—but only a part—is impotence.

Many men expect to become more or less impotent soon after they have attained the age of forty-five, or thereabouts, in the male 'change of life'. According to some authorities, there is a decline in sexual power at about the age of forty which is completely extinguished at about sixty-five. That no hard-and-fast rule is possible is proved by those who have become fathers when past the age of seventy.

One of the most remarkable cases on record is that of Thomas Parr. He reached the ripe old age of—one hundred and fifty-two years. When he was one hundred and twenty he remarried. His wife, according to the account given in *The Art of Prolonging Human Life*, by William Ebstein, which appeared in 1891, 'noticed no defects in

him on account of his age'. This, if true, which is unlikely, is an outstanding case. But it is a fact that complete
potency has definitely been observed in many men between seventy and eighty years of age.

It is a help to realise that our sexual capacity is not
certain to diminish greatly, or disappear, in early or late
middle age. Those who expect it to go, encourage it to
do so. Avoidance of extravagant behaviour in any form—
use and not abuse—together with a sound mental attitude,
help towards the maintenance of potency.

It is often asked whether tobacco aids or dulls the
sexual powers. Here, again, moderation is advised. Nico-
tine actually affects the genital secretions of those who
smoke to excess. Cases have been reported of men who,
while working in tobacco factories, have become impotent
only to find their powers completely restored with a
change of employment. Undoubtedly there is a measure
of truth in the following passage from the *Diary of the De
Goncourts*, quoted by Bloch in his *Sexual Life of our
Time*:

'There is an antagonism between tobacco and women.
The taste for the one diminishes the taste for the other. . . .
Passionate Lotharios usually give up smoking because they
feel or believe that tobacco diminishes their sexual appetite and their powers of love.' It must not be thought
from these references that there is harm in tobacco or
alcohol taken in moderation. It is *excess* which must be
guarded against. *Excess is the enemy of virility.*

Excessive smoking[1] does not only lead to reduced
virility—but of greater significance—to death, since it
appears that a relationship has been established between
heavy cigarette smoking and lung cancer. Indeed, no less
than one in eight of all heavy smokers are likely to die of
carcinoma of the lungs.

1 *How and When to Stop Smoking*, by Eustace Chesser, published
by Jarrolds.

A form of sexual weakness which is very common is premature ejaculation. Some men find it impossible to complete intercourse because love-play, or the slightest contact with the genitalia of a woman, brings immediate orgasm. If this occurs only occasionally there is no need to be unduly alarmed. Most men have at some time experienced this. Such unwelcome emissions may occur when, prior to the opportunity for congress, the man has been deeply stirred emotionally, or as a result of a lengthy period of abstention from intercourse.

It is when they become frequent that one needs to try to discover which factors are responsible. In the overwhelming majority the cause is psychological. Secret doubts as to potency, deep-rooted in some men, is one cause. Or it may be that a man loves someone with whom union is impossible, and that, whenever he seeks congress with another, the unsatisfactory substitution yields an unconscious distaste which expresses itself in premature ejaculation. On deeper emotional levels an unresolved Oedipal situation or an over-loving and over-possessive mother may be the cause.

Creative workers often suffer from this form of sexual weakness. Writers, artists, scientists, actors—all who 'throw themselves into their work' and spend their powers in this way—frequently seem too exhausted for intercourse, and may become impotent or suffer from sexual weakness. They are often extremely good lovers so far as love-play and, indeed, everything except actual coitus is concerned. There can be no doubt that creative work draws heavily upon the 'life force'. Men engaged in it may be impotent during heavy spells of work, but when relaxed their powers usually return.

This is so well recognised that some writers refer to 'literary man's impotence'. But it is not found only in artists and scientists. Intense nervous strain, a prolonged period of anxiety, may have much the same effect on others.

Such weakness can have an unfortunate effect on marriage and render the successful consummation of sexual contact impossible. Many a wife who has been stimulated by love-play into a state of expectancy and desire is exasperated beyond endurance when her husband proves powerless to complete the act. If this occurs again and again she may leave his roof, complaining bitterly that he is cruel to her. Yet the unhappy man's failure may be caused by anxiety to give his wife pleasure. His very eagerness to do so may result in fear of possible failure—and that, as we have seen, may induce premature ejaculation.

One piece of advice offered to men who suffer in this manner is that, after insertion has been effected, they should strive to withhold the orgasm by diversion of attention. Dr. William R. Houston, in his *Art of Treatment*, says: 'It is recommended that this be done by reciting the multiplication table and remaining quite still while the female conjoint is active in securing her own orgasm.' Needless to say, one should not perform this feat of memory *aloud*. The female conjoint is unlikely to be capable of entering into the spirit of the exercise—if, indeed, the male is. Another way for compensating for—if not overcoming—the difficulty, would be to indulge in after-play sufficient to effect orgasm, and so not leave one's wife dissatisfied. In some cases, this in itself, by lessening anxiety might help to overcome the premature ejaculation.

Frigidity in women is an all too frequent disorder. The term is often used to denote failure to achieve orgasm, but often such inability is present in women with strong sexual desire. They can hardly be regarded as 'frigid' when they are aflame with passion. Still they cannot achieve orgasm. Why?

It is important to find the answer to this question. Many

authorities maintain that one woman in every four *never* achieves an orgasm in the course of her sexual life. A hundred marriages carefully studied in the United States over a period of four years showed that no fewer than 46 per cent of the women never once experienced an orgasm during that time. In Britain the facts are no more encouraging.

In the Victorian era, when the 'Hush! Hush!' attitude towards sex was particularly marked, probably 75 per cent of British women never experienced orgasm. Even at the present time just over 50 per cent do so with any frequency, as was shown in the Chesser Report.[1] More than any other country, Britain has suffered from the effects of the false attitude to sex represented by the 'old morality', which nowhere was more strongly entrenched than in England, Scotland, Ireland, and Wales. Women had to pay a heavy price for it. They are still paying for it. It constitutes for men and women alike easily the greatest barrier to happy sexual relations.

Dr. Brunner, an eminent gynaecologist, has said that 'in the case of 50 per cent of the women in the eastern cantons of Switzerland, there is no question of passion in the real sense of the word . . . I can certify that half our women are ignorant of passion.' Inquiry among girls at Moscow University, made in 1923, showed that only 48 per cent derived any pleasure from their sexual relations. So one might go on citing evidence from country after country, all proving how few women really enjoy sexual intercourse to the full.

I add those last three words deliberately. For my experience has convinced me that *completely* frigid women are rare. Many a woman who never experiences an orgasm finds pleasurable excitement in love-play and coitus, although she is left 'high and dry', as one patient put it.

1 *The Sexual, Marital and Family Relationships of the English Woman.*

They enjoy intercourse up to a point. But they are never completely satisfied.

According to my own observation, most women who fail to experience orgasm can be classified in one of the following groups:

1. Those who seem quite unconcerned about sexual relations, whose minds are entirely occupied with domestic duties and the like, and who never expect to enjoy sexual union. Rather, they regard it as a duty—their obligation to their husbands, to be patiently borne.

2. The neurotic type. They often like kisses and caresses but dislike the final act. But in spite of this they are often concerned lest their dislike of coitus should imperil their marriage.[1]

3. Women of a warm and affectionate type, often vivacious and cheerful. They feel that sexual relations are not what they should be. They feel cheated. They seem vaguely to be groping for experiences which will compensate for what they feel they are missing.[1]

Those in the first group are usually good mothers, but poor lovemates, their thoughts being devoted to the children. They co-operate little or not at all in coitus, being content with an entirely passive role. Sexual congress is, for them, entirely a means of procreation. They are usually well content that it should be that and nothing more.

One-sided sexual intercourse is never particularly satisfactory. Both should play their parts. And here it should be noted that *simulation of orgasm* is within the power of most women. Eve, who proves so adept in the practice of femine arts which harmlessly deceive the male, can, once her eyes are opened to the need, simulate orgasm so well that it is almost impossible for the man to detect that genuine orgasm has not occurred.

Note, too, that if a woman is quite happy without orgasm there is not the slightest reason to fear that she

[1] See *Women and Love* by Eustace Chesser (Jarrolds).

will develop ill effects or frightening 'complexes'. I say this dogmatically, despite all that has been said to the contrary. Critics may say: 'Yes, but what about the husband? Even if the wife is happy without orgasm, and does not suffer from it, isn't he going to remain unsatisfied?' The answer is: 'No', unless his attitude of mind is such as to make him feel he is responsible—an insult to his virility.

These possible complexes have enjoyed far too much publicity. Today many people—particularly women—regard it as fashionable to have a complex. Only outsiders lack such a valuable topic of conversation. See the look of utter astonishment which often greets a denial that one has a complex! 'My dear—you simply *must* be joking!' But the plain—if unexciting—truth is that people who are happy do not develop complexes. It is those who feel irritated, discontented, who suffer in this way. Just so long as happiness and peace of mind are present, there is not much danger of psychological ills.

Various types are roughly grouped in the second division. Most conspicuous among them are women who seem to share the view expressed by Clement of Alexandria: 'A woman should expire with shame at the mere thought of being a woman.' They associate a sense of degradation with their genitalia, and with all that is in any way connected with them. They are victims of an upbringing which over-inhibits the normal expression of their sexuality.

Sometimes this sense of degradation arises from the absence of any sensible explanation when the menses first appear. They regard the menstrual function as something closely approximating the excretory system.

The third group consists of women who are suffering, in the great majority of cases, because of their husband's faulty technique—or lack of it. Generally, their problem can be solved only with their husband's co-operation. If the husbands can be made to see the error of their ways an improvement is usually effected.

Faulty technique, lack of love-play, and other faults of commission or omission on the husband's part are often offered as an explanation by the wife who has turned her attention elsewhere.

But what of the many husbands who realise that their wives do not desire abandon? Anxious not to 'inflict themselves' on their wives, yet fixed by strong desire, they may seek satisfaction outside the home. They may practise abandon with prostitutes. But in this way they only avoid the real issue. Far better to determine to overcome the difficulties.

Face them. They will grow worse if you run away from them. Too many people let love's joys largely escape them. They are unwilling to make an effort to retain them. Any effort demanded is amply justified.

The three groups of women dealt with cover most of the types—certainly the main ones. There are others, but they are not nearly so common as these. And often the others are extreme types—men-haters and other victims of psychological twists which go deeper than mere failure to experience orgasm in coitus.

Any man who has some understanding should, if married to a woman of the type mentioned in the third group, know how to bring her to orgasm. Usually the trouble arises from lack of adequate love-play by the husband, and from his failure to keep well in mind his partner's needs.

As for the others, the 'fault' may lie with the wife. No amount of stimulation of the clitoris, or other love-play, will overcome the deep-rooted inhibitions in some women. Indeed, it may but intensify their feeling of disgust and so make matters worse. Each case has to be studied on its merits. But it is well to remember that faulty upbringing, the root of so much trouble, can, with guidance, be overcome.

Whether or not a woman achieves orgasm can be quite unimportant. What is important is that she enjoys the sexual act at whatever level it is practised.

The question is not 'Do you achieve orgasm?' but 'Do you feel happy and contented with your sexual relationship?'

Undoubtedly, most men take it as a reflection on their virility if they are unable to give their wives orgasm, which is absolutely absurd. I am not, of course, referring to those husbands who only think of their own pleasure—*they* should feel ashamed—*they* are guilty. But a woman should not have to pretend to attain orgasm just because her husband's vanity is hurt and he is behaving like a big baby.

Over-anxiety to please sometimes results in sexual failure in women as well as men. A case in point is that of a woman whose erotic experience had been considerable, and who never experienced any difficulty until, following the birth of a child, she was ill for some time and then had to undergo an operation. Although restored to perfect health so far as careful physical examination could show, she still had bad headaches, and suffered much vexation because of her inability to enjoy her sexual relations as before.

Instruction in sex matters proved unnecessary, she was already well informed. One night, after her husband had attempted union with her and she had failed to respond, she almost fell asleep. While in that state of somnolence she faintly realised that her husband was trying again. She hardly bothered about it. The whole thing was 'beyond her'. And that very fact brought cure. For, since she was entirely unconcerned, utterly indifferent, her mind was freed at last from anxiety to succeed. The automatism which had prevented orgasm was released, and from then on she had no further difficulty.

Whenever a woman enjoys love-play, yet fails to enjoy

coitus, the probability is that the cause is psychological. How deep-rooted are inhibitions resulting from early experiences and, still more, early training, is proved by the manner in which women often reply to questions about their sex lives. They say that they are thankful that their husbands do not insist upon their marital rights too often. Or they adopt an attitude of utter disdain, and show plainly by their tone and manner they would much rather overlook entirely the sexual side of their lives.

More frigidity arises from early training which tends to put a stigma on sexual relations than from any other single source. Sex has been, and still is, represented as being something low and unworthy. The result is inhibitions which rob millions of people of their rightful measure of sexual satisfaction. Hundreds of thousands of people never know the joys of spontaneous union unless they have indulged in alcohol, which serves to break down the barriers. It is deplorable, but true, that people have to take alcohol to *enable them to be natural*. Surely this reveals how silly it all is.

Psychological factors lie behind both men's and women's inability to enjoy the sex act to the full except in specific circumstances, or with the help of some particular object. Detailed consideration of this aspect will come later.

Without going deeply into the matter here, it is enough to say that there are men who are potent only with girls who limp. There are women who cannot experience orgasm unless the partner is partly or fully clothed. There are others who can achieve erection only if certain odours are present. One could, indeed, list almost innumerable examples, some of them of a revolting character. And all are due to some early impression which has made its mark on the mind.

Nevertheless, while some fetishes are grossly abnormal many are harmless enough. But they limit the range of love in that certain conditions have to be fulfilled before full intercourse is possible. Without these essential conditions there is no potency.

Although the fear of being discovered performing the sexual act induces complete or partial failure in some cases, it may have the opposite effect in others. There are some women who *must* feel the danger of surprise if they are to attain an orgasm. There must be an element of *daring* in intercourse, as though they were defying authority. This attitude may have originated in early forbidden pleasures of a sexual nature. Often, once the whim has been satisfied and orgasm achieved, the sexual act can be fully enjoyed thereafter in the ordinary way.

Thus one woman who had not previously reached culmination had an intense orgasm when her husband, fully dressed, had intercourse with her in a secluded garden From that day onwards orgasm was attained without difficulty in more usual conditions.

Dr. Hirschfeld, in his book *Sexual Perversions*, tells of a young nobleman, who, in the interests of science and to further his ambition, vowed to abstain from sexual relations until he was thirty years old. He kept his vow and then appears to have decided that he would make up for lost time. He thought of love.

'But love did not answer his call. His most flattering seductions were wasted. Venus's capricious son continued to turn a deaf ear. Finally, he consulted me. I gave him treatment which, although lasting a long time, ended in his being cured.'

Mention must be made of *vaginismus*. This is part of the price some women have to pay for their husbands' mismanagement of the sex act. With others it arises from psychological factors. It is often associated with the idea of pain rather than pleasure in coitus. More often than not, however, it is resultant on a deep and unconscious fear of sexual intercourse. The body absolves the mind from recognising this fact.

The vaginal spasm is an involuntary contraction of the muscles of the vagina. The vaginal inlet becomes super-sensitive. Minor injuries—or rather, the memory of them —often cause it. The contractions may occur before insertion is effected. Or they may follow insertion. Women who suffer in this manner can usually be helped by psychological treatment.

What effect has 'change of life' in men and women upon the matters discussed in this chapter? Many men find the urge to copulate growing gradually less insistent after the age of forty or forty-five. Potency diminishes. But desire usually remains, although it is sometimes weaker than it was. Sexual pleasure—even orgasm—is often possible for many years after the capacity to achieve penetration has gone. Sometimes desire becomes more acute. This circumstance, coupled with the growing difficulty in satisfying the desire, may yield distressing consequences—as in those cases in which elderly men give expression to their desires in abnormal ways.

Many women retain their sexual appeal long after the menopause. Some whose love-lives have been marred by a constant fear of pregnancy really start to enjoy sexual relations when they know that conception cannot occur. Quite elderly couples enjoy intercourse, and there is no reason why they shouldn't.

1. *Do Not Frighten Your Powers Away.* Far too many people of both sexes do. Confidence—belief in one's powers—is as necessary in the realm of love as in any other sphere.

2. *Remember, Your Case is Not Exceptional.* Whatever your trouble, you are but one of a whole army. There are thousands as badly off as you, and probably thousands worse.

3. *Go to a Doctor You Really Trust.* The best doctor in the world is useless to you if he lacks your confidence.

4. *Wives should Visit the Doctor Alone.* Otherwise, the

husband will feel that his wife is simply carrying out doctor's instructions. No man likes his wife to base her technique on another man's orders.

5. *Patience is a Sex Virtue*—habit is a sin. Do not confuse the two. This book shows you the vital difference between them—the difference between expectancy and monotony.

6. *Do Not Choose the Second Best.* Substitutes are always unsatisfactory. Bring all your new knowledge of love technique to perfect physical union with the one you love.

7. *Quality—Not Quantity—Counts for Most* in Sexual relations. The supreme test for both men and women is the mutual satisfaction of the partners. 'Sexual athletes' often fail where the weakly endowed succeed. Love-technique can make the difference.

8. *Shun Sexual Stimulants.* They are mostly worthless 'remedies', marketed in the interest of 'get-rich-quick' manufacturers. Be guided by your doctor.

9. *Scientific Medical Remedies*—hormone therapy and the like—have come to the fore in recent years. They have their uses—and their limitations. Again, always be guided by a qualified practitioner. Sexual weakness and failure constitute a perfect gold-mine for quacks.

10. *Happiness is the True Test.* Bad effects occur when one or other of the parties experiences dissatisfaction. Never mind what books—including this—say you should do. If you are happy, and your partner is, too, *leave well enough alone.*

9: 'Youthful Pleasures' and their Effect

> Masturbation is a normal phenomenon which appears in the vast majority of healthy children, as well as in young adults who are, for some reason or another, unable to obtain the normal satisfaction of their sexual appetite for a long time after they have become sexually mature and ripe for mating.
>
> NORMAN HAIRE

Possibly when you were young you were told that 'self-abuse' leads to insanity and suicide. Most boys were. Many girls, too, were given the impression that dire ills must inevitably follow masturbation. Well, what is the truth?

The Kinsey Report, and indeed almost all investigations, have shown that almost 100 per cent of the male population have masturbated at some period or other in their lives. Very well, then. That brings us to this very striking point:

If All Masturbators Commited Suicide the Human Race would have Ceased to Exist Long Ago.

And if all who practised the 'solitary vice', as it is often called, really *did* become insane, there would be no sane people left in the world. An outstanding authority says: '*Everybody* masturbates. To this rule there is no exception, if we take into account unconscious masturbation.' But no one suffers the dire effects which the gloomy prophets have predicted.

The truth is that the absurd, and sometimes hysterical,

teaching against masturbation has done an enormous amount of harm. Parents, schoolmasters, and others, by warnings of terrible effects which must inevitably follow the practice, by cruel punishments imposed upon any found indulging in the 'vice', have themselves created deep-rooted impressions which have resulted in the very ills they attributed, utterly erroneously, to masturbation.

It is necessary to stress this because the false ideas which have been held for centuries cannot be removed by a few lectures, papers in scientific journals, or whole libraries of books. The evil the old-fashioned moralists did lives after them in many ways, as we have seen. But nowhere has their work left its mark more indelibly than upon the minds of people who, having practised masturbation, believe that the gravest ills must sooner or later afflict them.

The combination of ignorance and prejudice which formed the basis of the old, miscalled 'morality' accounts for a constant procession of men and women into the consulting-rooms of doctors and psychiatrists. One silly warning by an ignorant nurse in childhood days; one 'frank' talk on this intimate subject by a well-meaning but completely uninformed person; one violent punishment from a parent who, though he masturbated himself, firmly believed he must flog this vice out of his own children—these yield a harvest of ailments, mental, emotional, and physical, which often take months, if not years, to cure.

It needs to be stressed again and again that masturbation does *not* yield bad results. On the contrary, the practice is sometimes unavoidable, as we shall see. What we cannot avoid can hardly be labelled a 'sin'. And sometimes it is a *necessity*.

Most of the harm associated with the practice in the past has arisen through fears instilled by warnings about likely consequences. Scientific investigation has revealed conclusively that it is *these fears*, and not the actual masturbation, which have led to serious mental results.

Figures by experts show that the ages at which masturbation is practised most are twelve, thirteen, and fourteen. As to the frequency to which it is practised, the figures are remarkable. Very few cases exist of people who have masturbated once and never repeated the practice. One expert, indeed, tells how throughout many years of experience as a doctor he met only seven men and five women of whom this was true. Out of five hundred people included in a careful inquiry he conducted, 61 per cent indulged in the practice less than twice a week, and 39 per cent twice or more.

Contrary to a Widely Prevailing Impression, Masturbation is Never a Sexual Perversion.

Carried to excess it may be harmful, but so, too, may coitus, or for that matter eating and drinking. It is a normal phenomenon.

On the other hand, masturbation may be indulged in as a compensatory mechanism for discontent or unhappiness, or it may be symptomatic of problems relating to emotional growth and development. For example, let us assume that a boy is in poor relationship with his parents, that his father has, he feels, unjustifiably punished him—he may in these circumstances resort to masturbation as a release to his pent-up frustration and aggression.

Experts make a clear distinction between masturbation which is practised before, or simultaneously with, puberty, and adult masturbation. When a married man or woman, notwithstanding opportunities for intercourse, deliberately chooses masturbation or else indulges in mutual masturbation, it suggests a rather immature expression of sexuality. It is not, however, harmful or unhealthy, and often this is the only manner in which a woman can attain orgasm. Psychological considerations must often account for this withdrawal from normal intercourse. Of course, this does not apply to the unmarried adult; in his case masturbation might be the only outlet.

The psychological aspects are all-important. The child has a vague feeling of pleasure associated with the genital organs and often practises first masturbation with no sexual object at the back of his mind. Later, though, when the sexual idea is strong, masturbation invariably is accompanied by mental phantasies. There is usually a partner present—in imagination.

This is what Dr. Hesnard, whose researches into the subject have proved exceedingly helpful, says: 'The solitary pleasure is at first made up of a vague organic voluptuousness, a sort of sharp giddiness, hardly distinct from the satisfaction of a desire specifically localised in the genital organs. It is not accompanied by any psychological factors, nor by any mental representation. It is purely a conscious reflex.

'But it soon gives rise to reverie, first of all unconscious, and then vaguely directed towards normal erotic aims and objects or, less frequently, towards imaginary perverse complications.'

Many women have masturbated without deliberately choosing to do so. The highly arched seats of old-fashioned bicycles, men's saddles sometimes used by ladies when riding, and the old type of sewing-machine were all proved mechanical aids to masturbation.

Some married women masturbate because they fail to gain satisfaction from intercourse with their husbands. This is perfectly normal and healthy. Where there is complete freedom between the parties and an easy relaxation there is no reason why a husband should not masturbate whilst caressing his wife. Likewise, a wife can masturbate herself whilst being caressed. This removes the 'solitariness' from the act and at the same time brings the partners close together. Admittedly, not everyone can do this—it requires a great degree of emotional freedom. But in those cases where intercourse is difficult for one reason or another, or a wife can only obtain release through masturbation, doing so during a mutual embrace can be very satisfactory—physically and spiritually.

When either men or women indulge in masturbation in response to a natural urge ill effects are never discernible. But when the practice is linked with morbid fears the results are often unfortunate. Dr. Maurice Chidickel made a study of women in United States asylums. 'It is a strange and gloomy fact', he says, 'that the greatest number of girls who lost their minds through fear occurred among those who had a strict religious upbringing. Many of the inmates of the wards were profoundly religious.' He emphasises that many a woman's mental ill-health was aggravated by the fear of the consequences of masturbation.

One of the many cases he studied was that of a woman who first masturbated at the age of sixteen. She developed into a woman of a high intellectual level, but her life had been dogged by fears ever since a nurse had told her of the 'terrible effects' of masturbation. She suffered from all sorts of delusions and became psychotic.

One finds precisely the same sort of thing in this country. Time after time, when on the surface masturbation appears to have been the cause of mental derangement, inquiry reveals that the victim has been told or has read that fearful results must be expected. The old kind of upbringing, still not entirely gone, has cost a tremendous price by its insistence upon the wickedness of all sexual pleasure, and, particularly, its denunciation of masturbation. It has cost the suffering of millions of men and women.

It is said that a 'rose by any other name would smell as sweet', but the natural phenomenon of masturbation undoubtedly suffers from a name which has become closely linked with the idea of depravity. In this connection the amusing example given by Havelock Ellis springs to mind.

He tells of a lady whose life was devoted to propaganda in favour of social purity—as she conceived it. She was absolutely fanatical where this subject was concerned. One day, in order to gather ammunition for the fight against her enemies, she read a book about sex. To her horror she learned that for years she had been masturbating. The word stood for everything bad, to her; the practice, however—until she realised that this evil word applied to it— had seemed pleasant enough—all of which shows how ill-informed has been much of the fierce propaganda conducted on behalf of the old 'morality'.

From the practical standpoint it is important to bear in mind:

(a) That when a man or woman is in a state of sexual tension, without the opportunity of intercourse with a member of the opposite sex, masturbation can be the only outlet.

(b) That when such tension occurs—and not many are devoid of moments of intense sexual desire—definite psychological disturbances may result from continued repression.

(c) That nature usually defeats conscious refusal to meet her strong demands by taking matters into her own hands. Thus what are sometimes called 'wet dreams' or 'night pollutions' provide in possibly a less pleasant form nature's substitute for *deliberate* gratification and self-relief.

Those who wish to masturbate and deny themselves this means of relief may suffer later from sexual difficulties of one sort or another. Like all else, if we refuse to use our powers they diminish or depart. Those who strive against nature in this way are indulging in an unequal test, since nature ultimately wins. Their nights are often tormented and restless, and 'pollutions', if they occur, may give rise to a strong sense of shame and guilt.

References to erotic dreams must not be taken to indicate that they are abnormal. Exciting dreams accompanied by emission are frequent just before sexual maturity. There is no need to feel guilty about this.

In these dreams rarely is a loved person visualised, it is usually a stranger, or a vague figure which the dreamer feels he has met before, but cannot definitely identify. In the majority of cases the person is known by sight, but not the object of desire in the wakened state. Such dreams may even occur after sexual intercourse, and most commonly in young men.

With women the erotic dream may take a similar form, but it seldom results in orgasm. Whereas in men the result is often precisely the same as though intercourse had taken place, the erotic dream in women usually ends in sexual excitement and a strong desire for gratification, which is often relieved by conscious masturbation.

Daydreams are common to both sexes. They can be a constant source of psychological disturbance to some, for they arise from the demands of our sexual instinct. Our thoughts keep turning to sex, and concentration is rendered difficult.

There are few to whom the sexual urge does not come at some time or another and we may feel impelled to do something about it. Tension resultant on the congestion of our genital organs may be relieved by sublimation but masturbation in one form or another is usually more satisfying.

It is sometimes said that women who, prior to marriage, have grown accustomed to relieving sexual tension in this manner, tend later to become excited only through clitoral stimulation. There is something in this. Many undoubtedly show signs of lack of genital sensibility, and it is easy to understand that if they have grown accustomed to securing satisfaction by way of the clitoris, the vagina may become relatively insensible. But this is nothing to worry about.

This 'fixation of sensibility' in the clitoris arises from the fact that, owing to the presence of the hymen, masturbation is by way of the clitoris and not the vagina. And so it is that the external organs, the clitoris is particular, are the parts manually stimulated. Unless masturbation is practised for the wrong reasons there is no possibility of it making a girl unfit for marriage. An inquiry covering one hundred women who masturbated revealed that 95 per cent gave up the practice after marriage. Of the five who continued to do so, three were married to sexually inadequate husbands.

The very fact that nature makes physical intercourse possible long before society makes it permissible accounts for a good deal of conflict, with its resultant difficulties. Is it surprising that masturbation presents itself to the mind as the most natural, simple, and, indeed, innocent means of attaining relief?

In a work by Hirschfeld and Bohm there occurs this passage: 'The lies with which the phenomenon of masturbation has been surrounded must be destroyed. Youth must be liberated from the physical burden which is so hard to bear.'

The object of this chapter will have been attained if it has helped in that liberation.

10 : Sex Psychology

Psychology began as soon as man started to think. But only in recent years have doctors started to think much of psychology. Truth to tell, doctors are slow to adopt anything which develops outside of strictly medical channels. They deny—for as long as possible—that knowledge which comes from lay sources is knowledge at all. Which proves, I suppose, that doctors are human, just like other people.

Now, however, even the 'last ditchers' of orthodoxy in the medical profession realise the vital importance of psychological factors in health and disease. This means that they have added a very powerful weapon to their armoury. Of course, there are still some who tend to ignore it. Others accept it grudgingly. But, even so, the statement that 'all doctors are psychologists now' is not far from the truth.

Now, having covered most of the constructive side of love technique, we shall have to inquire into some of the dangers and pitfalls which surround the love-relationship. That means that we must be bold enough to face up to perversions which many people dare speak of only in whispers. We must start to find out how they arise. And that brings us immediately to psychology.

Psychological factors lie at the root of most sexual difficulties, and aberrations. And many of these psychological twists which prevent a happy sex life begin in childhood.

Sex does not come into being at maturity. It has a slow

growth from early beginnings in the baby. Obviously, as it develops through its various stages the mistaken attitude that any of its manifestations are shameful must inevitably affect our sexual expression.

The feeling that all sex impulses are bad gains in intensity throughout the years. In many adults it is strong enough to play havoc with their sexual activity. Guilt and anxiety go together. Small wonder, then, that the shadow of shame and fear is cast over the sex lives of millions.

When such feelings of anxiety or shame are excessive, psychological help may be necessary. Relaxation and healthy abandon are essential if sex is to be experienced as something natural and a part of total love.

Spoiled children frequently develop a 'mother- or father-fixation', which means that they will seek qualities which they admired in their mothers or fathers; they may even look for similar physical peculiarities, although they are totally unaware of 'why'. The search continues; thus boys tend to marry someone like their mother and girls someone like their father.

At first thought that may not be considered very serious, but in fact as a result sexual intercourse might well be felt as incest, which explains why many such marriages are never even consummated. The husband feels that all he needs is the companionship of his wife and her help in the home, and has little inclination for sexual intercourse, and vice versa.

Thus we find thousands of people, happily married up to a point, for whom physical union is out of the question. 'It would be like having relations with my own mother' was how one man put it. He had been a 'mother's darling' in childhood, had acquired a marked mother-fixation in consequence, and so had married someone who would *mother* him, not partner him in the sexual adventure which is what marriage should include.

It is our knowledge of psychology which has enabled us

to understand just how such ill-mating occurs, not to speak of the many sexual anomalies which we shall have to consider in the next few chapters. Psychology can give us the key which will clarify and help to resolve many of these problems.

Unwittingly, parents are often responsible for the development of sexual difficulties in their children. This is because many of the departures from normal in sex life spring from incidents which their children have witnessed. For example, a father's brutal or drunken sexual assault upon the mother can give rise to a severe psychological trauma in the child. And this, in turn, can in later years pervert adult sexual behaviour.

We have already seen how sexual experiences prior to marriage can provide psychological barriers to married happiness. Here is another example. It concerns a young woman of twenty-four. She was very much in love with her husband. Yet throughout a period of over two years she was unable to consummate her marriage.

Now what made this case so puzzling was that she had no objection whatever to intercourse. She eagerly desired it. Yet, curiously enough, no sooner did her husband attempt coitus than the young woman developed panic. There were no earlier experiences to explain this, and she was a virgin. Notwithstanding the panic which seized her on attempted intercourse, she was no 'bundle of nerves'. No, ordinarily she appeared to be a healthy, pleasant, normal young woman, of an affectionate type, and very much in love with her husband.

Naturally, her attitude was unaccountable to the three people most concerned—herself, her husband, and her doctor. The riddle was eventually solved by the doctor who by means of psychotherapy was able to ascertain something which, though quite unknown to her, was at the root of the trouble. It appeared that, although she was not 'damaged' physically in any way, she had been molested during her early adolescence.

That provided the key. This young woman, still a virgin, had locked up in her mind one idea which was very strong, and which revealed itself as soon as any attempt at intercourse was made. It was the idea of uncleanliness. The shock of that early attack upon her, although it was unsuccessful, had left its mark on her mind. How, and why?

Well, the experience had been a very unpleasant one. So she had repressed it, i.e. 'put it out of her mind'. But we cannot rid ourselves so easily of such things. We can push down deeper into the unconscious the impressions we do not like to think about. But we cannot get rid of them entirely. Quite true—she 'forgot' this unpleasant experience, but in the unconscious recesses of her mind the impression remained dormant—dormant until her husband's attempted intercourse which as a result was felt as an assault such as she had previously experienced.

In other words the emotional upset created in the first instance was felt all over again. There was a return to the same panic which had spurred her to fight frenziedly against the first attempt. Eventually when the repressed memory was recalled by psychological means she found it then possible to enjoy intercourse.

Now here is something which it is very important to note—something which is rarely realised:

The Premarital Factors which so Often Ruin Sexual Life are precisely those which we Find in Neurotic Individuals.

What are they? They are:

Spoiling . . . Fear . . . Anxiety.

These symptons usually have their foundations in early childhood, and are continued into adult life which explains the difficulties we experience in sexual intercourse. Thus it is clear that marital misfits are often made *in the home*.

The future married happiness of thousands is lost long

before they wed—lost under their parents' roof. Not a pleasant thought, is it?

Psychological reactions which prejudice the sex act are often produced by such bodily afflictions as halitosis, offensive body-odour, obesity, and so on. Take, for instance, an example of a man who returned from the war, with a suppurating wound in the face. It was accompanied by an exceedingly offensive odour. His wife, though she was devoted to her husband, was repelled by any sexual approach.

Anxious not to add to the terrible burden her husband had to bear, she was at pains not to let him know the true reason. The strain of the situation became too much for her, and ultimately her health completely broke down.

But enough of enumerating sexual difficulties arising from psychological causes. Besides those given in this and in earlier chapters, we shall have to consider others later on. Let us, therefore, turn to the available means of overcoming such difficulties.

Often a frank discussion with a trusted friend will suffice. Many a minor difficulty can be cleared up just as soon as the sufferer is able to take someone completely into his or her confidence. But the more deeply rooted psychological problems cannot be disposed of so readily. They involve a more searching probing into the unconscious mind. In this manner the real cause can be brought to light. Unfortunately, however, this is usually a lengthy procedure. More recently, shorter methods of psychotherapy have been practised with encouraging results.

In the past, the trouble has been that very few patients have been willing or able to discuss intimate personal difficulties freely and frankly, even with their own doctor or a psychologist.

The practitioner has been seeking to discover facts which the patient has tried to hide. There is a battle of wills.

Often, of course, the patient means to be as helpful as possible, but even when the desire to co-operate to the full is present, many a patient finds it impossible to discuss the intimate side of his life as frankly and clearly as he would, say, his business affairs. This is the reason not only for the lengthy treatment but for much disappointment and unsatisfactory results.

One method of overcoming reticence is to give some drug which keeps the patient just below the threshold of consciousness. In this state he can be induced to talk under conditions in which inhibiting influences are released. Those who, hitherto, had been most reluctant to describe the details of their intimate sex life, talk freely, without the slightest reluctance or shame. In addition, they often recall repressed experiences which have a vital bearing upon their difficulties.

It is curious that, while laymen often charge doctors with being slow to seize the benefits which psychological treatment can bestow—and the criticism is by no means always misplaced—they are apt to overlook the subtle ways in which doctors, often unconsciously, employ psychological aids. Quite apart from those sex problems which are our main concern here, it is remarkable how a doctor's assurance that all is well will often banish pains which are real enough to the patient. That oft-discussed 'bedside manner'—in spite of derision—is not without its value in promoting the recovery of a patient.

It is often of the greatest importance that the doctor should know the facts of a patient's sex life. Sometimes this is necessary when the patient comes to consult him about something which on the surface is not connected with this. Many who visit a busy doctor's consulting-room, complaining of a great variety of ills, are really suffering from the effects of sexual difficulties, although they may not know it.

If the doctor questions them upon that aspect of their

lives, they immediately display resistance, and so his efforts are defeated. Or it may take so long to overcome the patient's reluctance that sheer impatience with slow progress may prevent the doctor from learning the facts and effecting a cure.

Here is a story worth repeating. A County Councillor who was visiting a large mental hospital was impressed by the smallness of the staff responsible for the control of nearly a thousand inmates. Why, he wondered, were there not more frequent disorders?

'Tell me,' he said to the official who was showing him around, 'how it is that the inmates do not band together and overpower your small staff.' The official answered in a flash: 'Neurotics never co-operate.'

But wise folk do. And complete co-operation between physician and patient is never more essential to good results than during a search for the psychological causes of sexual ills. The right attitude to adopt is this:

Believe that a Cure is Possible.

Believe that You Can be Helped.

Believe that You Can Assist in the Good Work.

And after that, just stop worrying, since it does not help at all, and *Act on these Beliefs.*

For, in cases of psychological origin, the right psychological attitude to oneself, one's doctor, and life in general goes a very long way.

11 : Byways of Sex

Probably there is no healthy person in whom there does not
exist, at some time or other, some kind of supplement to his
normal sexual activity, to which we should be justified in giving
the name of 'perversity'.

FREUD

Our sexual development proceeds through normal stages
from infancy to adulthood when genital sexuality is the
main expression of our sexual instinct under normal conditions. It is not, however, the only method of sexual
expression in adults, for the habits from earlier periods of
development are still pleasurable and indulged in—as
well as sexual intercourse—for example, kissing, dressing
in order to attract, flirting both physically and mentally,
etc.

As Freud has said, there is no clear dividing line between
normal and abnormal sexual practices, or normality and
perversion. Most practices between consenting adults,
which are not harmful to either partner, and which lead
to normal sexual intercourse can be accepted as normal
variations. This, if only for the reason that we are all
made differently.

When, however, these variations are carried out as an
end in themselves, to the exclusion of sexual intercourse,
or when sexual satisfaction can only be attained in this
manner, then such practices can be regarded as somewhat
abnormal. These may take the form of homosexuality,

self love, or love displaced on to objects (fetishism), and many other deviations.

Deviated sexual practices can arise as a result of early upbringing and experiences, or from clear-cut mental illness. Often, however, no particular abnormality of upbringing or mental illness can be found, and in these cases it is likely that heredity is largely responsible for the sexual deviation.

It is possible that a small percentage of people, for example, are born with such tendencies, in much the same way that we are born with blue or brown eyes.

In other cases, deviations may be practised when there are no opportunities for normal sexual intercourse.

Most of us are tempted, every day, in many different ways. We cannot avoid being tempted. *What matters is how we handle our temptations*. We cannot be held responsible for our thoughts, because often these come to our minds without conscious volition. We must, on the other hand, be held responsible for our actions, except in certain rare instances when we might become the victim of an irresistible urge. This, however, is much less frequent than some would have us believe.

It is precisely the same with our sexual desires and phantasies. We cannot prevent their existence. How we deal with them is the real test of our character. We must not punish ourselves because some sexual deviated thought has thrust itself into consciousness. Those who mentally suffer because of dreams or conscious desires will be helped if they realise that, to a greater or lesser extent, almost every human being is confronted with the same difficulty. These tendencies within ourselves are most dangerous when, precisely as the result of our shocked reaction to them, we magnify their importance.

Look again at the quotation from Freud which heads this chapter. At first thought his words may appear alarming. But so complicated is the emotional make-up of each one of us, so full of legacies from the past—influences which have affected our lives—that it would indeed be surprising if there did not lurk within us all at least some slight tendencies towards those deviations from normal sexuality which, in their more pronounced forms, cause so much astonishment and disgust.

Mark you, a great deal depends upon what we are to regard as perverse and what is to be classified as normal. It is not my intention to list all possible practices, and to mark some as normal, some as perverse, some as borderline. I have my own ideas, but so have we all. It is surprising how hotly the 'admissibility' of various practices is discussed.

Freud made a vitally important contribution to our knowledge of the causes of sexual abnormalities. But in making the sweeping statement quoted he was undoubtedly using the term 'perversity' in a narrower sense than is usually understood.

On the other hand, it has been suggested that *anything* is permissible provided that one's partner enjoys it. Very little consideration reveals that this will not do at all. In the extreme case of a sadist and a masochist, even mutual murder might be held to be justified, which is clearly absurd. One must draw the line somewhere. But where?

That is the question. It is one which is not easily answered. Indeed, to lay down any hard-and-fast rule is exceedingly dangerous. So much depends upon the individuals concerned and their circumstances.

It is, however, worth observing that the dividing line between what is generally accepted as normal and what is clearly perverse, is an extremely thin one.

Almost every phase of normal sexual activity may be magnified until it alone matters. Thus we find all sorts of byways of sex taking the form of partial intercourse, in which a person loves another's foot, or breasts, or sexual organs, and performs acts which yield some degree of satisfaction but which, instead of leading up to coitus, becomes substitutes for it.

It would require a lengthy volume to describe even briefly *all* the factors which can lead some people along the byways of sex, away from the main course, until they find that they can no longer enjoy coitus. It is with these people that I am concerned in this chapter, not with those who, for some reason or other, have never been able to enjoy normal intercourse.

In a previous chapter I stressed the importance of variety. In doing so I have risked the condemnation of those who maintain that the sex act should consist of one thing, and that alone. But now we have reached the stage where I can indicate one of the reasons for such variety in addition to those previously given. It is this: There is more likelihood of indulging in perverse practices if our love technique is devoid of variety.

Many find their sexual life less satisfactory than it might be or even monotonous just because of this lack of variety, and so may experiment—'try anything once'. And, as we all know, the danger is that we may try again and again and again. Frequent repetition of a particular sexual practice often results in its gaining a firm grip. As Bloch says: 'The normal human being can become *accustomed* to the most diverse sexual aberrations so that these become perversions.'

But—and it is important to note this carefully—psychological factors very similar to those which, as we have seen, account for 'love at first sight', often lead otherwise normal and healthy people towards perverse practices.

You had no feeling of loathing towards those who fall in love with some trifling feature or mannerism in the beloved when you read earlier how such infatuations are produced. You may have smiled, but you were not shocked. Very well, then; you have no more reason to feel vastly superior or exceedingly righteous when you meet people who show a tendency towards abnormal sexual expression. For, in a great number of cases, their condition results from experiences which have left their mark on the unconscious mind. They can, however, produce tendencies which veer towards the byways of sex.

Unquestionably, love can be tinged with sadism or masochism—a love of cruelty for its own sake which represents a perversion of the sexual impulse.

The tendency to sadism is there. A campaign of violence, of outrages which at first shock, then become more or less customary, since they are so frequent, brings out this 'beast in man', as it is sometimes called. Tyrants who have practised cruelty have deliberately appealed to this baser side of man's nature. They have been fully aware of its existence.

Any regime which exercises cruelty towards opponents or helpless minorities brings sadistic tendencies to the surface. In the scientific books which delve deeply into the subject of sado-masochism many of the examples are drawn from revolutions, persecution campaigns, and the like.

Law keeps this tendency in check in normally regulated lands. But once law grows lax, or, worse still, actually encourages or supports such cruelties, sadism wins devotees by the thousands.

Striking evidence of this has been afforded by the fiendish cruelties perpetrated in concentration camps—and not only by the cruelties, but by the manner in which they were carried out. It has often been made a pastime, and as a result the basic sexual urge has, for many, become one of sadistic cruelty.

Cruelty is infectious. Many are attracted to practices which the instigators follow with such evident relish. And as a result the basic sexual impulse has become for many one of sadistic cruelty.

Once cruelty becomes 'the thing', once it is made

fashionable and restraints are removed, this invariably happens. It is not only in wars, revolutions, and campaigns of violence that we find this occurring. The same thing happens in other spheres where cruelty is permitted or encouraged, as we shall see in the next chapter.

The influence of fashion, too, is often seen when a perfectly normal person becomes a member of a 'set' devoted to perverse practices. The old saying about birds of a feather flocking together is true of perverts of every kind. They join clubs and other organisations where they know they can meet others similarly tainted. At certain schools, too, where perversions are practised, many innocent boys and girls are introduced to them.

Sexual abnormalities cover a wide range, and often a combination of them is present in the same person making classification rather difficult. We dearly love to label everything—and that is relatively easy so far as abnormality is concerned. What is difficult is to know how best to classify the individual patient. Often he does not fit into one grouping only, but presents a complex case in which a combination of anomalies exists.

One is reminded of the story, told by Mr. Alex Glendinning in *The Nineteenth Century*, of how a great queen was introduced to a famous American psychiatrist. 'This is Queen —— of ——', the psychiatrist was told. 'Oh, indeed. How interesting. And how long has she had this idea?' was his reply. He had become so accustomed to meeting people who thought that they were somebody else—and always somebody eminent—that it never occurred to him that he might actually meet a bona-fide wearer of a crown.

In much the same way, many experts can conceive of nothing worse than certain perversions which are abhorrent to them, yet they do not regard as nearly so terrible others which, in truth, originate in much the same way.

What they, and indeed all of us, have got to get firmly in our minds is this:

It may be as Cruel to Make Fun Of, or Despise, a Person who is Sexually Abnormal as it is to Laugh at a Cripple or a Hunchback.

When you read in the papers of how a man grossly misconducted himself in public do not immediately conclude, as do so many, that 'he ought to be flogged', but rather take the line: 'There, but for the grace of God, go I.' For, as likely as not, that man is the victim of circumstances which we do not understand, and which, possibly, the magistrate dealing with his case did not understand. It is true that in some cases imprisonment, flogging or some other form of punishment may make bad men good, but it would be more true to say that it makes bad men more bad.

Society's attitude to our emotional ill-health in general, and our sexual difficulties in particular, is such that it makes it difficult for the victim of a sexual aberration to seek medical advice. I think it would be safe to say that if only such people were able to do this there would be many fewer cases of gross sexual misconduct.

What we must realise, if we are to acquire a fair outlook upon such matters, is this: that sexual aberrations, however much we may deplore them, are not so much criminal acts deserving of hard punishment as maladies crying out for treatment. Let us be honest and admit that some are criminal acts deserving of punishment but the great majority of the sexually abnormal merit sympathy rather than punishment.

They are sick people. They dwell in the darkness. They are often extremely worried about their condition, and endure torments of the mind which are every bit as real as physical suffering. Forces which they cannot control compel them to perform actions which bring down upon them the contempt of their fellow men, and may lead them to prison. But, worst of all for many of them, there is the constant remorse, bewilderment and suffering, arising from a realisation that they are not like most people. They are not—but they are not all 'perverts'.

Now, that is a word which is thrown about very freely and ignorantly nowadays. Let us note what Dr. Hesnard, an authority on the subject, has to say about this.

'Perversion is a deviation of tendency in a normal sexual impulse, and can neither afford the individual any malignant pleasure nor appeal in any way to his desire for that which is forbidden; whereas perversity is a more or less abnormal quality in his character which impels him to do evil for its own sake, and to perform, or wish to perform, certain acts simply because they are forbidden.'

If you choose deliberately to experiment outside of the area of normal sexual activity, you run the risk of becoming perverted. It is the price to be paid for your perversity. But many find their sexual outlook and cravings perverted through no conscious fault of their own. The point to bear in mind is that not only does ample opportunity for variety of experience lie within the area of normal sexual practice, once the technique of love is mastered, but the highest pleasure is usually to be enjoyed within these bounds.

By far the most common sexual anomalies of our day are sadism and masochism. These are the positive and negative expressions of pain-craving. The sadist glories in inflicting pain, whether physical or mental. The masochist derives pleasure from suffering, the precise form it takes varying according to the individual taste.

In the normal sexual embrace, the man usually plays the active, aggressive, dominating part while the woman's role is generally more passive. She 'submits'—he 'possesses'. These expressions indicate accurately the normal relationship. Thus, to some extent aggressiveness in the male and submissiveness in the female are the general rule.

But in normal sex relations the man's aggressiveness and the woman's submissiveness are but means to an end —coitus. It is when these become the end itself instead of merely the means that the sexual impulse has begun to find expression along one of the byways. Then, a man may achieve ejaculation only after he has hurt his partner, either physically or mentally. A woman may be unable to experience orgasm unless she has been hurt. Or, as often happens, the man may desire to be hurt, humiliated, compelled to perform the most degrading tasks, finding in such pain and humiliation a substitute for normal intercourse. Some women can achieve orgasm only when they have 'mastered' a man, and this mastery may assume the form of pain-infliction, abuse, or mental torment.

I mention sado-masochism here because it enables me to illustrate how easily the well-recognised basic elements of normal intercourse can become the *main* consideration, so that one part of the whole becomes disproportionate, and ultimately replaces the sex act. In the next chapter I shall deal with the forms of sado-masochism which are the most common in this country.

We have seen how body kisses may play an exaggerated part in the sexual relationship. For those who replace coitus by this means of intercourse, cunnilinctus, as it is called, is often an act of self-abasement. It can be the sign of an excessively submissive devotion. A masochistic male, one with a tendency towards finding pleasure in suffering and humiliation, moves by way of the perfectly normal body kisses to one of the byways which lead him away from normality. Eventually he cannot enjoy full, normal union.

It is a mistake, however, to assume, as some do, that cunnilinctus is always a sign of masochism in the male. It may be a normal feeling of dependant devotion.

'SHE-MEN' AND 'HE-WOMEN'[1]

Homosexuality—love between individuals of the same sex, as it may briefly and roughly be defined—is not always, as some suppose, due to some fundamental defect. The he-women and the she-men, as they are sometimes called, are not born that way, at any rate in the majority of cases.

They become so because of the early experiences of life, and by events which are beyond their control. But here again there is probably a predisposition towards homo-sexuality, which experiences or events bring to the surface. Freud has said that to *a very great extent* homosexuality is acquired. I cannot entirely agree. Environment may produce a homosexual simply because a tendency was already present. Just as in the case of sado-masochism and other departures from normal, the experiences which will lead one person along a sexual byway have no similar effects on others. If it had not been for the original ten-dency towards homosexuality, the events which assume such importance, the contacts and experiences which loom so large when we study the individual case, might have yielded no marked results at all.

First of all, let us banish from our minds one very com-mon impression. It is widely believed that homosexual men are always effeminate in appearance; that all female homosexuals are 'mannish'. Some are. But appearances are often misleading in this as in other respects. 'He's so ob-viously homosexual' is often said of a young man who has acquired a somewhat feminine gait and manner. But you cannot tell as easily as that.

Because a woman's voice is low or hoarse do not assume that she is a Lesbian. The long, mannish stride of many modern girls is certainly no indication that they are homo-sexuals. Too many pride themselves upon being shrewd

1 *Odd Man Out* (Gollancz 1959), Dr. Eustace Chesser.

detectors of this and other abnormalities, and they are often wrong. Some homosexuals of both sexes are to all outward appearances normal.

Notwithstanding anything the law of the land may say, the genuine homosexual is suffering from a definitely pathological state. We need to exercise very great caution before we punish people for the inevitable consequences of that. Of course, this hardly applies to the homosexual who commits an act of gross indecency or who attempts to seduce the young.

Whatever physical acts homosexuals indulge in—provided they are genuine homosexuals and not fools engaged in 'trying anything once', or perhaps a second time to make sure—such acts are the outcome of the homosexual make-up. Your attitude will be kinder, more just and much more scientifically sound if you will always bear that in mind.

Just to prove how deep-seated the homosexual mentality is—male homosexuals dream of intercourse with other men, and women dream of love embraces with other women. Often a Lesbian dreams that she has become pregnant through intercourse with a woman. Is it surprising that the way of life, and particularly the sexual activity of such people, should follow the same course?

I have met more than one man who, previously apparently normal, has developed homosexual tendencies after being seduced. This term, applied to men, may surprise many. But it is literally true. Many a boy has been raped, for example, at our public schools.

There are cases, too, of women being raped by women. The victims, of either sex, often dislike the first experience intensely. In others it results in a tendency to seek a repetition of the act and so a strong desire for it is created.

Why go into this? Partly to show that many of us may be led along this particular byway of sex, and partly to answer the oft-asked question: What harm is done by a man who has relations with another? The answer is that he may change the whole current of the other's sex life. And this applies especially in the case of young boys. Like the heterosexual, the genuine homosexual—merely because he is a homosexual—has no right to seduce others and attempt to encourage them into a homosexual way of life.

Lesbianism (homosexuality in women) often begins with practices indulged in at school. Wherever women are brought close together, as in residential hostels, the staff sleeping quarters of large hotels, and so on, one may seduce many, and so the practice may spread.

But it must not be supposed that all boys and girls who indulge in mutual masturbation and other mildly homosexual practices become genuine homosexuals. In fact very few do. When girls have opportunities to meet men and experience normal relationships most of them abandon their former practices. The same thing happens when boys are able to enjoy heterosexual relationships with girls. But while for many the practices mentioned are substitutes until 'the real thing' becomes available, unfortunately there are some who never desire anything else.

It is clear, therefore, that some have a definite predisposition towards homosexuality. The tendency is there, but circumstances—often trifling experiences—bring it out.

Lesbians often have an urge which is directed not towards other Lesbians but towards normal girls. Indeed, they often admit that they intensely dislike other Lesbians. Thus they may deliberately seek to seduce normal girls, and win them over to their own particular practices.

It is sometimes said that homosexuals of both sexes worm their way into positions of authority in all sorts of organisations. There is no reason to believe that they do so more proportionately then heterosexuals. Belonging to a minority, however, they are more likely to be impelled into taking part in reform movements. Having suffered themselves, they are anxious to lessen the sufferings of others. Often a sense of injustice sits heavily upon them. They feel they are shunned, and resent it. They find that normal marriage is not for them, so once again they feel different. As a result of this there often arises a strong sense of injustice which finds expression in a reforming zeal. As a matter of fact, the homosexual on the whole belongs to a kindly and tolerant section of the community. Many are gifted, especially in the Arts. Of course, there are vicious persons among them, just as there are among other members of the community. But many homosexuals of both sexes seem to possess qualities which compensate them, to some extent at least, for the disability from which they suffer. I am, of course, referring to the genuine homosexual.

We have to remember that every individual has a measure of dual-sexuality. We are none of us *completely* masculine or completely feminine.

Sometimes homosexuals speak of their condition as being the result of 'accidents'. This is very largely true. The predisposition is there. Whether it becomes more than that or not depends very largely upon those outside factors which so often change people's lives.

'PEEPING TOMS' AND FEMALE 'WATCHERS'

From time to time cases are reported in the more sensational newspapers of men who have gone to the most surprising extremes in order to gain a glimpse of a woman undressing.

The abnormality known as voyeurism is, on the face of it, pretty harmless. But it often gets its victims into trouble. And it has given rise to quite an industry. The so-called 'blue cinemas', where private film shows are given, is part of it. The 'exhibitions' given in some brothels, and often witnessed by members of both sexes, are another.

From time to time word is whispered round London's West End that a 'blue' cinema show can be visited—at a high fee. The people who patronise such shows are not all deviated. Some are attracted by curiosity. More recently there has been a spate of theatre clubs in London, all specialising in shows which have enabled the artists to expose more of themselves than would be permitted in an ordinary theatre.

Linked up with this, too, is the indecent-postcard industry which operates all over the world. The League of Nations, through one of its committees, tried—without avail—to combat this traffic in postcards and photographs illustrating every form of sexual perversion as well as the normal act in its various positions.

Sometimes the witnessing of such scenes, whether actual or in pictures, still or moving, is an essential preliminary to intercourse. More often the excitement produced by seeing erotic pictures is sufficient to cause ejaculation. Sometimes, too, masturbation accompanies or follows the excitement produced by the pictures, or incidents actually witnessed.

Havelock Ellis has pointed out that 'to a certain extent' this tendency is absolutely normal. Indeed, this might be said of most departures from normality. Once more, what is usually a part of normal intercourse is magnified until it becomes the whole, or nearly the whole. Generally those who are victims of this abnormality are sexually weak, and need more than ordinary stimulation to provide any excitement. Or they may achieve nothing beyond masturbation, because of deep fears of sexual intercourse, and so they find visual aids useful in reinforcing their imagination.

Usually, voyeurism is regarded as solely a 'man's vice'. This is not wholly true. Many women like to witness sexual scenes, or watch naked men. But 'feminine modesty', or a desire not to seem lacking in it, generally causes women to make quite certain that they are not likely to be caught in the act. Moreover, women can usually explain their presence on such occasions. Indeed, when discovered watching men displaying themselves, women have been known (with a truly feminine lack of sportsmanship) to denounce the men for insulting them.

It must be noted that voyeurism can affect one's whole sexual life. Here is an illustration provided by Hirschfeld. It concerns an army officer, married, aged thirty-eight. His wife was fifteen years older than himself. Everything and everyone were against the marriage. His career, his relations, his high sense of dignity—all these he had to turn from to go to the arms of the prostitute he had married.

It was her walk that enchanted him. For hours he would follow the woman, watching her every movement as she was soliciting. He relinquished his commission in order to marry her, and confessed that for weeks he never even looked at her face. All that he desired was to watch her walk, and after marriage he insisted upon her walking about the room so that he could watch her. Once he had been thus aroused normal coitus was possible.

There you have an extension of voyeurism, and other examples could be cited.

Voyeurism is often linked with fetishism. In the case of the ex-officer it was the love of one particular kind of walk. Much the same thing often applies to garters, special kinds of underclothes—lace-edged, frilly, or plain —soiled linen, spotlessly clean linen, and a variety of other garments. Perversion is simply a matter of *diversion*. The basic sexual instinct is there but it is led away from its normal expression into a byway.

PEOPLE WHO LOVE THEMSELVES

When the love-energy is not directed to another person but is given to oneself we have what is called the auto-erotic or the narcissistic type. The child at one stage of its development, as we shall see later when we discuss how sex grows up in all of us, is interested almost entirely in his own body. Some people, however, remain largely at the infantile level of development in which interest in one's own body is natural and right, but hardly so when adults. They can be regarded as victims of an infantile sexual attitude.

They are usually extremely concerned about the cleanliness of their bodies. Often they have obsessional trends, such as frequent washing, fussing over themselves, and all manner of things. Whatever they touch—or touches them —must be perfect. They constantly seek medical advice in order to ascertain whether or not they are suffering from some illness or other. In extreme cases, these unhappy people lapse into mental illness.

As with other deviations from normal, pathological auto-erotism, or self-love, is found in varying degrees in different persons. The majority are shocked when they come across a marked auto-erotic personality and tend to forget that we are all endowed with some measure of self-love. It is as well to bear this in mind when considering the subject; the knowledge helps us to avoid a feeling of unjustifiable superiority over those who all too often are the victims of a set-back in their emotional development.

They go through life utterly self-centred. Whatever the cost, they demand satisfaction of their desires. Just as the baby, at a certain stage, is astonished if its wants are not immediately and fully met, these grown-up people with infantile self-love expect the world to give them exactly what they want. Of course, it does not do so, and so there may be mental and emotional upset.

As far as direct sexual expression is concerned, this usually takes the form of masturbation, even although they may struggle against it. Since, however, they are in love with themselves there is little, if any, other form of sex expression open to them. Narcissism was described by Havelock Ellis as 'the extreme and most highly developed form of auto-erotism'. It is generally accepted that this condition is more prevalent among women than men. Some assume that it is a feminine monopoly, but men too display all the marks of narcissism. The male narcissist usually chooses, if he can obtain it, work which gives him a good deal of the limelight.

Narcissistic men are sometimes described as nervous lovers. Here again their interest in themselves results in their striving to gain the love of women. But the first kiss of surrender is sufficient to change the apparently ardent lover into a completely indifferent person, at any rate so far as his love-object is concerned. He strives hard to win his lady, but, having won her, and thus pandered to his overwhelming vanity, he turns his attention to the winning of further triumphs.

The outstanding feature of narcissism is that sexual emotions are absorbed, and often apparently lost, in self-admiration. Girls who are narcissistic sometimes spend hours before a mirror studying and admiring every little detail of what they see. Needless to say, narcissists of either sex resent criticism. They make bitter enemies, and are bad targets for humour, although their own humour may be cutting.

There is, of course, a certain measure of narcissism in all of us. But when carried to excess so that self comes before all other considerations, and attention and admiration are exclusively on oneself, then the markedly narcissistic element is present.

Some narcissists have even been known to experience ejaculation whilst admiring themselves in front of a mirror.

STEALING AS A FORM OF SEX EXPRESSION

Reports of apparently inexplicable thefts, often of quite trifling items of small value by women who certainly did not need them, have drawn public attention to erotic kleptomania. Sometimes wealthy women go from store to store, stealing various articles at each one. When caught and brought into court they express sorrow at their conduct, and state that they were the victims of irresistible impulses.

There is no need here to go into details regarding the somewhat complicated processes which lead to such strange actions. Briefly, it may be said that some women, usually those whose sexual appetite has been aroused, but unsatisfied—those married to impotent husbands, for instance—find in such thefts a substitute for normal sexual gratification. It has been found that in some cases the women concerned have faced the risk of public trial, and possible fine or imprisonment, merely in order to steal a piece of silk, a glove, or some other trifle, *which they may even have thrown away shortly afterwards.*

Women who suffer in this way—and I think 'suffer' is the correct term—are indeed to be pitied. What makes their lot harder is the impossibility, in most cases, of showing that their actions are not common thefts. They constitute a difficult problem for magistrates, and let us admit that they also constitute a problem for many a psychologist, who finds it difficult to make a diagnosis of true kleptomania.

Surprising though it may appear, some women may even experience orgasm while engaged in stealing in this way. Others, however, gain no direct satisfaction, but experience a sense of emotional elation, followed by an easing of the tension which they felt previously. The cases which come before the courts by no means exaggerate the prevalence of this strange deviation from normal. Some are conscious that their difficulties have a sexual origin. Others, on the other hand, have no idea that sex enters into their problem. Inquiry, however, usually reveals that their sex life is not entirely satisfactory.

These, then, are some—but by no means all—of the forms which sexual deviations from normal may assume. It is desirable that we should know something of the devious channels into which the love-energy may be forced, for to be forewarned is to be forearmed. Later in this book we shall note how normal physical and emotional growth proceeds, and how deviations occur. We shall then go into greater detail regarding the influences which produce the departures from normality which we have noted in this chapter.

Meanwhile it is sufficient to say that in all such cases the first essential is to discover the cause of the diversion of the sexual instinct.

Once the cause has been found it is more likely that we can be helped. But since the causes of such diversions are many, it is clearly impossible to describe methods of treatment. The therapist must deal with each case along individual lines.

To understand how these various perversions and anomalies can arise is one thing, to suggest that we are the complete victims of such urges is another. It is true that there are some who unfortunately are so constituted that they are unable to exercise any control over their actions. They are the minority. For the great majority, at least a certain degree of control can be exercised and there can, therefore, be little justification for indulging in conduct which may bring them into conflict with the law.

We must also appreciate that what may be unnatural for

one may, in a sense, be natural for another. Furthermore, that the dividing line between normality and abnormality is a very fine one. The knowledge we have of sexual aberrations should help us to sense their possible existence in ourselves, and better enable us to fight against their expression if we should feel so tempted.

On the other hand, sexual perversions which are accepted by both parties and are mutually satisfying, need not give rise to anxiety, just so long as they are not socially injurious. For example, I knew a man who collected corsets, and from time to time wore one. He found it stimulating and this enabled him to have normal intercourse with his wife. She was, however, most upset when she made the discovery and behaved as if it were the end of the world. To have cured her husband of his strange desire might have been impossible, it was easier to get his wife to accept his love of corsets—and his love of her. And this was probably the best solution.

RIGHT ANGLES ON PERVERSIONS

1. *'Judge not that ye be not judged.'* Often two persons imagine each other to be perverts of some type or other, only to find, ultimately, that each is wrong.

2. *Remember that a little knowledge is a dangerous thing* when it is used in a sphere where *much* knowledge is required in order to be certain. What you have learned from the preceding chapter should be useful to you in many ways. But it does not qualify you to assess the precise failings of all and sundry. Experts often find it hard to get to the root of a perversion. *Don't you try.*

3. *Be honest with yourself.* Then be the same with your doctor. Tell him all the facts, and you will be on the path to improvement.

4. *The more you understand of sexual anomalies, the*

more understanding you become. The harsh critics invariably are ignorant. Generally, they have marked perverse streaks in themselves, but do not know it.

5. *Watch for this danger-signal.* It is when you desire to roam outside of your regular love union in quest of experiences that you need to be suspicious of yourself. The love relationship provides ample opportunities for variety and experiment. Make full use of it.

6. *See a doctor who specialises in psychology.* Perversions cannot be treated like pimples. Psychological in origin, they require psychological treatment.

7. *Don't say: 'I can't help myself; I'm made that way.'* You may be one of the many who have a predisposition to some abnormality or other, but that is no reason why you should throw in the sponge. If you have a tendency towards rheumatism you don't sit in a cold, damp cellar. Why rush into experiments likely to throw your sexual life out of joint?

8. *Always bear in mind that the highest joys lie in normal sex relations.* Run no risks of losing them. Be sorry for those who do.

9. *'He that is without sin among you, let him cast the first stone.'* The greatest of all authorities on men and morals said that. Act upon it.

12 : Painful Pleasures

Somebody ought to write a book entitled 'Problem Parents'.

We hear a lot about problem children nowadays. We devote much time, trouble, and money to trying to assist them. We might well go a step further and get right down to the real roots of the trouble—*faulty parental technique*.

With the parents we must group those other educators of the young—schoolmasters, governesses, heads of reformatories and of training establishments. For in their ignorance—and sometimes without that excuse—and in their selfish cruelty, these preceptors have been responsible for some of the most widespread sexual aberrations.

The hypocritical advocates of the 'old morality' were generally firm believers in the rod. Many gloried in its use. And they believed there was only one part of the anatomy to which it should be applied. Often child-whipping was indulged in not so much as a punishment of the child but as a satisfaction in itself. There is ample evidence to prove this.

The result is that today many thousands of men and women ENJOY flagellation. Some like to inflict it upon others. Some prefer to suffer chastisement.

It is safe to say that those who are not familiar with the less pleasant aspects of life would be astonished to learn how prevalent are certain sexual aberrations which are linked with the giving or receiving of punishment.

We have already seen how sado-masochism sometimes arises, but it is safe to say that few readers realise how widespread is flagellation, one form which this perversion assumes. It may seem surprising, but it is nevertheless true that there are thousands of people who find delight in chastising others. There are thousands more who experience sexual pleasure when subjected to corporal punishment.

The givers can be described as sadists; the receivers as masochists. The range is very wide. It extends from 'Schoolmaster's Sadism', which takes the form of an urge to cane or otherwise punish children, to the abhorrent sex crime, which can result in murder.

There are men and women who genuinely like to be humiliated and abused in every possible way. Some are even prepared to pay for this.

Because of the manner in which such byways of sex can grow up in us, it is a subject which needs to be frankly and seriously dealt with. It is also one which, in the interests of society, should be studied more carefully, particularly by those concerned with the administration of the law and the punishment of offenders.

Some years ago the police, in a large-scale 'clean-up' both in London and in certain provincial cities, raided various establishments which existed primarily to satisfy the cravings of such deviants. Some of the establishments which were closed in consequence had been making enormous profits for years. Not only did they provide girls who were willing to prostitute themselves in this way, but they satisfied the needs of certain 'clients', male and female, who *themselves* desired to be so treated.

It is vital that we should understand how such men and women acquire and develop their taste for these strange pleasures. The victims come from every social class. If we are to eradicate this deviated behaviour we must in the first instance have some knowledge of how it arises.

Here is an example which well illustrates how pain sometimes leads to sexual pleasure. This case history is in some detail because it brings out very clearly the transition from pain to pleasure, and is typical of hundreds of others. It is one cited in Hirschfeld's *Sexual Anomalies and Perversions*, a book intended for the guidance of judges, probation officers, psychologists, and criminologists.

The man concerned was masochistic—one who found sexual delight in experiencing pain. When he was a boy of thirteen, he was sent to an estate where there were two girls, aged fourteen and sixteen, and another boy of thirteen. The mother of the three children, an invalid, employed a governess to attend to their education. She was a strong woman, of the domineering type, twenty-eight years old.

One morning the visiting boy heard cries of pain and imploring words coming from the schoolroom. Looking through the keyhole, he saw Erna, the fourteen-year-old girl, lying across a table while the governess thrashed her with a cane. During lunch Erna fidgeted constantly in her seat and had great difficulty in sitting still, so severe had been the punishment.

Deeply stirred by what he had witnessed, the boy made friends with Erna. He learned from her that the governess seemed to enjoy whipping both her and her sixteen-year-old sister Elsa. Indeed, she beat them almost daily, sometimes using a cane, sometimes a birch. What he had witnessed, together with vivid first-hand accounts of whippings, given to him by the girl, resulted in his being sexually stimulated. He started masturbating with the other boy. One night the governess surprised them in the act.

She locked the door behind her and said: 'Now you're going to get a good whipping, and every evening, for eight days, you're going to get the same.' She fetched a stick, laid each of the boys across the arm of a sofa, and raising their shirts—all they were wearing—she laid on with the strokes until their buttocks changed colour.

But note carefully the effect. 'It burned like fire,' said the boy when a grown man, 'but at the same time it prickled pleasantly and in some strange way seemed to give me delight.' Actually the boy experienced orgasm during such thrashings. 'It was the blows that did it. It had never been so nice when we just masturbated.'

Various gestures, and the way in which she touched the boys during and after chastisement, revealed clearly that this governess experienced sexual pleasure from what she was doing. 'We were glad of the blows, and when the happy days were over, we longed for them again.'

There you have a revealing account of how masochists can be produced. Sometimes, too, witnessing a thrashing or receiving it, produces sadism—the desire to punish others. You may have observed press reports of cases which magistrates have found hard to understand. In recent years accounts of schoolmasters luring boys on to waste ground, then punishing them for trespassing—of husbands insisting upon beating their wives, and of establishments outwardly concerned with massage, but actually devoted to flagellation, have occupied the attention of our courts. Incidents such as those related by Hirschfeld may explain the origin of such abnormal behaviour.

The urge to flog and to be flogged has undoubtedly been greatly nurtured, to some extent at least, by our public schools. They unfortunately have a most unenviable reputation in this respect. Despite certain undoubted advantages of the public school system, both social and educational, the segregation of the sexes together with the incidence of corporal punishment undoubtedly encourages the growth of such abnormal practices. Of course, this applied much more in the past than it does to the present day.

Hirschfield's comments upon our public schools and other educational establishments are worth quoting.

'Flagellation constitutes a particular danger in the case of orphanages, boarding-schools, educational establishments, etc., where the large number of children in puberty or early puberty in any case creates an eroticised atmosphere. A centuries-old tradition in English schools has produced some very remarkable results. Already in the seventeenth century the English public schools and colleges had a number of sadistic masters whose names became proverbial.

'A well-known school was particularly notorious at all times. A rod made from apple-twigs was used. Two juniors were appointed as rod makers and it was their duty to supply the school with rods. The delinquent had to kneel down on a block with his buttocks bared. The master then gave him four strokes of the "Biblical" six. At one time a satirical paper on the subject was issued at this school. That the masters were not always acting solely from educational enthusiasm but partly from sadistic motives is proved by the case of one headmaster, whose supplier of rods was a man who had been cut off from the gallows and revived. He always took the rods from this man with "a pleased smile".'

In one of Thomas Shadwell's comedies, *The Virtuoso*, an old libertine visits a brothel and requests a whipping. The prostitute inquires how he came to possess such strange tastes. 'I became so used to it when at school,' he answers, 'that I can't give it up.' The same reply might be given by many others, male and female alike, from various educational establishments.

It is often remarked that every country has its special 'national perversion'. England has been regarded as the classic land of flagellation. Sadistic schoolmasters and governesses do not find it so easy these days to derive pleasure out of the suffering of their charges. But there can be no doubt that many still seek opportunities to do so.

It is not suggested here that an occasional smack or two is likely to have serious psychological after-effects. But parents should be on their guard against formal thrashings which in earlier times had as their object impressing upon the child mind that parental rule was absolute, and that disobedience brought pain inflicted while the child was helpless to resist.

These formal whippings are often desired in later years. Every detail which was insisted upon in childhood days has to be repeated. Thus a girl whose parents lowered her underwear before punishment, when a masochistic woman, may want her 'master' to do the same. Another, whose parents insisted upon her appearing in the punishment room with buttocks already bared, insists upon the same formalities when seeking a whipping for sexual pleasure.

These details, indeed, count for a very great deal with both sadists and masochists, as is clear from the literature which many of them eagerly read. Many pornographic magazines describe all sorts of whippings, with detailed accounts of the placing of the victim into position for the punishment, removal of dress, and so on. And, of course, each instalment finishes at some point where a new whipping is about to begin and the reader is urged not to miss the sparkling account of the whippings of Miss So-and-So in the next issue.

Doctors sometimes receive letters from parents who pretend to be concerned about their children's behaviour. They relate meticulously the punishments which have been imposed and inquire whether the practitioner approves the methods employed. Many—probably most—accept these communications as genuine requests for guidance. Those with a greater knowledge of sexual abnormalities, however, suspect that they are simply examples of 'graphosadism'. For many sadists enjoy writing accounts of whippings they have given.

Having read thus far, the reader who is a parent may well inquire: 'Have I, by punishing my children by means of chastisement on the buttocks, inevitably made them sado-masochists in adult life?' The answer is: No. It by no means follows that every child punished in this manner is going to become tainted. But the danger is real enough to deserve consideration.

When the question of the birching of child offenders has been discussed in Parliament, some members have puffed out their chests and said, in effect: 'Look at me. I've been flogged many times, but what harm has it done me?' Well, there are several ways of answering that question.

First, it is a fact that sado-masochists themselves are invariably firm supporters of the retention of the rod and of an extension of its employment. Second, even if it is true that a man has not been prejudicially affected by corporal punishment, it by no means follows that the same is true of others similarly treated. Indeed, we know for certain that in many instances, the opposite holds true.

Whereas one individual may be unaffected, another, because of some inherent or other imbalance, may have a predisposition towards sadism or masochism which corporal punishment will bring to the surface.

When someone of the old school pompously strives hard to retain the flagellation of children by the police, and produces no better evidence than himself in favour of this course, is he not arguing from the particular to the general? The love of chastising others, or being chastised, is far too widespread for us to ignore the psychological results which only too often accrue from 'old-fashioned' methods of maintaining discipline.

One authority, Wulffen, has said this:

'Boys after a sound thrashing are often surprised by the

subsequent pleasure arising from warmth in the seat. For this reason they sometimes endeavour to obtain a repetition of the chastisement which may ultimately affect them sexually. Chastisement on the buttocks is therefore in itself a dangerous thing, in spite of the fact that countless children have been and are still being chastised without becoming sadists or masochists.' For many people are conscious that, to some extent, they do experience pleasure by inflicting pain or receiving it, particularly in the course of the sexual embrace.

Here it must be stressed and made clear that the terms sadism and masochism denote an excessive desire in these directions. For it must be admitted that in love-play leading up to sexual union, and in the course of the sex act itself, pain is often inflicted by the delivery of 'love-bites', squeezing, pinching, and so on. These may give pleasure to both parties. That they do so is no indication of perversity. Such almost painful embraces are not exceptional and can be regarded as normal.

Sado-masochism thus has its roots in normal sexual activity, it is a byway, and the branching off is caused by the factors which we have observed. This chapter has dealt with one application of it—flagellation—because it is the most common. But there are many other avenues through which the same basic inclination finds expression.

Among the many forms which sadism may assume, for instance, is a desire to witness bullfights, all-in wrestling, dangerous circus or acrobatic performances, and the like. The strong emotions aroused in some spectators of prize-fights are unquestionably tinged with sadism.

Mental sadism may take the form of constant bullying of one's partner prior to the sex act. Some men cannot achieve ejaculation unless, by abuse of their wives, they have brought them to tears. In all other respects they may be model husbands and the sadistic tendency may reveal itself only in this way.

Some women, too, can experience orgasm only after having 'dominated' their partners. They may speak slightingly of them, or place them in a humiliating position. They may insist upon the man being dressed in a peculiar manner, or may even beat him. The curious cases sometimes reported in the newspapers of men who cannot resist the temptation to cut girls' hair are also partly sadistic in origin, though, in addition, an element of fetishism is present.

This, indeed, is often the case. The sado-masochist often demands some one garment, either worn by himself or his partner, or he may demand that his partner should assume some particular attitude.

Sadists and masochists usually suffer from some degree of anxiety and depression. On the reality level their desires are usually difficult or expensive to gratify. Often these inclinations bring their victims within reach of the law. It is not surprising that the great majority of sado-masochists regret their inability to enjoy intercourse without such stimulation.

Treatment along psychological lines can be helpful, since these deviations are psychological in origin. The main point of this chapter, however, concerns the preventive aspect, which, after all, is the most important one.

The responsibility of schoolmasters, parents, and others in authority over the young is very great. They can rise to it only by accepting fully something which most find extremely hard to believe. It is this: *that the child of today is the adult of tomorrow and that the seeds planted in childhood will flower, for better or for worse, in adulthood.*

A realisation of this, and the ability to act accordingly, should help to give us a greater understanding of how to prevent sado-masochistic tendencies from seeking abnormal expression.

13: How Sex Grows Up in You

So far as the sex side of his life is concerned, the individual child starts existence in this world at the identical point at which his primitive ancestors started. But by the time he has reached adulthood he has, by virtue of the interaction between his instinctual urges and his environment, developed certain mental and emotional patterns or types of thinking and feeling which prompt behaviour that is as different from primitive behaviour as the latter is different from that among the animals.

DR. WINIFRED V. RICHMOND

I have deemed it necessary in this edition to probe a little beneath the surface in our consideration of the psychological factors which influence sexual expression. But before we enter more deeply into the reasons for departures from normality in the chapter which follows, it is necessary to discuss the process of sex development. This is essential; for a knowledge of both the physiological and emotional aspects of sexual growth is a pre-requisite to the understanding of sexual expression and how deviations occur.

Sex is not something which suddenly appears at puberty. *Awareness* of sex may come then for the first time to some, while others find their consciousness of sex greatly intensified. It is natural that they should do so. But sex has been present all the time—right from the earliest days of infancy, in fact.

The fundamental misconception, still widely held, that sex makes its first appearance at puberty, has inevitably led to a great deal of misunderstanding. It has caused people to assume, quite erroneously, that sex education prior to puberty cannot yield the slightest benefit. It has resulted in parents dismissing the plainest indications of sex play among children as mere coincidence, in the mistaken belief that children of nine or ten years, let alone infants, must be completely devoid of all sexual feeling.

There is a measure of reluctance to accept the fact that sex plays a part in the life of even the youngest child. If only we would realise that it is something which is perfectly natural—like breathing, for instance—we would find it easier to accept the truth that sex is an inherent part of life, that the organs associated with it, the feelings which arise from it, and the curiosity which inevitably is left regarding it, are all perfectly normal and natural and in no sense 'nasty'.

In order to study sexual development as it proceeds from infancy to adulthood we must consider both the physiological and psychological aspects. In life the two are inseparable. They proceed side by side, and are so closely interwoven that it is sometimes difficult to say where the one ends and the other begins. More often than not they are considered separately, but this is for the sake of clarity and convenience. Both are so closely blended that, in life itself, the physical and emotional cannot be taken apart and looked at separately. I propose here to deal with them together. This method will help to emphasise their very close relationship.

The first point to grasp is one which the 'rational' man of mature years often finds hard to believe. It is this: *The beginnings of one's love-life take root in infancy.*

Undoubtedly there is a new awareness of sex at puberty, yet we have only to throw our minds back to our own childhood to realise that there was also a very definite interest in the subject much earlier. Every growing child asks, or wants to ask, his parents where he came from. His curiosity is aroused even in the nursery. He is puzzled by the problem, but is not as yet emotionally involved.

There is a big difference between mental curiosity about sex and the desire for sexual experience. You can feel desire without in the least understanding what it means. The child who asks where babies come from is not only ignorant of the physical facts, but unable to experience even in imagination the sort of feelings that become possible later. Even if he is given the right answer to his question, within the limits of his understanding, he still does not know he is being told about 'sex'. It is only when he is older that he becomes conscious of sexual feelings, and the word is singled out and placed, as it were, in inverted commas. Until then he displays the general curiosity he feels about so much of the strange world in which he finds himself. Where babies come from is no more a special question than where the moon comes from unless—and this is important—it is given abnormal significance by his parents.

If grown-ups seem startled and give an evasive answer the child is quick to detect something unusual in their attitude. Instead of satisfying curiosity they may merely whet it.

Once the child gets the impression that the subject is mysterious and forbidden he is no longer content to pass on with innocent inconsequence to the next question. Already sex has become 'sex'. The inverted commas baffle and intrigue him. He cannot speak of sex again naturally and without feeling self-conscious.

THE IMPULSE OF CURIOSITY

Psychologists have tended to neglect the enormous part played in our lives by sheer curiosity. They have stressed, rightly enough, the importance of the sex instinct and the desire to dominate and win approval. The instinctive side of our natures was formerly played down in favour of the rational element. The analytical schools in particular have redressed the balance by providing positive evidence that, in Hume's famous dictum: 'Reason is the slave of the passions.'

But like all epigrams, this is an exaggeration. To argue that reason—the desire to find out the truth about things—is no more than the inventing of ingenious excuses for what we *want* to do would make an impartial inquiry impossible. Even psychology would be an elaborate form of self-deception.

Nevertheless, the desire to know is closely related to our instinctual life. It serves a biological purpose. Curiosity may have killed the cat, but it has enabled the human species to outstrip its known rivals. Without curiosity our prehistoric ancestors would not have learned how to make fire or grow crops and so lay the foundations of the whole of civilisation.

Man is above all an inquisitive animal. His inquisitiveness begins almost as soon as he is born. It starts, as one might expect, with the object nearest at hand, namely his own body.

Obviously this is not an intellectual curiosity, though the latter may have its origin in such a simple beginning. The infant *feels* before he *thinks*. Thinking, in the ordinary sense, is a later development. It cannot arise until the child is conscious of himself; in other words, until the ego is formed.

We have no memory of this early phase. But it leaves a profound mark on the unconscious mind, and may exercise a decisive influence on our subsequent emotional life. Many character traits, such as stubbornness and even miserliness, have been tracked down to this dim period when the ego is in the process of formation.

But whatever else may be in the making at this time the impulse of curiosity soon shows itself. The first overt sign of its presence is a kind of experiment with bodily sensations.

Some parts of the body are more sensitive than others and therefore come earlier into awareness. Hunger is a primary driving force and because it is satisfied through the mouth the child is immediately conscious of the pleasure of oral contacts. He knows nothing about kissing, but he does know the delight that comes to him when he is at the breast and the warm milk flows into his mouth.

There is pleasure, too, in defaecating, and even withholding his stool. He relieves himself without inhibitions. He associates his mouth and excretory organs with pleasurable sensations.

FREUD'S THEORY

So much of our understanding of this obscure period is due to the pioneering work of Freud that it is necessary to consider his theory of infantile sexuality.

He was the first to show why experiences in the earliest years of life may have such far-reaching consequences. Until he pointed the way it was not realised that much of an individual's character which was usually attributed to heredity was, in fact, the product of early environment.

We are accustomed to think of character-training starting at an age when a child can talk and understand the difference between right and wrong. Freud showed that the foundations of character are laid very much earlier. The attitude of the mother in feeding him at the breast and training him in toilet is not a trivial matter. He needs emotional as well as bodily nourishment if he is to pass safely through the successive stages of growth that lie ahead. It is of overwhelming importance that he should feel the security of being loved.

The great contribution of psycho-analysis was to call

attention to the significance of these stages of development. The first stage is called 'oral' because the chief means of gratification is the mouth. Then, as the infant becomes more aware of his other bodily functions, he reaches the 'anal' stage.

It is easy to see that something remains of this infantile absorption in zones of the body all through adult life. It may play a preliminary part in sexual arousal, or it may, in some cases, become an end in itself. Most of the so-called sexual perversions show a regression to infantile behaviour. But it would be a mistake to jump to the conclusion that homosexuality, for example, is merely a return to anal eroticism. As we shall see later, homosexuals are not necessarily addicted to sodomy. The commonest practice is mutual masturbation which may or may not be accompanied by oral contacts.

Superficially, adult behaviour of this sort resembles the behaviour of a child, but the great difference is that it has a full sexual content. In an adult, sex in so far as the individual is concerned, is fully developed and the problem we have to solve is why it should be discharged in some unusual manner.

For some reason there has been a halt at one of the stages of development towards maturity. Given a good environment the child can usually succeed in jumping these hurdles even if he is constitutionally weak.

For the present we will leave aside the question of whether inversion is innate or acquired. In by far the greater majority of cases it is due to a failure to pass through the crucial stage that reaches its climax about the age of four years.

It cannot be too strongly emphasised, however, that success or failure at this period may depend very largely on what has happened in the preceding years. During the oral and anal stages the relationship between the child and his parents, especially the mother, provides the soil in which he is rooted. If the soil is poor he will have the greatest difficulty in meeting the demands which life will later make upon him. The most severe strain will be felt when he has to adjust himself to the first direct onset of the sex instinct.

THE MOTHER-CHILD RELATIONSHIP

The term 'Oedipus complex' has received wide notoriety and is only too often misunderstood. It is the name given by Freud to the intense emotional attachment that a boy feels for his mother during the third, fourth, or fifth years of his life. A somewhat similar situation arises between a girl and her father at this time, and it is called the 'Electra complex'.

These descriptions are unfortunate because they refer to Greek characters who were guilty of adult incestuous attitudes. Consequently, Freud made himself an easy target for the obvious criticism that a young child could not even desire such a relationship.

But Freud did not mean anything so crude as this. He held that the sex instinct develops in two great thrusts, the first occurring after the oral and anal stages, and the second at puberty.

This does not imply that the first stirring of sex is accompanied by desires of which an adult is capable. The child's body is obviously too immature for any such thing to be possible, but anyone who has had some experience in bringing up children knows that the young child becomes extremely interested in the purpose of his genitals.

As we have already pointed out, sheer curiosity is a sufficient explanation of the sort of questions he asks. Unfortunately the conventions of society focus his attention abnormally on the subject. Infantile masturbation is a completely normal phenomenon, but parents do not realise this when they make their children feel guilty of such behaviour.

A horrified mother may even threaten to mutilate the offending organ. She does not mean her words literally, of course, but to the child it is a terrifying possibility. The fear of losing his penis is increased if he happens to see a girl or his mother in the nude. For he then believes that they may have been actually castrated. These nightmarish fantasies are among the many fears of childhood which should be taken seriously if the child is to be helped to pass through the emotional crisis with which he is now faced.

THE GREAT CONFLICT

A new quality infuses the child's relationship with his mother when the Oedipal situation begins. The reason is that he has found a new *object* for his love. He has been gradually outgrowing the early pre-occupations in purely bodily sensations. Instead of the sole love-object being his own body it becomes the mother.

This is a tremendous leap forward. It is proof that he is now capable of far more complex emotions. He is no longer solely concentrating his attention on the pleasurable sensations he can derive from erotogenic zones.

He still finds these sensations agreeable, of course; but there are other, richer, possibilities. His mother is no longer someone who merely ministers to his bodily needs and gives him a sense of security in a dangerous world. Just as his own personality has developed, so his mother's is more definite for him. She seems as different to him from any other woman as a young bride appears to her own husband. Indeed, he will declare that when he is a man he will marry her.

There must be few small boys who have not made

some such remark. All they can possibly mean by 'marriage' is complete monopoly of the mother's affection. They cannot bear to think they must share her love with anyone else.

This poses a painful problem. The boy may be with his mother throughout the day, but he is usually supplanted when his father comes home in the evening. As a rare privilege he is sometimes allowed to sleep with his mother, but in the ordinary way he cannot share her bed.

He resents this bitterly. He is at an age when everything is felt with an intensity that a grown-up can hardly imagine. He has little experience of life, no ability to reason about what happens to him, and consequently there is no protection against the fierce emotions that rage within him. One moment he is in ecstasy; the next he is plunged into despair.

He cannot help regarding his father as a rival, and the primitive aggression he felt as a baby whenever his wishes were frustrated is again unleashed. Yet he knows that if he hates his father his mother will be displeased with him and he may lose her love—the very thing he desires to retain above all else.

He is now in the throes of the Oedipal conflict. Before considering how he can solve it, notice how similar this situation is to the later situations which occur when we can no longer doubt the presence of the sexual factor. The child is going through a rehearsal for the love-relationships of maturity.

It has the ingredients of romance—the same thrilling wonder, the same black jealousy, the same demand for exclusive possession. If all goes well a similar impassioned vow of life-long devotion will be addressed one day to another woman. This is what nature is carefully preparing him to do. But if he remains fixed in this stage of attachment to the mother he may find it impossible to switch to a different love-object and establish an adult-relationship in marriage.

That is why the Oedipal situation may prove the great turning point in his life. It may determine whether it is ever possible for him to enter into a satisfying sexual relationship with another woman. It may make a homosexual of him. The same kind of problems are met with as a girl grows to adulthood.

THE PHALLIC STAGE

When it is asked how this romantic attachment to the mother can possibly be associated with sex, one answer might be that if there were no such thing as the sex instinct it would not occur.

We can dismiss any idea of an incestuous relationship. Unhappily that expression was used rather loosely by Freud and seized upon by his opponents as a weapon of attack. Neither incest nor sex, in the ordinary connotation, have any meaning for a child of five. On the other hand, there is a potential sexuality which exists together with potential intellectuality.

We cannot say at what precise moment the shadow of the future development is first felt. Freud never suggested that it was manifested in the genital region before puberty. The Oedipal situation does not belong to the Genital Stage, but to what has been deliberately named the Phallic Stage.

The distinction is an important one. When the Genital Stage is reached the sexual instinct begins to serve the ends of reproduction, which is what we mean by sex in everyday language.

The Phallic Stage, however, has a peculiarity that would not have been noticed, owing to the fog of mystification in which the subject is wrapped, if psycho-analysis had not drawn attention to it. For both sexes in childhood only *one* kind of genital organ is taking into account—the male.

Thus a boy regards a girl exactly as he would another

boy whose phallus is missing. The girl, on her part, looks upon herself in the same way—as though she were a boy minus a phallus.

Such is the strange world of fantasy and misconception in which for a while the child lives. Most parents, forgetting their own childhood, do not even try to understand it. They do not believe it exists.

When a child betrays his naïve interest in bodily functions they are scandalised. They cannot seem to realise that fundamentally this is the very innocence they expect of him.

More ironical still, they often look upon these forbidden speculations as being a form of sexual precocity, whereas in fact they are no more than the natural and necessary curiosity to which we have already referred. Yet the romantic attachment to the mother (or in the case of a girl to the father), which is far more suspect, is openly encouraged.

The ignorance of parents only reflects the prejudices and conventions of the society in which they live. It is not that they do not honestly wish to do their best for their children, but they blindly accept a mass of false ideas and senseless taboos which have the very opposite result.

It is hard enough for the child to pass from stage to stage and finally attain emotional maturity without having artificial obstacles placed in his path. Yet that is what so often happens and the most serious harm of all is done to him at the Oedipal Stage when he is so desperately in need of wise handling.

From the sixth year until the onset of puberty there is a lull in the development of sexuality—to employ that term in the wide sense in which it is used by psycho-analysts. This is known as the Latent Period.

We must not suppose that all is peaceful at this time; on the contrary, there are emotional storms in plenty. But they differ in kind from the dramatic conflict which reached its peak during the Oedipal situation. Sex, as the layman understands it, is still far below the surface.

A moment's reflection shows that this must be the case. The glandular changes which occur in puberty have not begun. The primal energy (or libido) which is destined to serve the purpose of reproduction is still diffused and has yet to vitalise the genitals.

Consequently the Latent Period is in some respects a continuation of the pre-genital stage during which the pleasure of bodily contacts—kissing and caressing—does not have any obvious sexual content.

But the child, it must be remembered, is in a state of continuous development. His early delight in exploring the possibilities of his own body gradually becomes more complex. To the curiosity about his body is added an increasing curiosity about the world around him. It provides fresh opportunities for gratification, above all in that part of his outside world which is represented by his mother.

Apart from his own body, the nearest and most immediate object on which his attention is focussed is the person who cares for him. To put it in simple language, the child is first in love with himself and then with his mother. He remains very much in love with himself, but not exclusively so. If all goes well he loses his early self-absorption and becomes aware of a deeper need—the craving to receive all the love that his mother is capable of and to have her entirely to himself.

This is easier to understand if we think of it in terms of new relationships. As the infant grows he is restricted at first to relationships within the family circle, because that is the only world he knows. The demand for a monopoly of his mother's love cannot be considered 'selfish' in any blameworthy sense. It is egocentric because it is the inevitable accompaniment of the growth of the ego. At about the age of five or six, however, when the ego is established, the child is not quite so dependent on the home. He exchanges the nursery for the classroom.

This brings him into contact with teachers and schoolmates and loosens the bonds that have hitherto tied him to his parents. They are no longer the only people he has to please. He is made uncomfortably aware that he is not the only pebble on the beach and somehow he must adjust himself to more critical demands than were made upon him at home.

The work of millions of years of evolution is marvellously condensed into the brief span of this period of early childhood. From being a creature of instinct and reflexes, hardly distinguishable from an animal, the growing child turns with incredible rapidity into a civilised human being with a sense of right and wrong, feelings of guilt and shame, a capacity for genuine love and friendship.

This is not merely a change of degree, but a profound transformation. Emotions can now be experienced where formerly there was only a blind grasping for pleasure and recoil from pain. Instead of being limited to bodily sensation the child discovers a new realm of emotional experiences opening up before him. He is capable of feeling deep affection and of forming an ideal on which to model himself.

WHEN LOVE IS LACKING

He is growing up with a vengeance. His success, of course, depends very largely on what has gone before. The foundations of his character have been laid in the first three or four years of live. Provided he was then given the love he craved for he is secure enough to extend his relationships beyond the family without fear. However dangerous the outside world appears at first—and it can be very forbidding to a small child—he has the reassurance of knowing that his parents are there in the background.

If he is too dependent on them he will shrink from venturing forth. He will hide behind his mother's skirts, as the saying goes. Equally, if he feels that they have rejected him, the big world which he is forced to enter will seem a frighteningly lonely place.

It is no coincidence that sexual difficulties are almost always encountered by those whose early years were lacking in parental love.

Emotional well-being has its roots in the mother-child relationship. If its roots are not healthy a plant has a poor chance of growth, and this applies with just as much force to a child's development.

A good example is the more unfortunate type of institutionalised child. We are told that he frequently grows up cold, reserved, and outwardly unemotional because he has been deprived of mother-love. It is likely that later he will express his sexuality in a similar manner—or possibly in some deviated form.

These years prior to puberty are a preparation for the full awakening of the sex instinct. The manner in which it will ultimately express itself is mainly determined long before it is capable of physical expression. Whether the instinct is strong or weak in a particular individual depends on constitutional factors, but the type of relationship to which it gives rise may be fixed for life by the relationship between the child and his parents.

Undoubtedly this is one of the most important discoveries of modern psychology. The origin of sexual deviations is now seen to lie much further back than was previously suspected. And the reason it escaped notice for so long is that it belongs to a period of life which most people regard as free from any association with sexuality.

But the fact of a causal connection between the emotional disturbances of childhood and such adult phenomena as frigidity, impotence, and homosexuality has been firmly established.

MAKING A STABLE PERSONALITY

There are three factors to be taken into account: the strength of the sex instinct, the stability of the personality, the environment.

Just as some people are more aggressive than others, some are more highly sexed. We have all met people who appear to find no difficulty in remaining celibate for long periods, if not always. At the other extreme there are those for whom some kind of sexual outlet is an overwhelming necessity. If they are unable to satisfy the urge they are wretched. For them sexual experience seems as necessary as food.

The difference is probably genetic. The form of expression, however, is usually due to environment. But having said that, it is as well to remember that we cannot really separate heredity from environment. We may isolate the two factors for purposes of analysis, but what we observe in actual life as an interaction between the two.

Nature and nurture form an indissoluble whole. The instincts with which we are endowed are unalterable, but the manner in which they are expressed is the outcome of our conditioning; so is the stability or weakness of our personality apart from some physical defect or ill-health.

What, then, makes for a robust personality, able to cope with the stresses of growing up? The answer is, first and foremost, a good relationship with the family unit. If the child's need for love is satisfied he gains an inner stability which enables him to withstand the strains imposed at the successive stages through which he must pass.

The parents, therefore, are chiefly responsible for moulding his character and laying the foundations of his future behaviour patterns. It is only through these already existing patterns that his sexuality can eventually find expression.

From puberty onwards sex becomes woven into the patterns of behaviour and personality that have been built up during earlier years. The awakening of sex illuminates them and reveals their strength and weakness. It is the great testing time when we discover just how successful the child's upbringing has been.

LOVE WITHOUT SEX

Prior to puberty all love has a different quality. It is non-sexual in the sense of being pre-genital. This does not preclude a good deal of curiosity about sex or the quest for pleasurable bodily sensations. But the child's interest in his genitals and infantile experiments in masturbation are not measured by adult standards. The resemblance is purely superficial.

Nature guides us in the difficult climb to even more complex levels of experience, beginning with sheer bodily sensation and then leading on to the higher level of emotion. Love and friendship are not felt until we approach the top rungs of life.

It is part of nature's design to enable us to make the transition from self-love to love of parents, and finally to love of another person, infused with the additional force of the sex instinct—a totally new factor which only appears in its true form at puberty. To make this distinction quite clear let us regard as 'platonic' the kind of love which ripens in the Latent Period.

'Platonic' love can be defined in this context as the capacity to enter into and maintain friendly and harmonious human relationships of a non-sexual character. At school, for example, a boy selects one of his classmates as a 'chum'. They play together and share confidences. So, too, a girl chooses another girl—and this pairing is almost invariably with members of the same sex.

The affection that they feel for each other may be transient, but while it lasts it is often intense. Yet it would be far-fetched to read into this relationship the seeds of true homosexuality.

They may discuss sex and speculate about its meaning. If they have been brought up in ignorance of the subject they will compare their own guesses and phantasies. But this arises from natural curiosity—the desire to know rather than to experience.

There is an element of hero-worship in their regard for an older person or even some historical or fictitious character. A favourite teacher may be singled out—but not at all in the way that a teacher becomes the object of an emotional attachment in adolescence.

The outstanding characteristic of the Latent Period is the absence of sexuality. The instinctual impulses that besieged the newly formed ego in the preceding stage appear to die down. The conflict which reached its climax in the Oedipal situation is over.

Not that the issue has been finally decided. Before long the instincts will again make a shattering impact. But a period of relative calm is needed to allow other parts of the personality to develop. The child's intelligence must be given a chance to grow without too much emotional distraction. And if he is to be orientated away from the family circle and learn to live in society he must be capable of companionship and loyalty.

It cannot be doubted that the late awakening of sex in human beings serves nature's design. Man is unique among the other animals in experiencing an interval of sexual quiescence. We do not find anything like this even among the higher apes and Freud believed that the Latent

Period might be responsible for man's superiority in the scale of evolution.

He went even further and suggested that the cultural achievements of civilised man might be due to the abeyance of the sexual instinct prior to puberty. For, as is well known, many primitive peoples allow and even encourage erotic play among children.

Whether or not this is true, the pause before puberty enables the child to establish non-sexual relationships with other children and adults which are a vital preparation for choosing a life-partner. Platonic love—call it friendship, if you will—is not merely a prelude to the love which makes for a successful marriage, it is an essential ingredient.

Marriages based on purely physical attraction can quickly founder. Instead of a total relationship there is only a partial one. Love has been defined as 'friendship lit by passion', and unless the capacity for both is present there is no basis for a permanently satisfactory union.

Hence the supreme importance of developing platonic love before we are able to experience physical passion. Once the mighty drives of the sex instinct are felt it may be too late to begin. We may find that just because we have had no training in establishing a non-sexual friendship we are unable to do so. We have missed an essential stage of growth and the lack of it is felt all through life.

THE BISEXUAL STAGE

It is quite possible for platonic love to be charged with sexuality during adolescence and yet to have as its object a member of the same sex. That some men can be as intensely in love with a man as with a woman is unquestionable. This is why it is such a mistake to confuse homosexuality with depravity.

It is necessary to clear our minds completely of popular misconceptions about the nature of sex itself.

In everyday speech it is confined exclusively to genital experience, but, as we have seen, that is an over-simplification. The sex instinct does not spring full-fledged into existence at puberty, but it is true enough that certain bodily changes at that period canalise it into the genital area.

What name to give to the generalised instinct before it is localised in this way is a matter of convenience. Perhaps the more elastic term 'libido' is as good as any. Libido has all the potentialities of the sex instinct, and much more besides. It can inspire unselfish devotion as well as the desire for physical gratification.

We can think of it starting like a broad stream of creative energy which is capable of being diverted from its normal course when it meets serious obstructions. Before puberty it cannot possibly be directed towards reproduction and the energy is used in other ways. There comes a time, however, when it is sharply differentiated. In the ordinary course of events the adolescent becomes aware, as never before, of the opposite sex.

Until this threshold is crossed neither the boy nor the girl has a hard and fast sexual status. There is something of the other sex in both of them. The boy has certain feminine traits, the girl certain masculine ones. In short, they are bisexual.

During the Latent Period there is an evident attempt to overcome this bisexuality. The boy between the ages of six and ten—and often for much longer—affects a scorn of girls, although what he really despises is the 'girlishness' in himself. He finds that the best way to get rid of it is to mock such feminine characteristics and to bring out their opposite.

He boasts about his superior muscle and identifies himself with a sporting hero. Any boy at school who shrinks from many games and horseplay is scoffed at as 'sissy'. Similarly, girls of this age draw away from boys and repress the masculine tendencies in themselves. They look upon boys as rough, unruly creatures with whom they no longer wish to be too closely associated.

Some girls, of course, fail to repress their male side, but by continuing to be rough and share boyish pastimes they set themselves apart from most other girls. They are the so-called tomboys—postponing, perhaps indefinitely, the break with bisexuality.

With the girl, however, the maternal instinct is an additional complicating factor, nature has cast her for a special role. Even when she enters adolescence the onset of sex is not so directly genital as with a boy. It would be difficult to exaggerate the harm that results from failure to take heed of this elementary fact.

THE GENITAL STAGE

For both sexes the onset of adolescence is a profound experience. Step by step they have been prepared for it, but everything depends on the success with which they have been able to adapt themselves to the earlier stages of growth.

Their bodies are now the vehicles of a new, explosive force bursting to be discharged. Nature has done her utmost to build up the necessary strength to contain the imperious demands of the sex instinct, but only too often human interference ruins the long preparation.

The great stream of energy we have called Libido divides and follows the direction already foreshadowed by the grouping of the sexes in the Latent Period. The masculine traits of the boy are reinforced by glandular changes; there is a similar strengthening of femininity in the girl. Instead of displaying mutual suspicion and hostility they are powerfully attracted towards each other.

Boy meets girl on a new plane and with a new consciousness. Their emotional attitude is quite altered and they indulge in flirtations and experience 'crushes'—a form of incipient courtship.

The pre-genital period is at an end and for the simple reason that glandular changes have occurred, as can be seen in the changes that take place in the genitalia. Pubic hairs appear and the boy experiences nocturnal emissions. The girl's development is so dramatic as often to be frightening, for she begins to menstruate.

Boys and girls become capable of sexual intercourse before their schooldays are over and long before it is permitted by the laws of civilised countries. The customary age of marriage in Europe has become later and later for a variety of social reasons, although there is now a swing in the opposite direction. It was not always so postponed and the age of consent is still as low as sixteen. The story of Romeo and Juliet should remind us that passionate love in the early teens was not always socially unacceptable in itself.

Nevertheless, the adolescent is still emotionally immature no matter how mature he or she may be physically. This imbalance is the cause of so many of the tensions and disturbances which make adolescence such a testing time. The boy puts his childhood behind him and wishes to be accepted as a man, but the trouble is that he is neither a child nor a man: he is *both.* Similarly, this applies to the girl.

Whatever failures of adaptation occurred in childhood now begin to show themselves. Deep down in the unconscious there are traces left by the oral, anal, and phallic stages. For years they have lain dormant, but suddenly they are charged with sexuality and they may influence the form it takes.

Furthermore, there was the still more critical Oedipal situation. It was part of the normal development for a boy to become intensely attached to the mother at the age of four, but he should have outgrown that demand for a monopoly of her love before reaching adolescence. If he has not done so and the stage is prolonged, his sexuality will be unable to find a satisfactory outlet.

Any association of the idea of sex with the mother will seem repulsive, and the same recoil from sex may be felt when another woman is presented as a mother substitute. He will unconsciously see the reflection of his mother in all women and be more or less incapable of sexual relationship for that reason. He may find himself impotent with a woman and yet be attracted by his own sex because with another man he has no such inhibition.

On the other hand, if he has not learned to establish non-sexual attachments he may find himself caught up in a relentless drive for sexual novelty—a simulation of love with none of the enduring qualities of affection and understanding. He is searching all the time for mere genital gratification—the sensation-hungry 'wolf' type whose life is a succession of sexual adventures.

Numberless permutations and combinations are possible when we consider the many kinds of maladjustments that can occur and the varying strength of sexual impulses. Basically they all point to something that went wrong in the child's upbringing.

This lengthy digression on the nature of sex is a necessary preliminary to any understanding of sexual deviations. They arise because of some flaw in the personality which can usually be traced to early environment. The warping may not have serious social consequences if the basic character of the child is strong. Thus a man may be aware of homosexual tendencies and yet be sufficiently stable to resist them. Alternatively, of course, his character may not be unusually strong, but the impulses themselves may be so weak that they can be controlled.

But all sexual deviations due to psychological causes—and everyone has at some time been conscious of such impulses—are a sign of a certain degree and type of emotional immaturity. And now that the ground has been cleared let us consider more fully how sexual deviations occur.

14: How Sex Deviations Occur

We are all made up of thousands of different facets which go to make our own unique personality. Broadly speaking, we have two main selves, the real one, basically not far removed from that of our primitive ancestors, and the self that we would like to be, and which is largely influenced by what society expects of us. The real self—much of which resides in the unconscious—frequently comes into conflict with society, which is not surprising when one remembers that, although mankind has changed little throughout the centuries, there have been far-reaching social changes. The real self seems almost to have stood still while the outside world has rushed ahead. But the real self is constantly trying to adapt itself to the outside world—frantically trying to catch up with the ever-changing, complex world without.

In order to see precisely how this works out, let us take a quick glance at the situation in which a boy finds himself at puberty. He is capable of complete sexual intercourse. His sexual development has reached the stage at which nature intends him to be fully equipped for direct, full, sexual expression. Nature has a habit of reminding her creatures of what she expects of them, and to some, she speaks loudly and insistently. There can be no doubt

197

about that. Society also has something to say. The pro-creation of our kind is not regarded by society as a suit-able activity for a boy of thirteen or fourteen. Schoolboys cannot afford to maintain a family, even if society ap-proved of very early marriages. There, in simple terms, we have a clear example of the conflict between the real self and that other self upon which society insists.

Here, of course, the conflict is readily understood. It is not so easy to discern the struggle between self and the demands of the outside world at all stages of development. But it is there. From puberty onwards there is a constant clash between law, morals, public opinion, and instinctual desires. Before puberty, however—indeed, right from earliest infancy—we have the same *kind* of conflict. The young child knows nothing of public opinion, but what father and mother think, say, and do is of great importance. Their judgements carry as much weight with the infant— in fact, usually much greater weight—as do those of society with the adult.

This judgement of the outside world influences us all in varying degrees from birth until death. It is of immense psychological effect. We have seen that, ideally, we should live through the various stages of development with the physical and emotional sides growing smoothly and in harmony. Yet very few people succeed in achieving this complete, well-balanced growth. Invariably there are up-sets at various stages of the journey. The result is that the fully developed, ideally mature personality does not exist although, happily, there are many adults who display comparatively few infantile or adolescent traits of an un-pleasant or destructive character. On the other hand some infantile traits are not only harmless, but are pleasantly amusing and attractive. 'It's the child in him which makes him so attractive' we may say, with complete accuracy.

But if 100 per cent normality is unattainable, and even a reasonably close approach to it is exceedingly rare, we do not have to search far in order to find explanations. The journey which, ideally, should be smooth and free from wild alarms, is in fact rendered perilous at every stage. All the time adaptation is necessary. Society without, and the workings of our inner natures within our everyday setting, together present us with innumerable problems.

It is one thing to describe how the sexual instinct seeks expression—or how it should, if left more or less alone. But it is quite another matter to look at the sexual urge not only in its various forms, but against the background in which we live. As a practical problem, sex is always more than an instinctual urge. It is a social problem, an economic problem, a religious problem, and many other things besides, according to the individual concerned and the setting in which he lives his life.

One has, therefore, to be careful not to deal too much in generalities which will not apply in every case. All the same, while avoiding that very common mistake, it is possible to indicate how the self, reacting to pressure from the outside world, holds back from the demands of a new stage of growth, with the result that full emotional maturity is not attained. In adult life, so far as sex is concerned, deviations from normal (the so-called 'perversions') take the form of *substitutes* for direct sexual expression. We may well note that word. For *substitution*, used as a psychological term, provides an excellent starting-point for our study.

When the love-patterns do not unfold smoothly; when, in other words, the individual fails to pass successfully from one growth-stage to the next, there is either no sublimation, or else only partial sublimation. The time has arrived for a move forward, but instead of taking the necessary step on the emotional side, *we substitute something else for the new attitude or mental habit which the fresh stage demands.*

The individual concerned does not say to himself:

'This is a bit thick. Why should I be hurried in this business of growing up? I'll hang back and use my mind precisely as I do now.' If it were as simple as that, it would be possible in many cases to change the individual's attitude by reason alone. The trouble is that the process of substitution, like that of sublimation, is often an unconscious one—if it happens to you, you may be unaware of the fact.

Once a substitute has been selected by an unconscious process, it remains fundamentally unchanged. As the years pass, substitutions may produce various conscious tendencies, and these may change from time to time, according to the outlets available for their expression. The exact nature of the tendency may appear to change, but it is really the individual's experience and opportunities which have changed, not the basic tendency. Substitutions are responsible for a great number of tendencies and activities of a substitute character, many of which represent ways of running away from life. The fact that the basic substitution occurs on the unconscious level means that the individual concerned has no personal responsibility for his particular emotional propensity. No deliberate selection has been made. No conscious power of choice has been exercised. But it must be remembered that in some cases at least we must be held responsible for the manner in which we express unfortunate deviations. Some of us have the ability to exercise that degree of control which society demands, others have not and are to be pitied—not blamed.

This trick of the unconscious—as we may reasonably describe substitution—often occurs during our early years. It is not surprising, therefore, that many of the substitutes for normal sex expression found in adults are of an infantile character. They are forms of activity which, whilst appropriate at an earlier stage of development, should have been discarded long ago. For instance, the adult who wears nappies so as to save himself from going to the lavatory is doing something which is abnormal at his age but perfectly normal at an early age—in other words, when he was a baby. Activities of an infantile character include masturbation; homosexual practices; indulgence in various forms of love-play as an end in itself, instead of as a preliminary to full intercourse; fetishism, which assumes many different forms, and—just talk. For there are some people to whom constant talking about sex provides an acceptable substitute for direct sexual expression.

Reasonable emotional maturity includes an adult acceptance of adult responsibilities. Those who seek normal sex expression (using that term in its purely physical sense) without the responsibilities which should accompany it, are displaying infantile traits. They are still largely self-absorbed. Moreover, they have failed to attain 'acceptance' —that is the adjustment of oneself to the sexual expression in adult years. It might even render normal intercourse impossible, although the incident which produced the impression might have been forgotten long since. The shock which occurred was emotional, and its effects may be felt in the emotional make-up throughout life.

A boy, for example, may continue to grow, and attain full physical stature, develop mentally, and, indeed, become a splendid specimen of physical and intellectual manhood. But his emotional development has been arrested at the stage where the shock occurred. Although he is not conscious of the nature of the forbidding voice which calls to him to stop, what really is holding him back from normal sexual activity is the memory, in the unconscious, for example, of a parent's horrified cry, or the look of disgust, condemnation, or fear on a parent's face.

In an adult affected by such arrested emotional growth, the basic sex urge is, of course, still present. But long after the stage has been reached where intercourse is possible, the victim will find coitus either extremely difficult and distasteful, or perhaps impossible. The urge, demanding expression, may be just as strong as in others; but something within shuts and bolts the door leading to normality of sexual expression, and so the powerful basic, instinctual urge demands other outlets. It becomes diverted, for the normal channel is blocked. And this occurs in the course of the emotional upset at an earlier development stage. In adult life it may lead to a number of substitute sexual activities, or it may result in substitute tendencies and activities which, on the surface, are of a non-sexual nature.

In seeking to describe, as simply as possible, how emotional upsets often prejudicially affect adult sexual expression, I may have tended to give the impression that the unconscious consists of little more than a single, deep-seated impression which dominates the emotional life. This is not so. It is a store of innumerable impressions of different kinds; indeed, nothing is entirely without its effect upon the unconscious—every experience, thought, all that comes to us through any of our senses. But exceptionally vivid impressions, especially those linked with the emotion of fear, have a profound effect on our make-up and personality.

THE UNCONSCIOUS WAREHOUSE

Speaking very broadly, one may say that some of the items stored in the unconscious warehouse are close to the door on the ground floor, others are hidden away deep down in the basement. By an unconscious process we have thrust them as far away as possible, for we do not want to be troubled with them. Fear, feelings of guilt or shame, or some other emotion causes us to push them as far out of consciousness as possible. It is precisely these 'unthinkable' and 'unacknowledgeable' impressions which wreak havoc in many lives. They appear to dislike being thrust away, and seek every opportunity of making themselves known.

Let us, for the sake of simplicity and clarity, call this sum total of our *deep-rooted* unconscious impressions the Deepest Inner Self. This term will serve us better than any psychological expression. When this Deep Inner Self is largely influenced by infantile impressions, infantile it remains. It does not grow up. And so we tend to handle adult situations and problems in an infantile manner.

That is the point to note carefully for it applies to our sexual activities. The result is that we may have read a great deal about sex, and, on the conscious level, recognise fully that sexual expression is natural and desirable, yet be unable to participate in normal intercourse because of the interference of the infantile Deepest Inner Self.

It is important to realise that the Deepest Inner Self whilst it influences a pattern of behaviour does not necessarily completely determine it. A consciousness of its probable existence can help us to redirect or canalise its energies into more suitable adult forms of conduct. But if it remains infantile, it will exert a prejudicial influence. possibly of a profound character, upon our lives.

The goal which gives this book its title cannot be realised where the deepest part of our make-up is born of fear. Love without fear involves, among other things, freedom from the dictatorship of the untamed, infantile, unconscious self. Without that, all else—knowledge of sex, a correct social attitude, physical fitness—may be rendered largely useless, just when we need them most.

Directly the basic sexual instinct shows signs of seeking satisfaction, the Deepest Inner Self which has failed to grow up cries: 'Halt'. Although it is a part of ourselves, this tyrant within bullies us, interferes with us and prevents us doing many things which we know are perfectly right and desirable. The infantile, deep unconscious is not the same as our conscience. Often it forbids what conscience not only sanctions, but even urges.

With this in mind, we can begin to see why it is that sometimes we find husbands who are really in the infant class, and wives who are babes when it comes to the love relationship. Men and women, fully matured physically and mentally, are threatened and frightened *from within themselves*. They are terrified into impotence by a grim, warning voice which hints at the dire penalties which will follow if the deepest instinctual urges, and particularly the sexual instinct, are obeyed. Reason and conscience alike are powerless against this tyranny. What is the result?

The man or woman who is bullied and frightened in this way is often forced to seek some means other than normal for the expression of their basic sex urge. The warning voice from within forbids direct expression; the road which leads straight ahead is blocked, and there is a warning notice threatening severe punishment if one should venture farther along it. Numerous bypaths branch off the road of normality, and in an effort to relieve tension from the demands of our sexual urge some bypath is chosen. A roundabout route, but it may still eventually lead to the desired goal of sex satisfaction.

ROOT CAUSES OF HOMOSEXUALITY

In some individuals the substitution for the real thing may take the form of desire for intercourse with a member of one's own sex. During the earliest days of infancy the child finds how important his mother's ministrations are. She is always ready to ensure his comfort at a time when his sole interest in life is to secure bodily ease. The mother becomes the child's first love object. But very soon the child comes to realise that the delightful security he has known with his mother is threatened—or so it appears.

Father claims some of mother's time, attention, and love. This discovery comes as a great shock to some children.

It may result in a boy developing extremely bitter feelings of hostility towards his father. These feelings may be linked with a vague desire that harm should befall his father. He may even wish to be rid of his father. But as soon as such thoughts enter the mind, they are promptly repressed. Feelings of shame and horror result from such wishes and so they are immediately dispelled.

All this may appear trifling, but the boy is really passing through a period of intense emotional crisis, for deep within his unconscious mind, hidden away as unworthy, there is a latent hostility to his father. As the years pass the boy may have very good reasons for fearing the aggressiveness within himself. It may lead him into many difficulties.

The child's sudden discovery that his mother's love is not entirely his, but has to be shared with somebody else, often provides the situation in which the seeds of homosexuality are sown. Anger, and resentment against one of his parents; intense hostility towards his own father; a feeling that his mother is not faithful to him; a troubled conscience; fear regarding certain tendencies within himself, of which he is conscious; a sense of insecurity, after a period of pleasant, assured security; strong feelings of shame—here, surely, are all the ingredients of a serious emotional upheaval.

Most children soon adapt themselves to the new situation, recognising what the dual relationship—towards mother and father, instead of towards mother alone—entails. But some are unable to do so, and rebel against authority. In adult years they are the extremists, revolutionaries, and the advocates of destructive rather than constructive measures. Those who in infancy satisfactorily solve the problem of the dual relationship have passed the first real test of good citizenship. They have found a social solution. In a world in which no one can live entirely by himself, they have learned, at the right time, how to co-operate.

The boy who cannot solve this problem of infantile emotional growth may develop the most intense hostility towards his father, the feelings of guilt which accompany such aggressiveness serving only to intensify it. But his reaction may follow a different line. He may associate himself more and more closely with his mother. In this way he can, like her, accept his father's love. In this way, however, he may increasingly find himself tending towards a feminine attitude to life and love. Again, homosexuality may result, depending to some extent on his genetic constitution.

In some cases the child's solution to the problem may assume the form of close identification with the mother, not generally perhaps, but specifically as regards her relationship to father. Here, clearly, is an attitude which may easily develop into homosexuality in adult life. The child does not merely tolerate the father's love for the mother, but rejoices in it. Is it surprising that he tends to desire to share her role? The reader will be quick to appreciate the close connection between this desire and the inclination, felt by some in adult life, to assume a passive role in homosexual relations.

There, briefly, we have a simple explanation of the kind of situation in which the seeds of true homosexuality often take root. Genuine homosexual tendencies largely spring from such situations in infancy. We should, therefore, do well to remind ourselves that the true homosexual—as distinct from the dabbler in 'perversions' who seeks to ascertain 'whether there is anything in them'—deserves our understanding. He is the loser in a battle fought when he was very young, and had no choice. Something happened to him, and left its mark upon him.

THE CHILD IN US ALL

In endeavouring to explain how deviations occur I have described some of the ways in which emotional development is arrested. Happily, most people attain a reasonable degree of emotional maturity. But most, if not all, retain from earlier development stages certain attitudes, feelings, or activities which normally should have been left behind. Thumb-sucking in adults, for instance, is a 'left-over' of the oral stage. Many other comparatively harmless habits and tendencies could be cited. Some of these tendencies are so general that they appear to be—and, indeed, are, for all practical purposes—normal. The sucking of a pipe, even when it is empty; the chewing of gum; the sucking of fingers, or of one's teeth; the constant putting of a pencil or a finger to the mouth—all these are indications of the tendency which so many feel towards oral activity.

We have noted how the narcissist will spend hours before a mirror. Yet it is regarded as normal for women, in particular, to possess a measure of love of self-adornment. There may be few men who delight in standing gazing at their bodies for long periods before a mirror, but there are some. There is something of the narcissist in the kind of bore who is constantly telling his friends how clever he is, or who relates, to all and sundry, accounts of his athletic achievements. A very large proportion of men undoubtedly overrate their abilities and over-estimate their worth.

Then there are those who go to the opposite extreme—the shy, awkward people of both sexes who suffer so obviously in our presence that they make us feel uncomfortable. These, too, are victims of a failure to grow up completely, for they retain in adult years the backwardness, awkwardness, and shyness which are normal in adolescence. One could go on giving such instances; the list would become wearying. The truth is that there is something of the child in all of us.

The habits and attitudes of infancy, of puberty, and of adolescence are part of us, although, ideally, they may be sublimated and so become capable of serving us more efficiently at a later and higher level. But whether they enrich our lives—having been sublimated—or whether they produce in us childish or adolescent traits in adult years, they are there. They are never lost.

When you bite your nails, boast, spend too long before the mirror, or display any of the other almost innumerable childish traits, heave a deep sigh and say a prayer of thanks. For *your* little upsets on the march to maturity have left you with nothing worse than a habit or two which is not frowned upon by society, and which may not interfere to any serious extent with the living of a natural, adult life. But the others, the victims of deviations which yield social disgrace or even loss of freedom, owe their plight to practically the same factors which have made you a nail-biter, a boaster, or a gum-chewer. *It is a humbling thought.*

15: The Spacing of Children

Some deviations are practised for no other reason than that the couple concerned are afraid of pregnancy. Many a wife gladly submits to *anything* that her husband cares to do, provided that it will not lead to impregnation. Some, indeed, prefer abnormal intercourse because they fear that normal intercourse may lead to an unwanted baby. Yet those who are usually most severe in their judgement of 'perverts' are generally the very ones who oppose the spreading of knowledge regarding contraceptive technique.

Many women never enjoy sexual intercourse because of the constant dread of pregnancy. Many a marital relationship suffers just because of this situation, which all seems so unnecessary when peace of mind can be had so easily.

Why leave love to be a gamble, with the dice loaded, particularly against the poorer mothers? Why not, instead, apply modern methods so as to 'space' children, thus ensuring all these highly desirable results:

1. The planning of each pregnancy with a view to the best time and season, as regards both mother and child.

2. Keeping the size of the family within the limits imposed by the family purse.

3. Avoiding too many pregnancies, which may undermine the mother's health.

4. Meeting the specific needs of different families, which, of course, vary a great deal.

Volumes of statistics are available showing the need for

the spacing of children. I shall not go into the figures beyond pointing out that first babies die slightly more frequently than do second babies, and that after the second there is a steady rise in the infant mortality rate. When the seventh is reached in the scale the rate is 50 per cent higher. By the time the tenth is reached it is twice as high.

There is one other important point which is often overlooked. Little worse can happen to a child than the death of its mother, and the younger the child is when the mother dies, the worse is the effect. Thus, nearly five times as many children, whose mothers fail to survive their first year, die, as compared with those whose mothers live. This rate, impressive enough as it is, increases to seven times in the case of babies whose mothers die within a few days of their birth.

What has this to do with the spacing of children? A great deal. Anything which saves the mother's life helps all her children. Not only does it tend to increase their prospects of surviving, but it enables them to get a good start in life. The health of the mother will be largely reflected in the condition of her children, so that the least we can do is to relieve the gnawing anxiety and the fear of pregnancy.

It is a fact that infant death rates are high when there has been an unduly short interval between births. On the other hand, when there is at least a two-year interval between births, the infant death rate is about half as high. Such facts speak for themselves, and speak very loudly indeed.

Now before we go on to discuss the practical measures to be taken in order to achieve 'spacing' of births by replacing chance by deliberate control, let me demolish the two main arguments which are used by people who feel that there is something wrong in what is popularly called 'birth control'.

First, the patriotic one, which may be summarised thus

that control of conception must end in race suicide. The simple answer is that our problem today is not under-population but overpopulation.

The truth is that, if the race is to continue, and be strong and healthy, we must have regard for the health and well-being of mothers and children. The survival rates of young people up to at least twenty years of age closely affect the problem. Yet that aspect receives little attention.

The second argument against contraception is one which is, indeed, an argument against sex relations generally. It is not always advanced in the extreme form favouring *total* abstinence from sexual relationships. Often it is urged as a temporary expedient—a substitute for contra-ceptive measures. But, in either case, it represents an un-natural attitude.

I may, perhaps, quote from a lettter which I wrote to a gentleman who expressed annoyance at my suggestion that he and his wife should apply contraceptive measures. 'It is against my deepest principles,' he said, 'and I can't think how you can degrade your profession by advocating such things.' Here is part of what I wrote:

'Since you hold that sex expression is sinful, unless it is directed towards the procreation of children, I feel it my duty to warn you against various dangers which you will have to face if you are to attain your object.

'You must never caress your wife since nothing is more calculated to arouse desire. Do not sit too close to her, hold her hand or undress in her presence since this may have the same effect. In other words you must be utterly indifferent to your wife otherwise desire will disturb your peace of mind, and hers.

'While taking pains not to become friendly and inti-mate, be careful not to go to the other extreme. Quarrels end in reconciliations, which are the very devil for arous-ing desire in both parties. Never visit the cinema, for many of the scenes are sexually stimulating. The same applies to books, plays, and music. Avoid being stirred by strong religious emotion, which can have the same effect.

'If you should decide that this regime is too strict—though it is the only one consistent with your belief—two courses only are open to you. One is to indulge in the sex act, without any attempt to control conception. This may, of course, mean that you will have four or five children during your married life, in which case you may only have opportunities for sexual union five times.

'On the other hand, you may decide that, in spite of your present rigid beliefs, that measure of self-control which is conception rightly understood, is suited to your needs and to those of your wife.'

I had the pleasure, some six months later, of hearing from him, saying his wife had attended a family planning centre.

Before passing to a consideration of contraceptive technique, here are some of the main general grounds for *control* of births as against blind chance:

Prevention of conception can prevent the need for abortion.

Contraceptive technique demands a certain discipline, as does all other techniques. But results justify it.

It lightens the burden of motherhood, enabling mothers to enjoy more self-cultivation than would otherwise be possible, and freeing them to help the family more.

Happier sex relations invariably result from the use of sound contraceptive methods, which rid the sex act of fear, its biggest spoiler.

Contraception means pregnancy by choice and so preserves a woman's health and prevents premature ageing. Above all it saves them from becoming something which is very terrible—unwilling mothers.

Individual responsibility is strengthened when the family

population is deliberately planned—that is, the responsibility of an agreed number of children is assumed deliberately.

Control of conception is the only way to secure the highest good for all the members of the family. It is, therefore, the chief safeguard against race suicide.

16: The Technique of Contraception

Safeguarding involves taking thought. It therefore connotes intellectual activity whereby coitus is not merely a casual reflex or a mere impulse, with children as a by-product. Birth control is self-control under various aliases.

ROBERT LATOU DICKINSON

What the plain man and his wife want to know about contraception is this: is it possible to ensure reasonable safety? Most people know friends who have tried different methods which have proved a failure. What few people realise is that much depends not only upon the method but the *manner of its use*.

This chapter is intended to provide a clear, straightforward guide not merely to contraceptive devices, but contraceptive technique. In brief, it sets out to show you how to exercise GENUINE CONTROL OF CONCEPTION. And that means that you must master the technique as well as know something of the methods.

One of the difficulties facing those who try to estimate the relative values of different methods is the fact that many fail to use them properly. Thus a clinic may report that among its patients one hundred made use of one particular device, over a long period, and that it proved 80 per cent reliable. More careful inquiry might reveal that a proportion of the failures was due to faulty use of the method, or even to neglect of it on occasion.

But it is safe to say that where modern methods are

properly employed the degree of security is very high indeed. It is true that *complete* immunity cannot be guaranteed. But something around the figure of 96 per cent of safety is attainable, except in the case of the pill which is 100 per cent.

What are the essentials of a good contraceptive method? First, it must be *reliable*, otherwise it fails to achieve its main aim. Second, it must not be detrimental to health. Third, simplicity is important. The method should be within the power of the average person to apply. Fourth— and I attach great importance to this—it must not interfere with the course, and not unduly interfere with the pleasure, of normal sexual relations.

Every day several million people in this country have to decide whether or not to use a contraceptive method, and if so, which one. At least four-fifths of married people employ some means, whether good or bad, to prevent conception. But most of them have only the haziest ideas of how to achieve the best results. Most of them use only one method. To achieve the utmost security two methods should be combined, with the exception of the 'pill', and the Graffenberg ring.

Before going into the details of the various devices and methods available some general information regarding frequency and duration of intercourse must be given. For contraceptive methods must be adapted to the requirements of the individual. Therefore, we must know something of how individuals differ if we are to select the methods most suitable for the different types.

Reports, both published and unpublished, suggest that most couples indulge in intercourse twice a week, or, to be exact, slightly over twice a week on average. Of course, there are many who indulge far more frequently, while others rarely perform coitus. But the *average* is as mentioned.

How long do they take? Here again, individuals vary a

great deal. The average duration of the stay of the penis in the vagina is about five minutes. Many regularly exceed that time. The actual union sometimes lasts between five and ten minutes. Of course, cases of longer duration also occur. At the other extreme are men with quick emission. So far as can be ascertained, about 4 per cent ejaculate immediately upon entry. About 12 per cent do so within two minutes. I think it would be safe to say that the great majority of men ejaculate prematurely, i.e. before they really wish it.

What length of time does orgasm cover? Here it is difficult to be precise, but the evidence available suggests that most orgasms take between twelve and fifteen seconds. Some take twenty seconds or more. There are women who achieve 'multiple orgasm'—that is, achieve orgasm more than once in the course of a single sex act.

I go into these details because they affect the problem of which is the best method, or combination of methods, for any individual. As we shall see, some of the most popular preventive devices are not suitable in every case.

A lengthy volume would be required in order to list, and comment even briefly upon, the almost innumerable devices and methods available. My purpose is not to provide a catalogue of contraceptives, but to show the reader what use to make of them. Any man or woman who reads this chapter carefully ought to experience no difficulty in selecting the method, or combination of methods, best suited to his or her own needs.

It is very unfortunate that most contraceptives entail some interference with the sex act. The exceptions are the 'pill' and the Graffenberg ring—or some such similar device. Recently plastic intra-uterine devices have been used.

Caps and pessaries possess many advantages. But the method they represent, with all its advantages, has its drawbacks in some cases, even when there are no outward

216

indications against it. The girl who has been 'sheltered' throughout life, whose attitude to sex and to her own body is extremely 'delicate', may be conscious at all times of something strange, something which seems entirely out-of-place and objectionable, associated with the most intimate parts of her body.

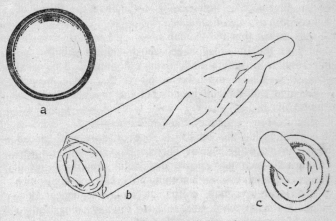

The condom (French Letter)

This applies equally to other contraceptive devices. When such strong disgust centres upon the genitalia, psychological factors may render all contraceptive steps by the woman exceedingly distasteful.

Then again, the condom—widely used as it is, and with so much to commend it—is often strongly disliked by women. They complain that when their husbands wear such a preventative they do not experience anything like the same sensation as they do when it is absent. This may in some cases be imaginary, but for many women the difference is very real. Furthermore, she is prevented from feeling the pleasurable sensation experienced during male ejaculation.

The importance of continuous love-play prior to coitus has been dealt with earlier. The use of a condom often means a break in the love-play, possibly with a lowering of passion. Indeed the rising flow of feeling may be changed abruptly to totally different emotions in which disgust may be prominent. The best plan is to include the fitting of the condom *as part of the love-play*.

This means that the woman fits it on her partner in the course of the love-play, when most couples will feel no interruption in the gradually rising emotional and physical sensations. But it must be admitted that some women would find this difficult because of the psychological factors involved.

The great advantage of the Graffenberg ring—placed as it is right inside the womb—is that, once inserted, it can be left in place for a year. There are no 'fittings', no preliminaries which may prove distasteful, no disposing of the device after use, and nothing to break the continuity of the ideal love-play, coitus, after-play sequence. Provided that no psychological distaste for any contraceptive exists in the woman, this in selected cases is the method of choice.

The cap, fitted when the partner is unaware of the proceeding, also has much to commend it. It leaves a greater degree of 'normality' than most devices.

Caps give a high degree of security, but by no means 100 per cent.[1]

Various purgatives, and other preparations are often consumed by people who believe that some mysterious contraceptive powers are attached to them. These are not contraceptives. They serve no better purpose than to enrich their manufacturers.

---

1 See *Which?* special report by Consumer's Association.

WITHDRAWAL

This involves withdrawal of the penis from the vagina just before ejaculation. It can best be employed by men who are capable of holding back until the partner has achieved complete orgasm. The method well illustrates one basic principle of contraceptive technique: namely, that some sacrifice has to be made in return for the security attained. That is why birth control can rightly be described as a form of self-control. Every step forward means that something must be left behind.

Clearly, withdrawal involves the surrender of a certain measure of gratification, since it fails to yield the intense, concentrated pleasure of uninterrupted coitus.

In fact, the method is by no means reliable. But when the man is capable of exercising the measure of control mentioned, a certain degree of security undoubtedly is attained. As we have seen, too, the ill-effects often attributed to this practice are greatly exaggerated.

Clearly, withdrawal can give no absolute guarantee of security. It is useless in about one-eighth of all marriages. The reason is that about one man in every eight emits quickly—premature ejaculation. It is not to be recommended in the many cases where its practice involves a feeling of either strain or fear. There are, too, some men who are never quite certain of the exact moment of ejaculation. These are few, but they do exist. It is not for them. Some, too, emit semen before actual ejaculation. This accounts for many failures in cases where this method is used.

Bear in mind also this vital point:

Contraceptive Measures, like all else connected with the Technique of Love, Concern Two People.

One must, therefore, always consider the effect upon the woman of any measures taken. Withdrawal should not be practised if the woman cannot attain orgasm before the man withdraws. Many women never feel satisfied unless they feel the rush of semen into the vagina. When this is the case it is unkind to practise withdrawal.

Millions of people practise this method simply because the couples concerned know no other contraceptive technique. Thus, as you would expect, it is often unsatisfactory. In a large number of cases the use of other methods would remedy this.

Why, in spite of such obvious disadvantages, is this method so widely practised? Undoubtedly, for two main reasons. It is the cheapest of all contraceptive measures—the only one that costs nothing—and it requires no preparatory manipulations. Psychologically, too, strange though it may seem, some men prefer this method to others.

THE CONDOM

This—popularly known as the 'French Letter',[1] or 'rubber preventative'—is unquestionably the simplest and most-used form of contraception. It is known to almost every adult. In the United States about one-fourth of married people look to it as their safeguard against unwanted pregnancy. In Great Britain the proportion is higher.

Much depends upon the quality of the condom. Provided the preventative is well manufactured, it is well suited to the requirements of men with good erection. Of course, 'coating' the organ with thin rubber slightly reduces the sensibility. Here again there is a price to be paid for the security given. But provided a man has an average 'surplus of sensation', this slight numbing of sensibility will generally be regarded as insufficient to offset the condom's security value.

1. See diagram, page 217.

The condom has often been attacked in the past on a number of grounds. These need not concern us now. Generally, the quality of condoms has improved in recent years. The makers have greatly reduced the proportion of faulty products, though there is still room for improvement.

The tested rubber condom is the one most used today. To apply it, unroll it *carefully* on to the erect penis. Try to avoid letting air in. The outside of the condom-tip should be lubricated with a contraceptive jelly. This is particularly helpful when the woman has a dry vagina. After the act withdraw promptly. Do so while the penis is still erect, in order to avoid a spill-over, or, worse still, the slipping-off of the condom. This is most important. Many failures occur through lack of attention to this point. A washable condom can be cleansed with soap and water within twenty-four hours after use, then left to dry. Avoid allowing it to become unduly dry, as this renders it likely to tear.

There have been many complaints that the condom method of contraception has failed. But inquiry reveals that a large proportion of failures is due not to the method itself, but to not paying attention to the points I have made.

CONTRACEPTIVE JELLIES

These are mostly used to reinforce other precautions, and, as we have seen, they also serve to provide lubrication. They are suited to use with either the pessary or the condom. Questions most asked concern the quantity to be used. In this connection a fairly safe rule is to use a teaspoonful. Various jellies, pastes, and creams are available, to which the same rule as to quantity applies.

There can be no doubt that, even when used alone,

chemical contraceptives of this kind are better than nothing; they should, however, be used as an adjunct to some other form of contraceptive.

Sometimes withdrawal by the man, together with the use of a jelly or paste by the woman, is the method adopted. The measure of security is thus increased. Dual methods generally are very successful. This applies particularly to the condom-plus-paste combination. The combined methods have the advantage of demanding no medical supervision or instruction, unlike some other methods to which I will refer later.

HOME-MADE CONTRACEPTIVES

These do not provide a high degree of protection, but they are better than nothing; that is about all to be said in their favour.

Medicated tampons consist of rubber sponge, cotton wool or animal wool, all in one piece. If more than one piece is used, part may be left behind in the vagina. A solution of common alum, household vinegar, and lemon juice is applied, and a string or tape is often used to facilitate removal of the tampon after use.

Sometimes the tampon is treated with fats and oils. When this home-made contraceptive is used, it is desirable to have a vaginal douche immediately after intercourse. Much depends upon how snugly the tampon fits into the vagina. Unless it is fairly tight, lying against the opening of the womb and even causing a little discomfort at first, it may be pressed aside by the thrust of the male organ. Tampons should be inserted as deeply as possible, just prior to intercourse, and never longer than one hour before.

I have said that the use of a douche is desirable after intercourse when a tampon is employed, but the very people who most frequently use the tampon method are the ones who lack modern conveniences—dwellers in the poorest sections of the community, or in rural areas. They do not always have a bathroom; warm water is never quickly available and, accordingly, a rough-and-ready method has to replace the douche.

This may take the form of *lathering*, which, for them, has the added advantage that no apparatus is required beyond a glass or basin. The best soaps for this purpose are those made with coconut oil, which, incidentally, possesses marked sperm-paralysing powers. People of all classes often rely upon lathering as a substitute for the douche when travelling.

DOUCHE TECHNIQUE

While I cannot regard the douche by itself as a reliable contraceptive measure, it certainly has a value when used with others. Moreover, it should be a stock toilet article. For many years it has been so in France. Increasingly, it is becoming so in Britain and the United States. Its value as an hygienic aid should ensure its general use, quite apart from any contraceptive value.

Ineffective flushing of the vagina obviously means that all semen may not be ejected. When syringing is performed while the woman is either sitting or standing the fluid tends to flow back. Often the passage is not cleared. It is essential that the vagina should be filled with fluid, which should then be permitted to run out. Always douche in the upright, preferably squatting, position.

Various chemicals are used—boric acid, lysol, vinegar, potassium permanganate, and others. Many women, having been advised as to the correct amounts, double them 'to make sure'. Too strong solutions are likely to irritate the mucous membrane of the vagina, and they certainly give no greater degree of safety. The simplest and best douche is one made by adding a small teaspoonful of salt to a pint of water.

Some authorities maintain that the sensitiveness of the mucous lining is diminished, and dryness of the vaginal wall produced, when douching is carried to excess. Certainly these results may follow continual douching and strong solutions. The dryness sometimes held to be due to this is, however, undoubtedly often due to totally different causes. Fatigue, excitement, over-work, nervous anxiety, and other mental and emotional states may yield this result.

Douching should never be regarded as a contraceptive method in itself. Used in combination with the pessary, pessary and paste, or with the condom, it can be recommended. When used in combination with pessary and paste, the douche may be used any time after intercourse. The presence of the paste makes no difference. Hot or cold douches are best avoided. The impression, held in some quarters, that cold kills the sperms is entirely erroneous. A warm douche should always be used.

VAGINAL SUPPOSITORIES AND GELS

For sheer simplicity the cone, or bolus, leads the field. There are three main types—glycero-gelatin, cocoa butter, and the soap suppository. These take the form of a small solid cone. They melt at slightly below body temperature.

For many years suppositories have been largely used in Great Britain. Among their advantages are the following: they do not have to be 'put away somewhere' like a condom, they do not require apparatus for their application, as does jelly or paste. Moreover, they are easily concealed —a point which will appeal to those who suffer from embarrassment about the use of contraceptives.

Suppositories do not interfere with freedom in the sex

224

act. But over-lubrication of the vagina may result and interfere with pleasure. Moreover, many dislike the smell of cocoa butter, and this may even make intercourse impossible. The objection to suppositories is that they are 'messy', and relatively costly. Suppositories have now largely been replaced by gels.

VAGINAL AND CERVICAL CAPS

These should be fitted in the first instance either at a birth-control clinic or by a physician experienced in this kind of work. An intelligent nurse who has undergone some special training for the work should be able to fit the majority of women. The large-scale help which is needed by those least able to afford medical assistance demands that nurses should be able to promote this valuable branch of preventive medicine.

When the cap is fitted at the doctor's or at a clinic the woman examines it in place, and is taught how to remove and replace it. She should then be left alone to put it in for herself, the doctor or nurse returning later to check her degree of success. Most women can be taught the technique of fitting within fifteen minutes. It is desirable that it should be fitted by an expert at the start to ensure securing the most suitable size, since a snug fit is essential to security. During intercourse the cap fits close along the anterior vaginal wall, thus shielding the mouth of the womb.

Those who live in out-of-the-way districts where instruction and assistance in fitting cannot be obtained should seek some other method of contraception. Obesity is also sometimes a bar to the use of a cap.

But the biggest drawback to the use of the cap lies in psychological considerations arising from that false morality which we have so strongly condemned for its other ill-effects. As we have seen, many a woman experiences disgust centring on her genital sphere. This may be so strong as to make her literally incapable of fitting a cap or, for that matter, of using any form of contraceptive.

There is no need here to go into the various kinds of caps available, since any suitable type, properly fitted, provides the necessary safety. Some general advice on technique will, however, prove helpful to many.

The actual introduction of the cap by a woman who has been taught how to fit it, should not take more than a few seconds. It provides a considerable degree of protection without interference with normal intercourse. Most patients with whom I have discussed the matter, men and women alike, agreed that during intercourse they have not been at all conscious of the presence of the cap.

Then again, no 'preliminaries' just before intercourse are demanded. This is important. Nothing tends to rob the sex act of its essential spontaneity more than the fixing of devices, or the taking of precautions which hold up love-play and distract attention, even if they do not occasion disgust. The cap should be inserted *every* day or night. If a woman makes a habit of fixing it in this way, it will always be there to play its protecting part, and there will be no unpleasant interruption of the love embrace. Moreover, repetition of coitus will demand no further preparation.

One word of warning regarding caps. It is not sufficient for a woman to buy a size which she thinks will suit her, as many do at various shops every day. An expert *must* advise as to size, and also instruct in fitting. Many failures arise through faulty fitting which results in the cap being pushed out of place during intercourse. Whenever caps are used, jelly or paste as an added precaution is advised. Some eight hours later the cap should be removed. Ideally, douching with warm water should both precede and follow removal of the cap.

ONE OF THE BEST METHODS IN SELECTED CASES

This is a modification of the Graffenberg ring. It is a spiral ring made of inert steel so that there is no chemical reaction between it and the womb. It is inserted in the body of the womb, past the internal opening and remains in this position for one year, after which it is removed and a new one is inserted. This should, of course, be undertaken by a doctor experienced in this work.

No other contraceptive apart from the 'pill' has yielded 100 per cent protection, but the ring comes as near to this as possible. It is entirely harmless, it can, however, in some cases be unsuitable for one reason or another. It is not always possible to know beforehand how a particular woman will react to the ring, but if unsuitable the ring of course should be removed.

When the ring is reinforced by a suppository, gel, or aerosol the combination can be regarded as absolutely fool-proof.

Those with least experience of the ring appear to condemn it most strongly without taking the trouble to investigate its value. Criticisms are made not only without knowledge, but as a result of bias and prejudice.

Very carefully over a period of nearly twenty-five years some thousands of cases have been watched and no worthwhile evidence against its use has been found. Scrapings from the womb show no sign of serious changes, nor is there any suggestion of malignancy. It used to be thought that the irritation caused by a foreign body could cause cancer; we now know that this is not true. There are millions of people going about with shrapnel in their bodies; millions who have had their bones plated; millions wearing loosely fitting false teeth; millions wearing pierced ear-rings, and yet not one of these by itself has ever given rise to cancer.

Of late plastic polyethylene coils, loops and other patterns have been used. These are inserted into the womb and usually no anaesthetic is required.

This method, however, leaves the mouth of the womb open so that there is a risk of infection. Unfortunately, the expulsion rate is relatively high—so too are its side-effects. None the less, some modification of the plastic coil could, one day, provide a real solution—especially in those parts of the world where a population explosion is threatened.

THE SAFE PERIOD

What has become known as the safe period is based on a knowledge of the days in a woman's menstrual cycle when there will be no egg (i.e. ovum) present to be fertilised by the male egg or sperm.

In every menstrual cycle the fertile days are those days when the ovum is present, waiting, as it were, to be fertilised. This corresponds approximately to the period from the tenth to the twentieth day—reckoned from the first day of menstruation. The infertile days—in other words the so-called 'safe-period'—are therefore the first and last ten days of the menstrual cycle.

It is necessary therefore for those who may be interested in the safe period as a form of contraception to know exactly when the 'safe' days occur. This is a task which, though comparatively simple, requires a lot of patience—patience which is beyond many a woman.

One way of ascertaining the exact time of ovulation is by taking the temperature once a day for two months. It must be taken at the same time each day—and taken very carefully. It will be found that, barring ill health, these temperatures will be the same each day except when ovulation takes place. It will then rise one degree and remain so until two to three days before the onset of the next menstrual period, after which it will go back to the previous level.

At the best this method can only be used by those whose menstrual cycles are extremely regular. Long and careful investigation is absolutely essential if one is to secure data of any real value. But even then one cannot be reasonably certain that the desired result will be achieved. So far as can be ascertained, conception has occurred on every day of the month, including the days of actual menstruation.

This method is not a particularly safe one, but it has the advantage as far as Roman Catholics are concerned of having the approval of their Church.

THE 'PILL'

This gives 100 per cent protection when taken according to instructions, but is obtainable only on a doctor's prescription. There is some doubt as to the long-term effects, also in some cases there are unpleasant side-effects—but these are the exception and not the rule. The wife takes twenty pills, one each day for twenty days, starting from the fifth day after the commencement of her menstrual period, and that month she cannot become pregnant. Equally, just so long as the pill is taken in this manner, pregnancy is impossible.

AEROSOL FOAM

This is a foam packed under pressure in a small bottle. It is manufactured in the United States under the title of 'Emko', and is now obtainable in Britain. It gives a very high degree of protection even when used alone. It is injected into the vagina and neither husband or wife are aware of its presence, and it is very simple to use.

IN A NUTSHELL

Double contraceptive measures invariably yield a high degree of security. Build a second line of defence.

Many dislike the artificial limitation of what should spring from a highly emotional state. The cap or the ring is recommended for 'normality' of intercourse.

The condom possesses one advantage over and above its contraceptive merits. It is largely a safeguard against disease.

Fully two-thirds of the failure of contraceptive methods is due to faulty technique.

In most families sexual intercourse which is happily adjusted in every respect demands contraceptive measures. The happy mutual response of both partners, the frequency and duration of the act—all depend upon a feeling of security.

To find the best in the sex life is a big step towards finding the best in life generally. That means selection. Contraception provides the conditions for selection.

SUMMARY OF METHODS

1. The Most Reliable Methods.
  1. The 'Pill'.
  2. The Graffenberg Ring.

2. Reasonably Reliable Birth Control Methods.
  1. Condoms.
  2. Aerosol Foam.

  3. Vaginal Suppositories and Gels.
  4. Vaginal Foam Tablets.

3. *Birth Control with a Doctor's Help.*
  1. The Birth Control Pill.
  2. The Graffenberg Ring.
  3. Plastic Coil.
  4. The Diaphragm—vaginal or cervical.

4. *Less Reliable Methods.*
  1. The 'Safe Period'—i.e. the rhythm method.
  2. Withdrawal.
  3. Douche.

17 : Abortion

Let me say straight away that this chapter is not intended for those whose religious beliefs or religion do not permit abortion under any circumstances.

Abortion. It is an ugly word, possibly, in part at least, due to its associations. For morally there is not a great deal of difference between contraception and abortion. The one prevents pregnancy, the other prevents its continuation. Now the trouble with abortion lies in the fact that, except in cases where the continuation of a pregnancy would result in severe ill-health, it is outside the law. This explains why quacks acting as professional abortionists, midwives who run grave risks for gain, proprietors of shady nursing homes, and manufacturers of certain so-called 'remedies' for pregnancy, and a host of other pests prey on human misery and make money out of procuring abortion, or of pretending to do so.

Termination of pregnancy is legal when in *good faith* the operation is done in order to avoid serious and incapacitating ill-health—physical, psychological or both—to the pregnant mother. In Britain, in all other instances, it is illegal, and punishable with heavy penalties. There is, however, a considerable—and growing—body of medical and lay opinion which favours a change in the law.

For one thing, in democratic countries the private life of the individual is highly prized. If, for very good reasons other than medical, a woman strongly desires to be freed of pregnancy, it seems unreasonable that she should be denied help. Of course, whatever changes are made in the law, proper penalties should always be imposed upon unqualified 'practitioners' who are prepared to risk the health of any woman provided they collect a fee. In fairness, however, it should be stated that there are some illegal abortionists prepared to help a woman for reasons of humanity alone.

I doubt if there is a doctor who has not at some time or other felt tempted to terminate a pregnancy on grounds short of legal sanction. They know, possibly better than most people, the kind of life which has to be lived in families capable of supporting two children, but where there are five or six. They know, too, that when there is a deep-rooted fear of having a child, the results can be disastrous. They are also aware of many cases where it is difficult to attach a specific label to the cause of ill-health; but where, none the less, another confinement would be the 'last straw'.

LACUNAE IN LAW

There are a number of cases where it should be legal to terminate a pregnancy, but which, as the law now stands, is illegal.

Firstly, in the case of the girl under the age of sixteen, it is a criminal offence to have sexual intercourse with her. If she should become pregnant, possibly as a result of rape, then surely the law should allow her to be relieved of her pregnancy.

Secondly, the woman who is insane, and becomes pregnent—should have the right to be relieved of her pregnancy —if she so desires.

And thirdly, when it is thought that the baby will be born deformed or otherwise severely handicapped, termination of pregnancy again, if requested, should be legal.

The law does not prevent abortion, all it does succeed in doing is driving it underground. This means that the overwhelming majority of abortions today are either self-induced or carried out by unskilled or little-skilled illegal abortionists. Fear on the doctor's part breeds fear on the patient's part, and only too often the vicious circle goes cruelly on, so that those who might have had relief within the law, find themselves seeking aid outside the law—often because they are afraid to consult their doctor.

It is true that in considering abortion the difficulty resides in assessing just what constitutes serious ill-health. Physical, psychological, and economic factors all play a part, and have to be faced by the doctor, for they undoubtedly affect health.

More often than not too much stress is laid on purely physical grounds, and too little on the psychological. This is strange when the emphasis today is on preventive medicine. We would think it quite right that a simple growth which might eventually become cancerous should be removed. But if there is a growth in the mother's womb, in the form of an unwanted pregnancy, which would, for a certainty, give rise to psychological ill-health, we are reluctant to do anything about it. In other words, preventive medicine is considered good in the one case, and bad in the other. Why this prejudice? Religious attitudes and legal prohibitions are probably the underlying reasons. Most of us know of cases where the birth of an unwanted child is tragic in its consequences. Yet if there are no grounds strong enough to satisfy the needs of the law, nothing can be done, except, of course, by the illegal abortionist.

It is true, of course, that termination of pregnancy can by itself be responsible for undesirable emotional disturbance. We must remember this when we are determining whether a pregnancy should or should not be terminated. The woman's background and circumstances must always be taken into account, and there is no one better qualified to judge than the general practitioner. The mother who feels that her doctor has genuinely considered every aspect of her case and decides that it is in her own best interest to continue with her pregnancy, will be more able to accept the verdict and make the best and not the worst of her situation.

It is only in recent years that the 'totality' of the patient has been recognised and that the interaction between the spirit, mind, and body at all times determines health or ill-health.

A word may be said here of the doctor who, through honest religious belief, finds himself unable in conscience to advise termination of pregnancy, even though there is legal justification. In such a situation he must acquaint his patient of the position in which he finds himself—and recommend a colleague.

Equally, of course, a doctor should not attempt to force upon a woman the practice of his own religious beliefs, neither should he try to force upon her a practice of his scientific beliefs where these conflict with her spiritual convictions.

His duty is to make an honest and sincere recommendation, the final decision rests with the mother. If she chooses to risk her life and health either from passionate desire to bear a child or from religion conviction, she has the right to do so.

THE SUMMING UP

Nothing in this chapter should be interpreted as indicating that a woman should have the complete right to have an abortion on request, since this can in some cases be detrimental to health.

Furthermore, what a pregnant mother feels is true at the time, but later she may feel differently.

One thing is certain, the removal of doubt and fear by a clarification of the law would enable doctors to make a more objective decision, and equally, women would be better able to accept an opinion, knowing it was given honestly and without prejudice. This, in the last resort, would, at least, result in fewer unwanted children being brought into the world.

FREEDOM TO SEEK MEDICAL ADVICE

And lastly, any woman whose health is suffering in consequence of an unwanted or wanted pregnancy should feel free to seek medical advice. She should not be afraid to inquire whether her condition warrants termination of her pregnancy

On the doctor's part, there is an onus to treat and judge every case on its individual merits. Indeed, the doctor who turns down such a request out of hand without bothering to examine his patient or give due consideration to all relevant factors in so far as they might affect her health might find himself guilty of negligence if, as a result, his patient's health suffered.

I have no desire to minimise the difficulties involved in making a psychiatric assessment as to the justification for the termination of pregnancy. Only a fool, or someone possessed of super-human powers, could predict with absolute certainty the short- and long-term effects of an unwanted pregnancy. We must have the humility to appreciate that our views are based on probabilities and possibilities. We are, of course, helped in making our judgement by the patient's past history and her present reaction, but again, how can we say with absolute certainty that this will be permanently damaging? This difficulty, however, is no reason for attempting to opt out of our responsibilities. We do not do this in any other branch of medicine, but when the termination of pregnancy is considered our readiness to express an opinion against this often seems to be in inverse ratio to our knowledge of all the possible consequences of an enforced continuation to full term.

Let's face it, there are pregnancies which are terminated to the eventual detriment of the patient's health. There are others which are not terminated, with equally disastrous results. Since there is no such thing as human infallibility this may be one of the occupational hazards in the practice of medicine.

There are cases, however, when to refuse help to a woman with an unwanted pregnancy, is completely contrary to human rights and to the humanities. To attempt to force anyone into accepting the unacceptable is bad medicine, for it must seriously affect health. So whether we like it or not, we must recognise the therapeutic need, in certain cases, for termination of pregnancy. Naturally, in making a decision, we will have to weigh the possible consequences of termination against the possible consequences of continuing to full term. If we decide that termination is the lesser of the two evils—then the question arises—is there legal sanction? The destruction of a woman's soul as a result of her being forced to continue her unwanted pregnancy into the birth of an unwanted child—is one of the greatest tragedies a mother can suffer.

18 : Sex Superstitions and Myths

In no department of life is superstition so hard to die as in the sex sphere. Half the world is still guided in its sexual conduct not by knowledge but by half-truth, traditions, superstitions and old wives' tales.

DR. WINIFRED V. RICHMOND

That the subject of sex should be surrounded by superstitions is not in the least surprising. The great majority of adults discover as soon as they become aware of sex, that it is something hardly to be breathed about. Many of them can recall how, when they inquired how they came into this world, they were informed that the doctor brought them in a little black bag, that they were discovered sleeping comfortably in the basement of a large department store, were brought by a stork, or appeared in some mysterious way under a gooseberry bush.

What appalling prevaricators parents can be—even the most honest among them—when answering their children's questions about sex. We may well wonder that anybody eventually attains anything approaching a sane outlook on this subject, and in fact few do.

Even great teachers have sometimes said things which must have exercised a profound and prejudicial influence upon millions. Consider, for instance, the words of St. Paul, he who wrote so beautifully about love in its wider sense: 'It is better to marry than to burn!' he said. It is to be doubted whether those words carry a great deal of weight these days. But no doubt, in the past, females who failed to find a husband must have suffered agonies contemplating the fiery furnace which awaited them.

Nowadays most people adopt a somewhat superior attitude regarding superstitions; but a remarkably large number secretly order their lives by reference to what the stars are alleged by certain seers to foretell. Books which deal with 'fate and fortune', the alleged influence of the planetary forces, and the like, sell in enormous numbers. They can do a vast amount of harm.

It is true that a great many people read such books, or follow the astrologers more for fun than for any serious purpose. But there are also many who take the prophecies of these seers seriously.

It is amazing how some otherwise intelligent men and women allow themselves to be guided in such a manner. Many a woman has been convinced that her forthcoming baby would be a boy, because she herself had been born under the influence of some planet or other, that she had chosen his name in advance. But when 'Frank Robert Surname' was born, and proved to be a girl, did her mother stop believing in astrology, lucky signs, magic and the rest? Not for one moment.

The truth is that such people do not *want* to disbelieve in these things. They like to feel that they can peer into the future and know what is coming to them. They feel happier for the knowledge that they possess some lucky charm or other which will serve as an ally if danger threatens. All these are crutches which serve to support the ill-adjusted—those, that is, who have failed to come to terms with life. And sex superstitions, at any rate those which are the most dangerous, also arise from a failure to come to terms with one's own sexuality.

The thousand or more superstitions concerning pregnancy—how to ensure that the baby shall be either a male or a female, how to influence the child before birth so that it will be brilliant intellectually, gifted artistically, or of outstandingly attractive appearance—need not concern us here. Nine times out of ten, experience reveals that the people who believe in such superstitions, and refuse to allow anything to shake their faith in them, are neurotic. But we must face the fact that almost everybody—indeed, it may be truer to say *everybody*—is to some extent a victim of superstition where sex is concerned.

In the appendix at the end of this book I stress that menstruation is an entirely normal process, and one which should not be regarded as an illness. There is one very common impression, which arises no doubt from the fact that menstruation involves an apparent 'draining off' of impurities. It is thought that the whole reason for menstruation is the need of the body to be thoroughly cleansed at regular intervals.

This totally false notion is widely held all over the world. It is regrettable that women should have a wrong impression regarding a normal functioning of their bodies.

As is well known, sometimes the menses are suppressed for a time. This may occur for one of many reasons—and there is seldom anything to worry about.

There are, however, many women who suffer mental agony because they are convinced this means they are 'going bad inside'. There is a good deal of truth in the saying: If you *think* you are ill, you are. And women who think they are ill because of a temporary suppression of the menses sometimes worry themselves into illness.

Men as well as women are victims of superstitions and phobias, although they are less likely to visit palmists and fortune-tellers, or experience fear if there are thirteen sitting at table.

Men cling to some beliefs which, if they are not of a superstitious character, are very close to it, just as women do to their faith in fortune-tellers. The man who sees all the virtues in blondes, or in brunettes, and fails to recognise that both blondes and brunettes include all kinds of females, is surely the victim of a foolish superstition.

One has only to mention the matter in this way and the absurdity of insisting upon blondes, brunettes or red-heads, when selecting staff members or partners in marriage, is at once apparent. There are other widespread beliefs which are held by men, and which are equally absurd. They persist in spite of constant propaganda designed for their banishment. Who has not met the man who is convinced that the frequency and strength of his sexual desires are a sign that he is a splendid specimen of his sex? He may not describe himself thus. But his whole attitude reveals what he really believes. Sometimes this outward obsession with sex arises from a feeling of inadequacy. Indeed, the man who talks a great deal about sex, especially when there is no particular reason for discussing the subject, is usually sex-hungry, if not starved.

The man who is well-fed does not constantly feel hungry, nor does he talk and think about food most of the day. He enjoys his meals, then turns to other matters. He probably does not devote a single thought to the subject of food until another meal-time arrives. It is the same with those whose sex life is healthy and satisfactory. The victims of the old, but apparently undying, belief that to be 'full of sex' is a sign of virility and manliness, merely cry out to the discerning: *'There is something wrong with my sex life.'*

It is easy to laugh at some of the more obviously absurd old superstitions, but more profitable to examine ourselves carefully in order to ascertain whether or not we are replacing them with new ones. The increase in sex education, together with the growth of knowledge regarding the physical and psychological aspects of sex—all good in themselves—have produced a crop of strange ideas with a marked superstitious flavour.

In Victorian days it was customary to assume that, from

soon after puberty until he had reached advanced years, a male should indulge in sexual relations more or less regularly, otherwise his health would suffer. It was also believed, curiously enough, that the precise opposite applied to females. They must on no account have sex experience until they were married. 'Women', it was said, 'are different'. All this was part of the double moral standard —the view that sexual indulgence was necessary for the male, and wicked, foolish and harmful for the female. But with the growth of knowledge regarding sex matters there has come a sweeping change.

In so far as there has arisen a demand for an equal moral standard, one which applies to both sexes and does not give to men a freedom which it denies to women, this change is to be welcomed. But some of the more extreme advocates of 'women's rights' have sought to take from men their foolish superstition, and make it their own. Their argument runs something like this: 'Men have had a very good innings, now it is time for us to bat. They have claimed sexual freedom and have denied it to us for centuries. Now, let us claim complete freedom to do as we choose. If men can enjoy freedom in their sexual expression, then so can we.'

At first thought, there appears to be soundness in this argument. But consideration soon reveals its weakness. If it is pointed out to the women who advocate complete sexual freedom for themselves that they are now proposing to do precisely what they have condemned in men, they are unmoved. If it is suggested to them that, after suffering injustice, they now tend to overcompensate by going to extremes which will not benefit them, they are not impressed. The old, foolish superstition which held men in its grip for so long now has hold of them.

We know enough of the biological and historical aspects of sex to realise that women are not 'different', or not markedly so, where the urge to sex expression is concerned. They are different, however, in the manner and framework within which they will express it. We know that they experience desire, just as men do. But one has only to look closely, or, indeed, even casually, at the lives of women who follow to its logical conclusion the doctrine of complete sexual freedom, in order to observe that it does not always bring happiness to those who adopt it. On the contrary, every big city, and many a village, contains women who have gone out boldly to claim and enjoy 'Women's Love Rights', and have broken themselves by doing so. The practical test: *How does it work out?* reveals conclusively that it can bring unhappiness to those directly concerned, and, often, to others as well.

But that is not all. Some authorities in the past maintained that men and women possess a similar psychology. At every stage of physical growth, in both the male and female, physiological change is invariably accompanied by enotional change. It is difficult to imagine that physical changes can occur without some corresponding psychological repercussions. This being so, is it likely that women, whose physiological make-up is different from that of men, will not differ in their emotional make-up?

It is, of course, somewhat dangerous to generalise regarding the psychology of any group. It is even more dangerous to do so regarding the psychology of a whole sex. No two individuals are precisely alike in their emotional make-up. Even so, it seems that, *taken as a whole*, women differ emotionally in some respects from men, in other words, there is, in fact, a feminine psychology.

Apart from this, however, we must realise that women are what they are, just as men are what they are, *at this moment*. Even if there is no separate psychology of women in the true basic sense it is absolutely certain that today, as the result of the influence of the past, and other factors, the emotional make-up of women differs from that of men. For all immediate practical purposes, then, it is a mistake to regard men and women as being the same psychologically. Men may do certain things and suffer slight hurt in consequence. Women may do the same things and suffer much greater hurt, and vice versa.

Licence in the sexual sphere can deeply wound a fundamental part of a woman's nature. This may arise partly from the fact that women, unlike men, carry the responsibilities and privileges of maternity. That in itself, surely, is sufficient to account for a different attitude towards life in certain respects. The condemnation of conscience felt by the man who indulges in sexual irresponsibility arises mainly from his departure from conventional standards which have been imposed by society in order to ensure the ordered growth of community and family life. This applies equally to the woman who casts off sexual restraints.

It would seem that the struggle for sex freedom is like that of nations which cast off various yokes only to find that they have established fresh ones, so that the struggle for liberty has to continue along new lines. We secure a measure of freedom from some false impression or old superstition, but too often put in its place a new one which, closely regarded, looks very much like the old in thick disguise. This is true of the claim of the more extreme feminists who demand a sex equality based not on raising the male standard to a higher level, but upon lowering the female standard.

This chapter is headed by a quotation from an American woman doctor. Dr. Winifred Richmond also says, in her *Introduction to Sex Education*, that 'the idea that the adolescent girl is not troubled by sex thoughts or feelings, that until she is awakened by actual experience the normal girl's love-life is purely romantic and sentimental—an idea upheld by the majority of masculine writers on sex— probably merits the term superstition'. It probably does.

She goes on to say that in the cultures which accord equal freedom to both sexes, and according to studies which have been made in recent years in America, girls do not appear to be much behind boys in their sexual interest. Dr. Richmond has made a study of the sexual lives of many races, and her conclusions are, therefore, of more than usual interest. She maintains that, while it is true that girls do not carry their sex desires into action so often as boys, this is due 'as much to our social standards as to any slowness of awakening on the girl's part'.

This point of view is interesting and is worthy of careful consideration. It affects our attitude to sex education in certain respects. But, of course, we have to take girls as they are today when giving advice on practical issues. The girl may, fundamentally, possess as strong a sex urge as the boy; but at present, in the majority of cases, it has to be 'brought out' by suitable action on a lover's part.

Girls have sexual dreams, just as boys do, and indulge in sexual phantasies. Round about puberty they pass through a masturbatory period. There is much to be said, therefore, in favour of Dr. Richmond's view that, if the same amount and type of stimulation to which boys are subjected were applied to them, girls would be found to behave very little differently from boys.

It may be argued, for instance, and with much truth, that, for a woman, sexual intercourse does not consist of the single sex act as in the case of a man, but, when Nature's full purpose is achieved, it continues throughout the process of gestation, pregnancy and childbirth. Indeed, we may agree with Canon T. W. Pym and regard the 'sex act', in women, as something much more than a single copulatory act—a series which embraces courtship, wooing, sex act, conception, gestation, childbirth, lactation and maternity.

Now we are able to look back to Dr. Richmond's remarks about the superstition attached to the girl's sexuality, and to consider whether or not a fresh superstition is making its appearance in the guise of 'sexual equality'. For, while it may be true that sexuality in girls is equal to that in boys, immediately we consider the expression of that sexuality we are brought up against the fact that the girl's sexual nature is different from the boy's.

Men are men and women are women. It would be silly if men were to seek sex 'equality' by acting exactly like women. And when women try to achieve sex equality by behaving like men, they find themselves defeated, not by anything men do, but by their own nature.

Another myth which has grown up in recent years is that a woman who sows her 'wild oats' before marriage is no more affected than are the innumerable men who have indulged in sexual relationships prior to wedlock. I accept the contention that woman's sexuality is comparable to men's so far as its strength is concerned. But its nature is different. The woman does not play precisely the same role as the man in a sex relationship. She may engage in the sex act with as much ardour as her partner. But if this act is outside of the fuller relationship, then because of her feminine nature, even though largely environmentally determined, she may be giving away something much more than she has bargained for.

Next, let us consider the fantastic idea, once very commonly held, and even now by no means dead, that sexual intercourse is a cure for various mental and nervous ailments. If, for example, a young man or woman suffers from sleeplessness or anxiety, or displays symptoms of restlessness and inability to settle down to the tasks in hand, the remedy proposed is: *Get married*.

Anyone would suppose from this that marriage provided a cure for immature traits, or else that marriage was designed for neurotics, infantiles, and ill-adjusted people who cannot come to terms with life. Of course, the result of advising people to marry in such circumstances is simply this: *two* people are made to suffer instead of one. The victims carry into marriage their emotional disabilities, and inflict upon their partners their own immature personalities. Marriage alone will not heal a neurotic. But many a neurotic has wrecked a marriage.

Superficial observers have often believed that sexual difficulties or 'sex starvation' are the principal causes of mental breakdown. I have seen it stated that the psychoanalytic school has been mainly responsible for this belief. Nothing could be further from the truth.

It is true that sexual difficulties are frequently experienced by people suffering from mental or nervous ailments. Because of the disabilities from which they suffer, such people are unable to handle their lives competently. Is it surprising that they fail to secure a sound adjustment to sex, or to their partners in marriage? They are sick people. Their sexual difficulties usually arise from their emotional illness or lack of adjustment—rarely the reverse.

Many erroneous ideas are held regarding the menopause in women. Just as puberty marks the beginning of woman's reproductive phase, so the menopause, or climacteric as it is often termed, marks the end. The dangers and difficulties of the period of 'the change' have been grossly exaggerated in the past. Now, however, there is a tendency to go to the other extreme and to dismiss the symptoms which sometimes accompany the change as being purely imaginary.

It must be confessed that the almost superstitious belief that 'the change' means the end of all that is worth-while in a woman's life is responsible for more harm than any other single factor—if not *all* other factors put together. I do not propose to go into details regarding the menopause, all that need be said here is that whilst it is true that so important a change may constitute a psychological difficulty, acceptance of the fact that the change is natural, and, above all, that it brings fresh opportunities for the enjoyment of life, is of vital importance. With the right mental attitude, the majority of women acquire the necessary adaptation to the changed physical state. Here the oft-quoted words of W. J. Fielding are worth stressing:

'Among countless numbers of women the climacteric has been the beginning of a golden period of achievement. Nor is there any reason why women, normally constituted, should lose their sexual attraction at this time. As a matter of fact, many women are more attractive at fifty then they were at twenty-five; and if their personality has been developed and enriched by the passing years, they may be more charming at sixty than they were at thirty.'

Finally, always bear in mind that there is no magic in marriage. It will not in itself solve your problems. It is something which depends for its success upon two people —husband and wife. All the lucky charms, good omens, the hard-working planets and the rest, will prove useless if the constant effort needed to secure adaptation of each partner to the other is lacking. Even within marriage there is no 'free love'. We buy it with intelligent effort.

That is why charms, belief in magic and the like, are dangerous. They promise us something for nothing. They serve as substititues for the effort which is needed. The price to be paid for success in marriage is small compared with the benefits which a truly happy marriage can bestow. But it is as well to realise that there is a price to be paid.

19: Making Love Last

Omar Haleby was a great believer in sexual stimulants. He played the part of sexual adviser to the prophet Mohammed, founder of Islam. And he prescribed aphrodisiacs because, as he said, 'the prophet is a human being, affected by the fatigue entailed by his activities, and also by the temptations to which he is continually subjected by his numerous wives and slaves, each of whom aspires, of course, to the supreme honour of uniting herself to God's emissary'.

Haleby advocates a word of prayer at the beginning of coitus, somewhat along the lines of grace before a meal. He even urges that the name 'Allah' should be shouted at the moment of ejaculation. Perhaps it is not surprising that Eastern races have contributed much to the vast store of aphrodisiacs.

For all practical purposes, there is one safe rule for you to follow regarding sexual stimulants which take the form of powders, tablets, or beverages. *Shun them*. When they are not positively dangerous, they are useless. They serve only to yield profits to their makers.

They have a vast sale in this country. 'Weak men' eagerly pay a high price for them. Women, too, sometimes persuade their husbands or lovers to take various concoctions which are believed to possess love-arousing powers. Many old superstitions centring around love potions are still widely accepted, especially in rural areas.

'Spanish fly' is often mentioned as being a reliable

aphrodisiac. *Cantharides,* or *Lytta Vesicatoria,* which is the same thing under its correct names, has been thoroughly tested by the medical profession, and rejected. Small doses proved useless. Large doses yielded marked ill-effects. Possibly this concoction composed of insects still has its adherents because of its high reputation, though most of its advocates would speedily revise their opinion were they familiar with the full story of what happened when, during the sixteenth century, some women gave their husbands a large dish of cantharides in order to cure them of fever.

The close connection between drugs—opium, cocaine, and hashish, for instance—and sexual stimulation is well known. The brothels of some countries—particularly China—depend largely upon the effects of opium and other drugs for their revenues. Many such drugs stimulate sexual desire and increase the sexual faculties at the start. But, in time, they lead to mental and physical demoralisation.

It is often said that there is little drug-taking in Great Britain.

In recent years one drug, Indian hemp, has been sold in cigarette form, and introduced to large numbers of people. The cigarette is smoked in the ordinary way. In some, the most erotic phantasies can be produced by this drug. Undoubtedly its availability—especially in the form mentioned—renders detection of the suppliers extremely difficult.

The anaesthetics administered for surgical operations and dental extractions often produce erotic dreams. Surgeons and dentists have been accused of rape or indecent assault, and the evidence has clearly shown that the patient must have dreamed the events related.

Now what of the more promising, and constructive, aspects?

Without going into details on the progress made in

what is popularly called 'rejuvenation', some reference must be made to gland therapy. Although still in its experimental stage, in the sense that there is much to be discovered, some progress has been made in recent years. It has been established that the secretions of an old organism are very different from those of a young one. Experts can ascertain the age of an individual by carefully examining the secretions from his endocrine glands. This provides the key to rejuvenation.

Operations sometimes take the form of grafting, a method in which Voronoff has specialised. Steinach evolved a method which does not necessitate surgical operation, but is confined to electrical measures. For men, a hormone implant is a form of rejuvenating operation now practised. The operation is simple and there are few contra-indications. In a certain percentage of cases no marked benefit results.

THE PROBLEM OF LIVING TOGETHER

Possibly you have heard the joke about the girl who remarked: 'Matrimony is a great institution'. To which her friend replied: 'Yes, but who wants to live in an institution?'

Cynics have observed that matrimony is an institution which is always in a stage of seige. Those within long to get out. Those without strive to get in.

The first thing to bear in mind is that marrage is for two. Far too many people think of it in terms of one—themselves.

If a young man starts out in the world hoping to make money, the first thing he needs to realise is that there is no such thing as the *perfect* job. Search where he will, he can never find a perfect business, or any kind of organisation which cannot be improved in some way or other. It is the same with marriage.

Marriage is what you make it. Just as our ambitious young friend may turn the most humdrum of jobs into something worthwhile, so with marriage. You have to make the best of it. You have to co-operate. The institution of matrimony can be a prison or it can be a wide field, full of opportunities for the mutual enrichment of the lives of two people. You make your choice, if you are wise, and act accordingly. You get out of life precisely what you put in—no more and no less. The same is true of marriage.

One of the advantages of knowledge of the technique of love is that it inevitably yields a wider sympathy and a deeper understanding. The man whose wife is a nagger may well wonder whether the cause does not lie in sexual dissatisfaction. All that has been said of the technique of coitus—what leads up to it and what follows—and everything connected with the physical side of marriage is closely related to the less intimate sides of marriage which all the world can see.

But over and above all this we have to remember that husbands and wives are *people*. That rather obvious statement needs emphasising. For it means that we have to apply to our partner in the love-relationship the methods which enable people generally to get along well together. Far too often husbands and wives take each other for granted.

People of every class, colour, and race need encouragement. To require constant praise before one can do one's best in anything is a sign of immature development. But *all*, even the most self-reliant, feel better and work better for being appreciated. 'Be hearty in your appreciation and lavish in your praise', is an old saying. This exhortation might well be taken to heart by all married lovers.

The woman who finds herself developing the nagging habit can hold herself in check by trying a new technique in which praise plays a part. Of course, she will not be able to pretend she is pleased when all the time she is intensely annoyed. There is not the slightest need for her to be dishonest. What is needed is that she should look out for the many chances which are bound to arise for her to express *honest appreciation*.

Men sometimes accept all their wives offer them with nothing more than a grunt of approval—if that. The business man who prides himself on the belief that no worthy effort of his staff escapes commendation may allow his wife to struggle for years on end with household worries and the care of the children, yet never say one word to show that he sees it all and appreciates it to the full.

Instead of adopting towards your wife or husband the attitude of the old proverb, 'Give a dog a bad name' try the opposite for a change. Give a man or woman a reputation to live up to, and they will strive to deserve it. The flower-girl in Shaw's *Pygmalion*, whose whole outlook on life was changed because a gentleman called her 'Miss', illustrates what I mean. The wife who knows that her husband admires her personality, her work, her cooking, everything about her, rarely becomes slovenly. And the man whose wife sincerely encourages him is unlikely to stray very far.

Constant carping criticism is one of the biggest enemies of marital happiness. The victim often learns to respond in the same way. Things go from bad to worse, then much worse. By looking for what is good and praiseworthy we go far towards remedying this. If criticism there must be, then let it be made in a form which will not offend.

Never have I seen the technique of criticism-without-wounding better illustrated than in the story which is told of one of America's steel kings, a man worth millions of dollars, who controlled thousands of employees—Charles Schwab. One day he was walking through his works when he saw a group of his employees smoking. Just above

253

their heads was a sign with 'No Smoking' written in huge letters.

Schwab did not sack them on the spot. Neither did he utter a quiet word of reproof. He did not even point up to the notice and pass on. No, he did better than all these. He went up to the men, produced his cigar-case, and said: 'I'd be obliged if you fellows would smoke one of these outside.'

He had learned how to criticise without giving offence. More than that, he had acquired the happy knack of getting people to do what he wanted and really like it. To those men Schwab was never again merely 'the boss'. He was a human, friendly person whom they could understand and appreciate—a gentleman, too, who, even when he was in the right, took pains not to offend. *In marriage it is more important not to offend than it is to gain your point.*

Excesses of every kind are bad, and lead to satiety. Moderation in all things—and this includes sexual activity.

The man whose business is worrying him or who has to face intense strain for a long time may find himself restricting his sexual life. He may even, for a time, abstain from all sexual contact. It is not surprising that his wife may feel slighted at the absence of familiar embraces. She may even feel that her husband's love for her has ceased, but of course this is not necessarily so.

Moderation goes hand in hand with regularity. Just as with meals and bathing and most other activities of life one must avoid extremes, yet acquire regular habits, something of the same is true of the sexual life. I say only 'something' of the same, for anything like a regular routine, a keeping to a time-table, is undesirable. The point is that moderation must on no account be confused with total abstention.

MOST COMMON FAULTS

'An American study covering fifteen hundred marriages yielded nearly five hundred pages of facts. An analysis showed the most grievous faults of married life—apart from sexual difficulties such as we have discussed in detail—to be as follows:

Poor wives	*Poor husbands*
nag;	are inconsiderate;
are not affectionate;	are bad money-managers;
are selfish;	are 'untruthful';
interfere with hobbies;	do not show affection;
are slovenly in appearance;	do not talk things over;
interfere with child discipline;	are harsh with children;
are conceited;	are very 'touchy';
criticise their husbands;	are uninterested in home;
neglect the children;	lack ambition;
are poor housekeepers;	are rude;

That is a very obvious list. Yet it has been carefully worked out on the basis of the fifteen hundred marriages investigated, and the various faults are given *in their order of frequency*—which makes the list interesting. Go through it, be absolutely honest with yourself, and see just where you have a tendency to work against the happiness of *your* marriage.

If it seems very unlikely that *you*, of all people, could possibly acquire the nagging habit, become inconsiderate to your love-partner, or be guilty of any of the other failings listed, please bear this important point in mind; that such habits grow on people, and grow slowly. Nearly all the naggers, the rude ones, the child-neglectors, and the rest, have *drifted* into their present state. Yes, and there was a time when such things would have seemed just as unlikely for them as they do for you.

People drift into these sorry states so gradually that they are usually completely unaware of what has happened. Half the world's naggers have no idea that they are so. Brusque, domineering men have a shock when some brave or distraught person tells them the truth. How do such curious changes occur?

One way in which people drift into these faults is by overdoing things. The nagger starts, often enough, by trying to improve her partner. The tight-fisted stingy husband begins by trying to be economical. The conceited of both sexes simply carry a proper pride too far. All of which proves, once more, the importance of moderation in all things, including the good.

When we reflect upon the thousands of marriages which completely fail and, still more, upon the much greater number which are only partially successful, we see how faulty technique can ruin the best-laid plans. For it is a fact that not one person in a hundred marries with bad intentions. In the overwhelming majority of cases, high ideals and the best of motives are present. Mr. A cannot trace the steps which changed him from a generous lover in courtship days to the miserly old skinflint he is now, at any rate towards his wife. Mrs. B has no idea how it is that she cannot bear her husband to complete a single sentence without interruption—she who, at one time, devoured every word which fell from his lips. They just drifted.

TRUTH TREATMENT

A surprising number of cases of marital woe yield some improvement as soon as the partners can rid themselves of deception. I am not referring to deliberate deception due to ill-intent. No, in marriage there is often much deception which has its origins in the slightest motives but which leads, step by step, to all sorts of difficulties.

All married people indulge in little white lies—even those who have been married for many years. Loyalty, in all truth a desirable quality, accounts for many lies. The real trouble is that most of us lie to ourselves because we do not like to admit to ourselves, far less others, the truth of what we see in ourselves.

We must remember, however, that there are occasions when silence is golden, and when it would be unfair to tell our partner of some incident in which we felt we had failed them. In other words, we must not ask our partner to pay the price for our sense of guilt and shame, but should attempt to atone for this and pay the price ourselves. I know there are some who believe that a husband and wife should tell each other literally everything—I am afraid I cannot agree, since I am sure that this would not be conducive to the best in human relationships; and that it would only succeed in super-human beings—not ordinary ones.

Deeply buried in such deception lie the roots of discord. And discord kills love. One woman told me that she must leave her husband or she would go out of her mind. She painted a detailed picture of the man—a drunkard with evil habits, uncleanly in person, bullying in his attitude towards her, and so lazy that he was likely to lose his position before long. In fact the man appeared from her description to be so bad that I thought that I should like to see him.

The wife assured me that he would not consent to see me. Nonetheless the next day he telephoned for an appointment. He was a quiet-spoken, pleasant man, and we soon became friendly. When I carefully brought the conversation round to his wife, he said he was thoroughly ashamed of the way he had treated her, for he loved her dearly.

She was all that a good wife should be. It was only in the course of some general talk that I gained the impression that, if he were free to do so, he would gladly leave his wife.

When I put it to him directly, he thought for a minute or two, then admitted it. 'Yes, I suppose it's true,' he said, 'I should like to get away from her.' Further questioning revealed that constant nagging was the trouble, but even so he felt that most of his wife's bitter criticisms were justified. In truth, he had a guilty feeling arising from his desire to get away from it all, a desire which, hitherto, he had been unwilling to admit even to himself.

There is no need to go into further detail. Suffice it to say that similar self-deception was present in his wife. They had both been making one of the commonest of all marital mistakes—that of sugar-coating their faults, or what they believed to be faults. It was said of old: 'Know the truth, and the truth shall make you free.' So far as lovers are concerned, the application of the test is: 'Don't lie, and your love will last longer.'

J. Pierpont Morgan used to say that a man always has two reasons for everything he does: a good reason, and the real reason. The same is true of women. And where marriage is concerned it is necessary to distinguish the real reason from the false.

Nine out of ten lovers' lies arise from good intentions. Or, at any rate, that is how they start. They are designed in the first place to spare the feelings of the beloved. But deception soon results in a tangled web. More and more lies have to be spoken or acted in order to keep the first intact. Soon deception becomes a habit.

To know the truth is to understand, in most cases, how to set about effecting an improvement. The object of the score cards which follow is to help you, if you are married, to check upon your success as a marriage partner. They are not comprehensive. They are rough-and-ready tests. But they do tend to bring the truth to the surface, provided that absolute honesty dictates every answer.

A low score is not a distress-signal. It does not mean that you must sit back and cease your efforts. These score cards are intended *for guidance*. If your score is low, you can see just where weaknesses lie and take steps to remedy them.

SCORE CARDS FOR HUSBANDS

Score

1. Do you realise that your wife is a separate individual with opinions and interests which may not always be yours?   ...   .

2. Can you honestly say that you recognise that your wife likes 'courtship' just as much as before marriage, and do you see that she gets it?   ...   .

3. Are you quite certain that your wife and children do not have to climb over a wall in order to reach you—a wall of unapproachability you have managed to build?   ...   .

4. Do you manage money and think of the proverbial rainy day, so that money does not manage you, and give rise to financial worries?...   ...   .

5. Do you exercise control on your behaviour? Smoking, drinking, and your sex life come into this. ...   .

6. Do you talk things over with your wife—the 'two-heads-are-better-than-one' idea?   ...   .

7. Are you sure that you are not domineering towards her?   ...   .

8. Do you allow her a free hand in the household, including control of housekeeping money?   ...   .

9. Has she some part of the family income, however small, which she can spend as she chooses?   ...   .

10. Have you recently praised anything she has done, or shown appreciation of her efforts in some way?   ......

11. Do you remember her birthday, wedding-day, and

other anniversaries, with some token, however small? ... ...

12. In the intimate relations are you always as mindful of her well-being and pleasure as of your own?... ......

13. Do you gladly accept the responsibilities of married life, entertaining, attending to the bother of the children's education, and so on, cheerfully?... ......

14. Do you refrain from criticising or abusing your wife in the presence of others, including the children? ... ...

15. Are you able to face the complete truth about your real attitude and behaviour towards your wife?... ......

16. Is some part of your free time regularly spent in joint recreation with your wife? ... ...

17. If both of you feel that a frank talk on an intimate subject is necessary with one of the children, are you willing to undertake the task? ... ...

18. Are you still deeply concerned that she shall have a good opinion of you? ... ...

19. Can you say without hesitation that jealousy plays little part in your attitude towards her? ... .

20. Are you willing to permit her as much freedom as you claim for yourself? ... ...

Total

How to score

Give yourself from 0 to 5, according to the degree to which you can answer 'yes' to each question. If your score reaches 100, it is too good to be true. Try again.

Pass this test to your wife and let her answer the questions in the light of her knowledge of you. Take her total and yours, add them together, then divide by two, and if you have both tried to be fair and honest something like the real truth will emerge.

SCORE CARDS FOR WIVES

Score

1. Do you try to encourage your husband in his work, without, however, demanding too much of him? ... ...

2. Is it your aim to appear as attractive and 'well turned out' as you did before marriage? ... .

3. Are you courteous to his relatives, and refuse to allow interference in your home from his mother or other relatives? ... ...

4. Are you careful not to nag or make a fuss over trifles? ... ...

5. Are you a good sport—meaning by that willing to accept the ups-and-downs which may affect your financial position without putting the blame for every setback upon him? ... ...

6. Is the sex side of your married life free from morbid self-consciousness or childish fears on your part? ... ...

7. Do you take a lively interest in his business, while refraining from offering advice or criticism of associates, unless asked? ... ...

8. Has your interest in him and in his recreations made you a really good companion for his leisure hours? ... ...

9. Are you capable of entertaining his business associates with confidence and efficiency? ... .

10. Is your handling of housekeeping finance business-like? ... ...

11. Think! Have you run up any debt of which he has no knowledge? ... ...

12. Do you feel that the home is as comfortable, interesting, and attractive as your means permit? ... .

13. Are you certain you have not left your husband 'out in the cold' in favour of one of the children? ....

14. Can you say without hesitation that jealousy plays little part in your attitude towards him, and that you never seem to arouse jealousy in him for any purpose? ... ...

15. Are you able to discuss intimate matters without awkwardness? ... ...

16. Do you try to be pleasant to his mother and other relatives? ... ...

17. Can you honestly say that you never make demands which must add to his difficulties or decrease his pleasure to increase yours? ... ...

18. Do you put at least as much thought into housekeeping and being a wife as you would if striving to hold down a well-paid job? ... ...▪▪▪

19. During the past week have you made it plain that you love your husband, and do you always do this however tempted you may be to 'keep him guessing' at times? ... ...

20. Can you face up honestly to your true attitude towards him, without an awareness that you have given him a 'raw deal'? ... ...

Total

How to score.

Give yourself from 0 to 5 according to the degree in which you can answer 'Yes' to each question. A score of 100 means perfection, so try again if that is your total.

Pass this test to your husband and let him answer the questions in the light of his knowledge of you. Take his total and yours, add them together and divide by two. If you have both been fair and honest, something like the real truth will emerge.

20 : Some Definitions

A

Abortion

This is the termination of a pregnancy, either deliberately induced or through natural causes. It is not the same as premature birth, which means the birth of a live baby any time after the twenty-eighth week. Many women, married or unmarried, seek an abortion on economic, health, or social reasons, because they do not want to bring an unwanted child into the world. Abortion is legal in this country, when done on medical grounds, physical, psychological, or both.

Adoption

This is a procedure whereby a husband and wife can act as parents to a child unwanted by its real mother, i.e. by adoption.

Aggression

Psychologically, this word is used to denote our aggressive instinct, without which we would not be able to attack or defend ourselves. Without this capacity—physical or mental—mankind would have made little progress from his primitive ancestors. With social progress we are able to exercise a certain degree of control, and express our aggression in more constructive and socially desirable ways. Aggression when associated with our sexual instinct, as it often is, can be dangerous.

Ambivalence

Is the word used when we find ourselves feeling one way at one time, the opposite at another, about the same thing. We often experience this sort of dilemma in our sexual relationships.

Amoral

A person lacking a sense of morality, in other words, a sense of right and wrong. This is distinct from the person who has a moral sense, but acts contrary to it, when he is said to be immoral.

Anal Intercourse

This is sexual intercourse either between man and man, or woman and man, where the penis is inserted into the anus and not the vagina. In this country it is illegal even between consenting parties, or husband and wife.

Aphrodisiac

Anything which will increase sexual desire and performance. There is no known drug which will safely do this. Alcohol helps to reduce our inhibitions, and thus gives us greater freedom of expression.

Artificial Insemination

The fertilisation of the ovum (female reproductive cell) not by sexual intercourse but by introducing the male sperm into the vagina by means of a syringe. The husband's semen, or that of another man, can be used. This method is practised when the husband is unable to obtain an erection, or for some other reason is unable to make entry into the vagina. Likewise if the husband's sperms are inadequate, those of another man (donor) can be used. A woman who is not prepared to pay the price of marriage could avail herself of this method of having a baby—supposing she did not want to enter into sexual congress.

B

Bestiality

Sexual relationship with an animal—it is a criminal offence in Great Britain.

Bidet

A small bath not unlike a lavatory basin, used for washing one's genital organs—usually before or after intercourse. It is most common in France, but is now fashionable in this country for those, of course, who can afford it.

Birth Control

The use of a chemical, mechanical, or other barrier to prevent the sperm from reaching the ovum and fertilising it. In this way it is possible to plan one's family, although accidents do happen, since every method carries some risk—if only the risk of not using it properly.

Bisexual

Every man has something of the woman in his make-up, and every woman something of the man. We may not always be conscious of this, though it is none the less a fact. When we have more than our fair share of the opposite sex in our make-up, we may be unable to have sexual intercourse with a person of the opposite sex.

Buggery

See Bestiality and Anal Intercourse.

C

Cannibalism

The eating of human beings by human beings—doesn't sound very civilised, but nor is war with its wholesale slaughter of man, woman, and child!

Carezza

The name given for prolonged intercourse—usually without climax for either sex. In this manner the closest physical and spiritual relationship is possible.

Castration

The removal of the testicles from a boy or man. Eunuchs (slaves in a harem) were often castrated so as to desexualise them—though, in fact, it did not always have this effect. Castration before puberty does remove the sexual urge —after puberty, not necessarily so.

Celibate

Someone who of his own volition abstains from sexual intercourse. This was regarded as a recognition of the baseness of the body and worldly pleasures. Generally speaking, one can regard this as an unnatural way of life.

Chastity

Abstinence from premarital sexual intercourse, an attitude proscribed by many religions—and also encouraged by social pressures—largely on a fear of enjoying sexual expression and its possible consequences—e.g. pregnancy, emotional trauma, etc.

Circumcision

The removal of that part of the foreskin which surrounds the glans penis. This is a Jewish religious ritual—but it is now common all over the world. It is hygienically healthier, but the penis, as a result, is a little less sensitive. This can be a help for those who ejaculate too quickly.

Clap

A colloquial term for gonorrhœa.

Climacteric

This is the period during which a woman ceases to mensurate—after which she cannot have children. The climacteric is commonly referred to as the 'change of life'. In many, there are mild psychological changes, since at this time we are likely to take stock of ourselves, as it were, look back on the past and peep into the future, wondering what is in store for us. Men, too, go through a similar, though less well marked phase, between the ages of forty to fifty. Many of both sexes try too hard to hold on to their youth, instead of going 'with it'. A lot of nonsense is spoken of loss of sexual vigour and desire, as if this were completely lost to us. In some, the very opposite is the case, in others there may be lessened performance, but not necessarily desire.

Clitoris

The small organ just above (though inside) the lips of the vagina. It is the counterpart of the male penis, and, like it, becomes erect on sexual stimulation or excitement. Masturbation of the clitoris usually ends in clitoral orgasm.

Coitus

Sexual intercourse—the insertion of the penis into the vagina and the subsequent friction resultant on movement leads to orgasm and ejaculation.

Coitus Interruptus

The withdrawal of the penis during coitus, just before ejaculation, so that the semen is not lodged in the vagina.

'Come'

A word commonly used to indicate ejaculation on the part of the man and orgasm in the case of the woman.

Conception

The fertilisation of the female egg or ovum by the male sperm. Hence contra-ception means the prevention of this.

Condom

Commonly known as a 'French Letter'. A fine tubular sheath of rubber or some other material which fits on to the penis, not unlike a finger stall. The ejaculate is deposited inside this and, barring accidents, pregnancy cannot occur.

Continence

Sexual temperance.

Cunnilingus (cunnilinctus)

Kissing of the clitoris with one's tongue. This is much more common than we imagine. It is one of the ways a woman can be sexually stimulated and, indeed, achieve orgasm without the need of an erection on the part of a man. Many of both sexes find this method of sexual expression quite satisfactory.

Curettage

Scraping of the wall of the womb either for medical reasons, or to remove an early pregnancy.

D

Defloration

Rupture of the hymen—loss of virginity, often referred to as loss of maidenhead.

Detumescense

Relaxation of the sexual organs after sexual excitement is over—usually following orgasm.

Discharge

Vaginal secretion often coming from the mouth of the womb. This is quite usual between menstrual periods and is not abnormal. If, however, it is infected, it will be a yellowish colour, and possibly have an unpleasant odour, in which case it is as well to see one's doctor.

Douche

Rinsing and washing out the vagina by means of a vaginal syringe or some other method. Very commonly used for hygienic purposes.

Dysmenorrhoea

Painful menstruation—usually just before, during, or after the menstrual period.

E

Ejaculation

This occurs at the height of sexual feeling when the penis discharges the semen as a result of muscular contractions. It can happen even when the penis is not erect. Premature ejaculation happens when the semen is discharged too quickly and possibly even before the penis is inserted into the vagina. A large number of men, largely due to faulty sexual upbringing of one sort or another, suffer from this. It usually implies nervous tension and an inability to be fully relaxed in the intimate relationship. Others, a minority, may experience difficulty in being able to ejaculate—i.e. retarded ejaculation. These conditions are almost always psychological in origin—and can often be helped by psychiatric treatment.

Emission-nocturnal

This is perhaps better known as a 'wet dream and is the result of ejaculation during sleep. It may, or may not, be accompanied by a pleasurable sexual dream, often the only evidence is soiling the bed sheet. It is incredible the number of people who feel guilty and ashamed of such an occurrence—when it is, in fact, perfectly healthy and natural. Society seems determined to make us feel that any evidence of sexuality prior to marriage is sinful!

Environment

This represents the world in which we live, as distinct from the world within us, i.e. our constitution, physical and mental make-up, etc., which is, more or less, fixed at the moment of conception, i.e. when the male sperm unites with the female egg or ovum. We refer to this as genetic inheritance (heredity). From the day of our birth there is an interaction between ourselves and everything that impinges on us from the outside world. At first it is mother —then father—then other members of the family, and so on and on, until, in a sense, everything and everybody in the outside world has some bearing and influence on the sort of person we are, and are going to be. Our upbringing, i.e. the way our parents love and look after us, the home we live in, school, the people we meet and are in contact with, all play a part. The manner in which we react to these influences will eventually determine our sense of values, our way of life, and our character.

Erogenous areas

Those parts of the body which are susceptible to sexual excitement and stimulation. In point of fact, almost every part of the body has this capacity—but it varies from individual to individual. Women in particular enjoy most forms of love-play, although, not surprisingly, the genitals, breasts, and mouth are particularly sensitive.

Excess

Is a word often used in relation to our sexual conduct. Actually, since no two people are alike, what is excessive for one can be too little for another. For example, some enjoy sexual intercourse two or three times a day—others once a week or once a month. Much harm has been done by silly talk of sexual excess, for it can give rise to an unwarranted sense of guilt, whether it be in regard to masturbation, intercourse, or any other sexual activity.

Exhibitionism

To display a part or the whole of our body, clothed or unclothed. We are all, to some extent, exhibitionists—mental or physical—in the sense that we want to show ourselves off. Usually the word is used in those cases—usually male—where there is an urge to display the naked penis, often to children. This in itself gives satisfaction, and there is seldom any need for us to be afraid of such a person. Children, however, quite understandably, bearing their upbringing in mind, are frightened when something like this happens to them. Exhibitionism of this nature is a legal offence—although the unfortunate sufferer may be unable to resist the urge to behave as he does.

Experience

This is the way we feel rather than think about something that happens to us. No two people feel exactly alike about an objective reality. Our way of life is to some extent determined by our subjective experiences. Even words have different meanings to different people, since the feelings that a word conjures up within us are unalike, because of the differing associations to the word.

F

Faithfulness

This usually implies sexual faithfulness, meaning that once we are married we do not have intercourse with anyone other than our wife or husband. How far we succeed in this depends largely on the strength of our sexual urge, our compatibility, sexual and otherwise, and the need we have of variety, together with many other factors. In Britain there has been some recent recognition of the fact that faithfulness is not always easy (particularly for men), and that an act of unfaithfulness by either party does not necessarily signify lack of love. Indeed, it can occur within the framework of a very happy and successful marriage. After all, we cannot be held responsible for feeling sexually attracted to someone outside of our marriage—admittedly, we can be held responsible for what we do about it. But let's remember, human nature is frail. The isolated act of unfaithfulness, although grounds for divorce, should never really break up a marriage. It is really rather an infantile way of dealing with an adult situation.

Family Planning

The prevention of pregnancy in order to plan the number and timing of our family.

Fantasy

Is a form of daydreaming. We think of, or visualise, situations imaginatively and mostly with pleasure. Most of us indulge in this at one time or another in regard to our sexual desires and activities, often during masturbation. This is perfectly normal—indeed, without fantasies of some kind life could be very dull.

Father fixation

This is a continuation of the close ties we have with our father during the earliest years of our lives, and applies to both sexes. When we carry this through into adult years and fail to free ourselves as individuals in our own right, we remain emotionally dependant. This is what is understood by 'father fixated'. We can be so on both conscious and unconscious levels—and it can influence, if not determine, our way of life and sexual patterns.

Fertilisation

This is the union of the male and female reproductive cells. The male cell is very active, not unlike a tadpole. On ejaculation, during sexual intercourse, some one hundred to five hundred million are deposited into the vagina, despite the fact that only one fertilises the egg. We see how extravagant nature is in order to ensure the continuation of the species. And also, as a result of nuclear weapons, how extravagant man can be in order to ensure the destruction of the human species. In a manner of speaking, the male sperm is manufactured when required. The female cell, however, is present from birth and generally is released at the rate of one a month from the age of puberty (this is called ovulation). The female egg is released from one of the two ovaries, and is caught in the open end of the Fallopian tube (there are two of these), from where it slowly travels into the womb (uterus). The egg is fertilised in the tube and not in the womb. The latter prepares for reception of the egg each month by thickening its lining membrane and increasing its blood supply. If the egg is fertilised, it becomes embedded in the wall of the womb and over a period of nine months grows into the baby to be born. If, however, the egg has not been fertilised, it passes out of the womb, together with the thickened lining membrane, and blood, which is no longer needed. This is called menstruation, and as we have seen occurs approximately once a month.

Fetishism

We refer to a person as a fetishist when he or she is sexually stimulated by a part rather than the whole of the body, or when some article (usually clothes) has a similar effect. Normally, we are all, to some extent, fetishists, but we usually use the word when it plays a disproportionate part in our sexual satisfactions or when it replaces sexual intercourse. Fetishism is practised more by males than females. The condition is due to a fault in our growth towards sexual maturity. Unless it gets us into trouble with the law, there is nothing really to worry about—although obviously, in some cases, it could interefere with one's marital relationship.

Frigidity

A woman is said to be frigid when she is sexually disinterested. Of course, when we consider the manner in which women have been brought up, and masculine attitudes, it is not surprising that many women come to fear sexual intercourse. And when we consider how sexually inadequate and selfish many men can be in their love-making—we cannot be surprised that some women are not impressed with the 'pleasures' of sex and regard it as a much over-rated pastime. Frigidity has little to do with whether a woman does or does not achieve orgasm—if she is able to enjoy the sex act and love-making then she is not frigid. Many men, because of their conceit and ignorance, think that if a woman does not attain orgasm, she is frigid. This in fact is absolute nonsense. Few women exist who are without sexual feeling—in a large number of cases their inability to express or enjoy sexuality could be overcome by a sympathetic and understanding partner.

G

'Giving'

This is the slang term used when a man or a woman has orgasm.

Gonorrhoea

This is a venereal disease and is usually transmitted through intercourse. The organism responsible is the gonococcus. The man is usually aware of being infected, since there is a yellow-green discharge from the penis. Obviously, to have intercourse before being cured would be the height of immorality and irresponsibility. Unfortunately, a woman is less readily able to know whether she is infected—but if she has the slightest suspicion she should immediately see her doctor. In both cases delay can be seriously detrimental to health. Gonorrhoea is no different to any other disease—we do not feel ashamed if we become infected with tuberculosis, for instance, as a result of cuddling and kissing someone who has tuberculosis. Why should we in the case of gonorrhoea?

Guilt

This means a sense of shame or embarrassment when we do something or think or feel something which our conscience tells us is wrong. Guilt is perfectly natural when not excessive and not unjustified. Without a sense of guilt to help us behave in a manner not harmful or destructive to ourselves or others, we might remain very primitive human beings. It is *abnormal* when it is excessive and not justified, so that we are hampered in the living of our lives and are afraid of that of which we should have no fear. In our upbringing parents and social convention seem to do their best to condition us into a way of life through fear rather than love.

H

Happiness

There are perhaps fewer words in our vocabulary less understood. We seem to think of happiness (a state of contentment) as something which we can achieve through material comforts—something which can be bought and sold. Indeed, something which the world owes us. Whereas the fact is, we can only experience happiness as a result of a full living of our lives and the expression of our individual potentials within the social framework. That is why blind conformity—the need to imitate and keep up with the Joneses can be so destructive to the human personality. In so far as the affluent society helps us to live the life that is uniquely our own—it is conducive to human happiness. If, on the other hand, it makes it more difficult for us to live our own life, then it is conducive to unhappiness. Happiness is a consequential gain resultant on the full living of our lives.

Heterosexual

This is our attraction, and the desire to express our sexual urge with a member of the opposite sex, not with a member of our own sex. Every man has something of the woman in him and every woman has something of the man, but this is something very different from homosexuality, the opposite of heterosexuality.

Homosexuality

The love and sexual love for members of our own sex. This occurs as a result of something having gone wrong with our emotional growth during the early years of life. We find ourselves unable to enter into sexual relationship with a member of the opposite sex. This must not be confused with the ability of a heterosexual to have a homosexual relationship or the homosexual to have a heterosexual one. Because, for example, we have all in our life-time told lies, that doesn't make us liars—any more than having stolen makes us thieves. We must distinguish be-tween this sort of behaviour and that of the genuine homosexual who has no choice in the expression of his or her sexual urge other than with a member of his or her own sex. The homosexual component which is present in all our make-up is usually at unconscious rather than con-scious levels. It is those with the greatest degree of un-conscious homosexuality who are most likely to be loudest in their protests against homosexuals. Homosexuals can-not be held responsible for their homosexuality any more than we can be held responsible for the colour of our eyes. Unfortunately, there is little we can do to make a homo-sexual heterosexual by any present known means—assuming this were desirable.

Hormones

These are substances secreted by glands known as en-docrine glands. They circulate in the blood stream and affect the activities of other glands and organs in the body. They play a large part in determining the kind of person we are, such as our reaction time, our mood, our ability to defend ourselves, fight back or run away, etc. They also, by means of our sex glands—the ovaries in the female, testicles in the male—largely decide the measure of our sexuality and its degree. It was thought that to give a male homosexual female hormone would redress the imbalance and produce a heterosexual. Unfortunately, this is not so, although we can reduce one's sexual urge in the case of the male by giving feminine hormone and vice versa in the case of the female.

Hypnosis

This is a state of mind induced by the hypnotiser in his subject as a result of which the subject can be made to think and behave according to the wishes of the hypnotiser. To be properly effective, the subject must willingly give himself up to the hypnotiser—but he is unlikely to do anything which would run contrary to his true nature. In some cases it can be used to help people, for example, to stop smoking, blushing, being excessively shy and so on. It is, however, unlikely to be of permanent value unless the person deeply and truly wants to rid himself of his embarrassment or habit. It is not a form of treatment to be lightly undertaken, and there is much that we do not understand about its mode of action.

Hysteria

This really is the behaviour of the person who uses infantile reactions to cope with adult situations. This explains the uncontrolled and violent nature of the hysterics outburst, and the fact that it can often be halted by treating the person in similar manner. It is one thing for the child to stamp his feet and shriek in anger—another for the adult. In psychological hysteria we can transfer our mental condition into a physical one—what we call psychosomatic symptoms. For example, it is thought to play a part in such illness as asthma—hay fever—stomach ulcers, etc. In reality, few conditions are 100 per cent physical or 100 per cent mental, all have overtones of one or the other.

I

Identification

This is the process whereby we imaginatively try to feel like someone else and perhaps behave in a similar manner. Perhaps the best example is when children look up to their parents and attempt to behave like them. When we watch a film we often, if only for a brief period, escape from the realities of our own lives by identifying ourselves with one or another of the characters in the film. Indeed, it is through the power of imaginatively putting ourselves in the position of the other person that we can understand how they are thinking and feeling. In growing up— boys tend to identify themselves with their fathers and girls with their mothers. If, however, a boy should identify himself with his mother, or a girl with her father, then we have a situation which could, for example, result in homosexuality, sexual impotence or an inability to marry.

Immorality

This is conduct, or indeed thoughts, contrary to the accepted code of the community in which we live. Of course, with some exceptions, there is no such thing as an absolute morality—for this differs from one community to another —from one time to another—and from one place to another. What would be regarded as sexually immoral for some at one time or place, could be moral for others at another time or place. To some extent we all create our own ideas and standards of what is and what is not moral. And this will be dependent on how far social conventions and prohibitions are compatible or incompatible with the image we have of ourselves and the sort of person we would like to be and think we should be. In other words, conscience will largely determine the morality or immorality of our behaviour.

Impotence

This is used to denote the inability on the part of the male to obtain erection and have sexual intercourse. It exists in women who are incapable of accepting the entry of the male penis into the vagina—but this is relatively rare. In both cases it is almost always psychological in origin. In the man there are varying degrees of impotency. There may be absolute failure to obtain an erection, or after obtaining it the erection is lost just before attempting vaginal entry. Or else, ejaculate, what is called premature ejaculation, before actual intercourse has taken place. As a result of failure many men subsequently suffer from the fear of further failure, they feel ashamed, embarrassed, and lacking in masculinity. If to this we add the scorn or criticism of our partner, then that is the last straw. Most cases of impotency can be relieved by love and sympathetic understanding on the part of the woman—and similarly female impotency can be relieved. A sense of humour can go a long way in altering our attitude to impotency and making us feel less selfconscious. Nearly all have experienced isolated incidents of impotency, but this need not create concern.

Incest

This is sexual intercourse between close relations—e.g. father and daughter, sister and brother. In Great Britain it is a criminal offence. It is much more common than many would believe. An interpretation of our dreams shows the wish to be in such relationship exists in our unconscious minds. This explains much of the awkwardness of father-daughter, mother-son, sister-brother relationship in adolescent and adult years.

Indecency

Sexual conduct unacceptable to the society in which we live. Indecent exposure is an example of this which we see in certain forms of exhibitionism (see Exhibitionism).

Infanticide

The killing of children immediately after birth. This practice was not uncommon in Britain in the nineteenth century and was used as an alternative to birth control. Today, of course, we would regard such a practice with abhorrence—although oddly enough some of us feel less strongly about the destruction of the world with nuclear weapons or nuclear fall out!

Infantilism

This means physical or mental childishness—in other words, a failure to grow up into adulthood.

Inferiority

This is a sense of feeling inferior in one way or another. We feel that we cannot match up to others in some direction or other and as a result tend to retire from what we regard as an unequal contest. When the sense of inferiority resides in the unconscious, we might attempt at conscious levels to redress the imbalance by appearing brave and confident on the surface, for instance, the extroverted hail fellow well met type. Or we might gradually withdraw into a world of our own (introverted) and so save ourselves the trials and tribulations involved in coping with our sense of inferiority. A certain degree of inferiority is universal and acts as a spur to growth and progress—it is when it exceeds this that it can act as a brake on the living of our lives.

Inhibition

This is a process whereby we prevent ourselves from fully expressing ourselves as we would like to—either because of external or internal pressures. Naturally, we are afraid of behaving in a manner grossly contrary to social requirements, and this is not entirely surprising. It is when we blindly follow convention—good or bad, right or wrong—and in so doing limit our emotional growth that inhibition can be positively harmful. For example, false ideas of sexuality can prevent us from entering into a full and meaningful relationship. In many ways we have to inhibit putting some of our wishes into action, it is the price we pay for the benefits of communal life. But when we do this unnecessarily, resultant on faulty social attitudes and out of keeping with individual needs, then we can run into trouble, and interfere with healthy and purposeful living.

Intolerance

This is perhaps the greatest curse of mankind, and it means that we are unable or unwilling to concede to others the right to think, feel, behave, hold religious or political views different to our own. We are not satisfied to agree to disagree and understand and appreciate difference as difference—we see it in terms of superiority or inferiority. Thus white is not different to black but superior. Christianity is not different from other religions but superior—which incidentally is a negation of Christianity. And so one could go on cataloguing a list of such intolerances. Class distinctions and educational systems in Great Britain give rise to intolerance. We are moving towards a greater tolerance, it is true, but the journey is a slow and painful one. It seems strange that with all the advances made in science and our greater understanding of human mechanisms and motivations we have not progressed more rapidly. On the other hand, when we consider how we are made to believe in our own superiority in one direction or another, from the cradle to the grave, we can hardly be surprised. It is not so long ago that the Englishman in a foreign country regarded the inhabitants there as the foreigners. In fact, we only begin to fully live our lives when we attain a degree of tolerance which makes us receptive to views—wishes—ways of life, other than our own. Just so long as we imprison ourselves in a cage of superiority of our own making we shall never be free to live and love.

J

Jealousy

This is not easy to strictly define—in general terms it means the desire to possess someone. When we are children we feel jealous of others, including our father, brothers, or sisters, who we feel take some of Mummy's love. We should outgrow this as we get older, but most of us don't fully do so. When we marry, for example, we are much more anxious to possess our partner than to enter into a partnership. We are jealous of those who we feel will take love which belongs to us. Actually, it is a vote of no confidence in ourselves, for if we felt secure in our relationship, say with our wife or husband, we would not experience their relationship with someone else as a threat to our own security. A certain degree of jealousy is helpful in the living of our lives, since it helps to keep us up to scratch—beyond this, however, it is destructive. Indeed, there can be little more destructive to a human relationship than blind, irrational jealousy.

K

Karezza
See Carezza.

Kinsey
An American professor of zoology who set himself out to discover the sexual behaviour of male and female without regard to moral judgements. In other words, he was interested in what people actually did with their sex lives, irrespective of what one thought they should or should not do. He published his findings in two monumental works —*The Sexual Behaviour of the Human Male* (1948) and *The Sexual Behaviour in the Human Female* (1953), Saunders. This rather shook the world and timid souls were sceptical of his findings, so accustomed had they become to evasion of the truth and double talk where sexual behaviour was concerned—in other words practice fell short of precept. The Chesser Report, published in 1956 by Hutchinson, was, unlike the Kinsey Report, an

attempt to discover what the average Englishwoman thought and felt about her sexual, marital, and family relationships—and the book was published under the title of *The Sexual, Marital and Family Relationships of the English Woman*. The total number of women who completed the questionnaire was 6,251. In a broad sense this report could be regarded as complementary to the Kinsey Report.

L

Lesbian
The term used for a female homosexual.

Loneliness
A feeling of being alone in the world and not in significant relationship. We can experience this at all ages, even when young, as a result of an inability to make contact with others. We can feel lonely and alone when we suffer from severe depression, and we can suffer loneliness when we are older and retired from work. Loneliness seems to be more prevalent in the affluent society. Whether this is due to the gap between the generations in the case of the older people or to emotional inadequacy, or to material comfort amidst spiritual poverty, there is nothing more destructive to the human soul than a feeling of aloneness.

Love
There are many kinds of love. There is sexual love—mother love—love of one's country—love of possessions—love of pleasure—love of self—love of the theatre and of things, etc., etc. The capacity to love varies from individual to individual. It is difficult to love others if we don't love ourselves. Which is what Christ probably meant when he said: 'Love thy neighbour as thyself'. Sexual love is the expression of our sexuality, and in this sense it can

be a limited relationship. Within the framework of a totally loving relationship sexual love is enjoyed at its best, but we must be honest and admit that sexual love is at all times, or at least should be, more than ordinarily pleasant.

Love-play

This is cuddling, caressing, and all forms of petting, either as a prelude to intercourse or as an end in itself. We use love-play as a form of sexual stimulation, and this can be induced not only by physical contact but by the spoken word and all forms of communication, visual and otherwise.

Lust

This refers to the expression of our sexuality, when we are not in a truly total loving relationship, but one for the purpose of release of sexual tension. Lust, which is one of the deadly sins, has an unpleasant meaning, one which makes us feel guilty whereas, in fact, release of sexual tension by itself is neither moral or immoral. It is the manner in which we express our needs, which can be immoral. Just so long as we are honest in our relationship with a willing partner, lust, as we call it, is perfectly healthy and normal. Some of us will be more lustful than others depending on the strength of our sexual urge. To indulge in rape or sexual assault of any description or force ourselves on an unwilling partner, are forms of sexual release which could be more rightly described as lust.

M

Maidenhead

This is another name for the hymen which is a thin fold of mucous membrane partly covering the opening of the vagina. Today, as a result of using tampons, deep petting, and masturbation, the hymen is often ruptured. Loss of virginity is, therefore, by no means indicative of having had sexual intercourse.

Masochism

This is a desire to be hurt mentally or physically. The great majority of us experience this at some time or other, although not always consciously. By being punished we relieve ourselves to greater or lesser extent of thoughts, feelings, or behaviour of which we feel guilty. Usually masochism refers to an excessive need of hurt or punishment, often related to our sexual expression. For example, the desire to be flagellated or sexually humiliated. Psychologically, the martyr may be such a person, so too the celibate. In the first case through deeper feelings of unworthiness, in the second because of a sense of guilt in regard to unconscious sexual desires which the conscious mind cannot accept. During love-play and sexual intercourse many are stimulated by, and even enjoy, a degree of pain which they would not in other circumstances tolerate. This is perfectly normal, for it is only when masochism plays a disproportionate part, or replaces sexual intercourse altogether, that it can be regarded as deviant. There are some who seem to obtain mental satisfaction by being humiliated, in the ordinary living of their lives, this, too, is masochism.

Masturbation

Sexually stimulating ourselves without being in physical relationship with another person, and thereby attaining orgasm. We discover this ability usually after puberty, although many of us play with our genital organs long before this. It is a phase of sexual growth and as such is perfectly normal and harmless. Indeed, few, if any, men have not masturbated at some time in their lives, whilst probably a majority of women have also masturbated. Unfortunately, due to fear, prejudice, and ignorance, most of us have been made to feel guilty and ashamed of masturbation, another name for which is self-abuse. Young people are often frightened out of their wits by the silly idea that they will go mad or injure themselves permanently in one way or another if they masturbate. One would think that the older generation, many of whom have suffered as a result of such absurd talk, would have the sense to tell their children that masturbation is not only harmless but pleasurable. The degree to which this is practised will vary from individual to individual—once a day could be too little for some, once a month too much for others.

Member
Another name for the penis.

Menarche
Another name for the first menstrual period.

Menstruation
Approximately once a month an egg is released from the ovary and is caught up in the open end of the fallopian tube (there are two, one on each side of the womb) and slowly passes down the tube. It is here that the egg becomes fertilised—and if so usually becomes embedded in the wall of the womb, which has prepared itself for its reception. In which case, a pregnancy is started. If, however, the egg is not fertilised it passes out of the womb, together with the extra blood supply and thickening lining membrane—and this is menstruation. It is as simple and natural as that. Most girls start menstruating in Great Britain at about twelve to thirteen years of age—some sooner, others later. The start of the menstrual period means that a girl is capable of motherhood, certainly in a physical sense, and this is something of which she should feel proud. No man can become pregnant, yet in some

strange way all too many girls feel embarrassed or ashamed of this evidence of their femininity.

Monogamy

This means being married to one person—i.e. one person at a time. In years gone by polygamy was practised—this permitted a man to have more than one wife. There appears to be something inherent in our natures which fundamentally impels us to attempt to be in deep, meaningful and significant relationship with a partner of the opposite sex. This despite the fact that we may at times desire variety—but few of us who break our marriage vows have any wish to break our marriage.

Morals

This is a code usually set up by society by which we attempt to regulate human behaviour and human relationships. There are few absolute standards of right and wrong—and, indeed, what can be right for an individual or a group at one time and place could be wrong for another individual or group, or indeed the same individual or group, at another time and place. Apart from conventional and social moral standards we all, consciously or otherwise, have our own moral standards or ideals. In the main moral standards are man-made, not divine, so that what man can do, he should be permitted to undo when change demands this. Different peoples have different moral rules, and, of course, life can be easier for most of us if, broadly speaking, we know the rules—so that, at least, we can know when we are breaking them. This is especially important when most of us have a set of rules for ourselves, and a different set for others. It explains much of the 'double talk' prevalent in our society. Perhaps this is nowhere better exemplified than in our sexual morals where there is one rule for the man and another for the woman!

Mother fixation

This is the description given to those who have not suc-
ceeded in gaining their own freedom and emotional independence but remained tied to their mothers. As a result,
they are hampered in living out their own lives. Since they
are, as it were, imprisoned with their mothers. The tie is
usually stronger on unconscious than conscious levels. A
classical example of mother fixation is the son who is unable to marry, since he is, in a sense, married to his mother,
or if he does marry, he chooses someone very like his
mother.

N

Necrophilia

Is the word used to describe those who have a desire to
give release to their sexuality with a dead person.

Needs

This usually refers to our instinctual urges, such as the
need to love, eat, drink, etc., etc. We experience a hunger
if these needs are not satisfied. What is more, failure to
satisfy our hunger directly or indirectly means that we
are not fully living out our lives, even although we may
not be consciously aware of the fact.

Normal

This is the idea we have, in practice often very remote
from the truth, of how we should think and behave. There
are a set of rules laid down by society to which most of us
pay, at least, lip service. In fact, there is really no such
thing as normal, for what is normal for one person could
be abnormal for another, since it depends on the make-up
of the particular individual. The word is a very confusing
one, particularly when we apply it to our sexual behaviour.

Nuaism

This is a movement whereby people can meet each other, not dressed, but undressed. It is really a rebellion against the absurdity of being ashamed of the human body and the fear, socially instilled, of exposing the naked body, in part or in whole. There would be no need of such a movement were it not for the excessive prudery which exists in regard to our bodies.

Nymphomania

This applies to a very highly sexed woman, who finds it difficult to satisfy her sexual appetite.

O

Obscenity

The name we give to anything which we regard as sexually offensive, indecent or unpleasant, whether this be pictures, sculpture, painting, literature, etc. What is and what is not obscene is always a very controversial matter, since it is largely a matter of individual taste and susceptibility.

Oedipus Complex

This is the attachment which exists at unconscious levels during the first few years of life between a father and daughter and a mother and son. According to Freud the manner in which we live out this early relationship determines our future emotional growth and ability to live our own lives freed from such parental attachments.

Onanism

Another word for masturbation.

Oral Erotic

The ability to enjoy sexual feelings through the mouth and tongue.

Orgasm

This is the climax we experience at the height of sexual release. For men this occurs at the moment of ejaculation, and there is little doubt as to the intensity of feeling with which this is accompanied. In women it is not necessarily so clearly defined, and orgasm can be felt in a more generalised manner, and with relatively little feeling of intensity.

Ovary

This is the woman's sexual gland (there are two) which contains the female reproductive cells, the ova or eggs. Ordinarily one egg is released approximately every month.

P

Passion

This refers to the strength of our sexual feeling: we are said to be passionate when we are actively very highly sexed.

Pederast

This refers to adults who have sexual relationships with children. More often than not it applies to homosexual adults.

Penis

This is the male sexual organ. When erect it is capable of being inserted into the vagina (sexual intercourse) and ejaculating sperms (the male reproductive cells).

Penis envy

This refers to the envy some women have for the male genital organs. The young girl when first she realises the boy has something (a penis) which she hasn't got often feels envious of the fact, unconsciously if not consciously.

Period

Another name for menstruation.

Personality

This is something which it is easier to recognise than define. Briefly, it refers to a person's total make-up and the
manner in which it is expressed. Character—heredity—
way of life—conscience—morality, the strength of our
instinctual drives together with the image we have of ourselves and the sort of person we would like to be, all these
determine the sort of person we are going to be, and our
personality.

Perversions

These refer to sexual attitudes and behaviour regarded by
the particular society in which we live as unnatural and,
therefore, abnormal. For example, sadism, masochism,
pederasty, fetishism, etc., etc. But of course, what is normal for one person could be abnormal for another, depending on whether we were going *with* our nature or
against it. Furthermore, the great majority of us have
sexual perversities in our make-up even though we are
not aware of the fact. This often explains our irrational
attitudes towards those who practise what in our unconscious minds we too would like to practise but daren't.

Petting

This is another word for flirting and love-making, short
of orgasm or sexual intercourse.

Deep-petting

This is petting short of sexual intercourse—but which
permits of masturbation, mutual or otherwise, so as to
attain orgasm if desired. Contrary to general belief this
can be satisfying in itself, and has the great merit of avoiding the psychological and physical risks involved in pre-

marital intercourse in our society. Furthermore, we can make a fair judgement of our sexual compatability in this manner—it is a means of communication between the sexes.

Phallus
Another name for the penis.

Pimp
A man who lives on the immoral earnings of a woman. This is a criminal offence in Great Britain.

Polyandry
This applies to the woman who has more than one husband at the same time.

Polygamy
The practice of plural marriage—in other words, one person can be married to many wives—or one woman to many husbands.

Ponce
The same as Pimp.

Prejudice
An emotional and irrational bias against some one, some thing—or some idea. It is probably the greatest curse in the world's civilisation, and productive of much human misery and destruction. Until mankind is capable of shedding his irrational prejudices there is little hope for him.

Private Parts
A name used for the female and male genital organs. In a society which makes us feel ashamed of our bodies, or at least certain parts of our bodies, it seems more delicate to use such a term.

Prostitute

Those of either sex who live by the sale of their bodies. It has been said that we all have something of the prostitute in our natures, but, of course, this is something different from prostitution. Female prostitution is regarded as the oldest profession in the world. Society tends to exaggerate the immorality of prostitution, and, indeed, all too often makes a scapegoat of the prostitute for its own deeper unconscious desires for a part of them to behave similarly.

Psychiatry

This is the study of disturbances of the mind, and doctors who specialise in this subject are known as psychiatrists.

Psychoanalysis

A way of treating mental disorders discovered by Freud by which the person being analysed relaxes and allows himself to say everything which comes to his mind, whether it makes sense or nonsense. This is an exercise known as free association. In this way unconscious motivations are gradually exposed. The psychoanalist need not be a doctor but he must have gone through an analysis himself in order to be aware of his own unconscious mind and in doing so understand the universality of the workings and nature of the unconscious. Psychoanalysis is usually a lengthy process since it takes time and needs patience.

Psychologists

Are those capable of making use of their knowledge of psychology to understand the workings of the human mind.

Psychology

This is the study and science of the normal mind as far as we know it. In reality there is no such thing as the normal mind—and, indeed, we often learn much of the so called normal by a study of the abnormal.

Puberty

The time in life when boys and girls are capable of sexual intercourse and reproduction. The girl starts menstruating and the boy is capable of having an erection with ejaculation. In both sexes there are emotional and mental changes, there is a growing desire for independence—the need to assert one's own individuality and an awareness of sexual feelings and desire. In addition, the boy becomes more manly and the girl more womanly.

R

Rape

Sexual intercourse against a woman's wishes, i.e. by force, either physical or mental, as a result of fear or threat.

Rationalisation

An attempt to justify our behaviour, thoughts, or feelings by giving reasons which in fact are excuses for our attitudes. Everyone makes use of this technique at some time or another, for we want to see ourselves in the best light, and others to see us in a similar light.

Relaxation

The ability to be physically at ease, with no muscular or mental tension. The usual method is to lie on a couch or bed and consciously attempt to become aware of our muscles and then relax them. We may start with our leg muscles and gradually work upwards. It is not possible to be fully mentally relaxed if we are not physically relaxed and vice versa. That is why in psychoanalysis total relaxation is so important.

Romance

This is the feeling we have for others which is largely resultant on sexual desire and attraction. We are often reluctant to admit the truth of this and endow it with finer feelings of mystery and love. This romantic idea which society is so insistent on has done much to make marriage more hazardous than it need be. The theory that all that marriage needs is romantic love, usually of the sexual variety, is nonsense. Love is all very well, but we have to love the right person, i.e. the one who is right for us. Otherwise we will find it difficult to enter into a deep and meaningful relationship—a relationship which will help both partners to express their unique individualities within the framework of marriage.

S

Sadism

Is the pleasure we have in hurting others, physically or mentally, it is the opposite of masochism. Within limits most of us at times enjoy the pleasure of hurting our partner during our sexual relationship, although we may not be conscious of the fact. Sadism is related to our aggressive instinct—and if it gets out of hand can lead to much cruelty.

Scopophilia

The satisfaction we derive from looking at the naked body. There is nothing abnormal in this unless it reaches the stage when it replaces our desire for sexual intercourse.

Self-abuse

Another name for masturbation.

Semen
See sperm.

Sexual glands
These are the two testicles in the male and the two ovaries in the female. The former contains the male reproductive cells (sperms), the latter the female reproductive cells (ova or egg).

Sexual hygiene
Physical cleanliness and everything which encourages mental and physical health as far as our sexual needs are concerned.

Sexual technique
This is the manner in which we make love—what we do and how we do it. It not only applies to our physical approach but the mental, which is often the more important. Many positions have been described for sexual intercourse, and there is no such thing as one position being normal, another abnormal. The point is that there should be mutual willingness and pleasure. It is essential to be relaxed when making love—self-consciousness, a feeling of shame or embarrassment, is hardly conducive to free and uninhibited sexual expression.

Sexual urge or needs
These are the demands of our sexual instinct, on both the conscious and unconscious levels. This shows itself not only in our sexual desire but in all activities of life, although we may not be aware of it. In other words, sex not only expresses itself through our sexual organs—but becomes integrated with our total physical and mental make-up. The sexual appetite is just as important as any other appetite, such as eating or drinking. Society, however, would like us to believe otherwise, and behaves as if our

sexual needs can be harmlessly suppressed. It is one thing to exercise control and have regard for others, quite another to attempt to unduly restrict the requirements of such a basic instinct.

Sexuality

This refers to the quantity and quality of our sexual needs, some have more, others less.

Simulate

This is to pretend we are enjoying some sexual activity when in fact we are not. In order to please their husbands many women pretend to attain orgasm. The average man is so childish that his pride is wounded if he thinks his wife has failed to respond fully to his sexual prowess.

Sissy

An effeminate type of boy or man. It is not a pleasant term and is often wrongly used when a man is being no more than sensitive, affectionate, and kindly. In this masculine-dominated world, however, a premium is put on suppression of emotional feeling with all the harm that can result from this.

Society

Groups of people who, broadly speaking, conform, more or less to the same ideas, thoughts, behaviour-patterns, etc. This will vary from one group to another—and there are smaller groups within larger groups, and smaller societies within larger.

Spectrophillia

Sexual intercourse not with another human being, but with a supernatural being, ghost, or spirit. This occurs in those who in some way or other are mentally unbalanced.

Sperm

The male reproductive cell.

Sterilise

To deliberately operate on a person or in some other manner to make him or her sterile. This is often done when there is a risk of pregnancy being harmful either psychologically or otherwise, and it is also used as a form of contraception. Not many men or women like to feel they are no longer capable of propagating the species, even when this could be harmful. It is one thing to say to a woman: 'You should not become pregnant', quite another to say: 'You can't become pregnant.'

Sterility

The inability of a man's sperm to make a woman pregnant, or the inability of a woman to become pregnant.

Sublimation

This is a psychoanalytical idea whereby energy related to an instinct can be canalised along channels not directly concerned with the instinct. For example, if we are furious with a person we may release our fury, not by striking the person, which would be an understandable reaction, but by banging our fists on the table. It was thought that we could satisfy our sexual appetite by, for instance, playing games, which, if it were true, would be a form of sublimation.

Superiority

The opposite of inferiority. We feel ourselves to be better in some way or other from another person. The white man may consider himself superior to the coloured man, the Christian to the Jew, the rich to the poor, the doctor to the layman and so on. Feelings of superiority may be a compensation for deeper feelings of inferiority. If we saw ourselves as being different but uniquely ourselves, and took pride in the fact, we would have little need to see difference in terms of superiority or inferiority.

Symbol

There is much in life which is expressed in symbols: the alphabet, for example, symbolises sounds. Words are symbols for thoughts, ideas, and feelings. Pictures are a symbol of the reality. In our sexual behaviour and language we may make use of symbolism. In our dreams we certainly make use of symbols, many of which we do not understand.

T

Titillation

This is the physical or mental stimulation of sexual feelings. Physically, perhaps, touch plays the greatest part, whilst, mentally, the spoken word and sight sexually stimulate. Our bodies and minds are sensitive to sexual excitement, in this manner titillation plays an important part in love-play, and all kinds of sexual communication.

Transvestism

The wish or need of a man to dress himself in female garments. Although such men may have homosexual tendencies the desire is by no means confined to homosexuals.

Trial Marriage

Two people living together in order to discover whether they can make a success of marriage.

U

Unfaithful

We rather tend to make a mountain out of a mole-hill where sexual unfaithfulness is concerned—i.e. a married person having sexual intercourse outside of marriage without the wife or husband's knowledge. There are many instances in the living of our lives where the breaking of a contract can be much more immoral and disastrous in its effects. The *desire* for sexual change or variety is fairly universal, certainly on the part of men, whether the desire is put into practice is another matter. Human frailty is very real and a lapse should not be regarded as if it were the end of the world. For an isolated act of unfaithfulness to be grounds for divorce seems silly. In fact, it is more often the excuse than the reason. A good marital relationship should stand up to the hazards of living. Where there is a mature and meaningful relationship sexual unfaithfulness is less likely.

Upbringing

This means all that has happened to us in our early years. Our home, whether we felt loved and wanted, our relationships with brothers and sisters, school influences, our physical and mental health, parental and social attitudes. All these determine the kind of upbringing we have had and the kind of person we are likely to be.

V

Vaginismus

Contraction of the vaginal muscles on attempted sexual intercourse, which make penetration of the penis difficult and may be impossible. In the great majority of cases this is due to unconscious resistance to sexual intercourse, largely resultant on early faulty sexual attitudes on the part of parents and society. Most women with this condition suffer from excessive anxiety. It is relatively easily remedied by a kindly, understanding, loving but firm, approach on the part of a husband. Above all, patience is required.

Virgin
A woman who has not had sexual intercourse.

W

Wet dreams
Another name for nocturnal emissions.

Whore
In Great Britain it is another name for prostitute.

21 : Postscript

In marriage a cold approach during the day is certainly not conducive to a warm one at night. The inner fire although banked should glow continuously, for if it is allowed to go out, it cannot be suddenly re-kindled at the whim of either partner. Equally, in our day to day activities a warmth of feeling is essential to a meaningful and worthwhile relationship.

It is not sufficient to have a fire only in one room in the house—any more than that we should be warm in only one room. Mutual affection demands that we be warm-hearted as total persons, not just in one part of our being. If we are cold, we cannot be relaxed, and we cannot be physically relaxed if we are not mentally relaxed.

Looking attractive often produces a warmth of feeling which radiates out beyond oneself. If, however, our attraction is a camouflage, a façade, a gimmick to make us look what we are not, then we are playing with fire and there is a grave risk of disillusionment. A proper pride in our appearance is one thing—carried to excess, however, it defeats its own object.

A man can be helped by his tailor and barber to look better, but neither can make a new man of him. So that if a relationship is founded on admiration of surface markings, the fire presented during the day will at night, when his bluff is called, be something very different. Even a warm room will be poor consolation, and the relationship will be one of uneasy co-existence.

The same applies, perhaps with greater force, to a woman. Her camouflage is usually heavier and the change may be overwhelming. The beauty salon and the dressmaker cannot produce a new woman—only one that looks new. Her natural attributes can be enhanced, but essentially she remains the same person. And if, in her efforts to delude others, she succeeds in deluding herself, then she is no longer a person in her own right. She is playing in a charade so whole-heartedly that she may not recognise her real self.

Too much in the shop window suggests that there is little behind.

Of course, a good appearance boosts the morale, but in a cold bedroom it takes more than that to fan the flames of an intimate relationship. To be natural is the pre-requisite of close-togetherness. The more fully we are our true selves, the deeper and more meaningful the relationship. What's more, the more we discover our partner—the greater the knowledge we have of ourselves.

Incidentally, no nightie, however alluring, will help the intimate relationship if it interferes with closeness and physical communion. And no hair style, however becoming during the day, compensates for its being rolled, pinned and hidden under a cap during the night. To shine at the party, to be flattered and envied, will not count for much if, when the glitter is removed, the sparkle disappears.

It is amazing, too, how many people, newly-weds in particular, pay so much attention to washing machines and all manner of kitchen equipment and gadgets, and forget the needs of the bedroom. It is here where approximately a third of their lives is spent. It is not enough, therefore, for it to contain the basic pieces of furniture, for it is a room in which we not only sleep, but live. Surely, the double or twin beds are, or should be, the greatest gadget of all. Nowhere is comfort more important. History owes much to the bed—it has been known to determine war and peace. It is a refuge from the storm—a healer of emotional sickness or difficulties, but above all, creative, both literally and metaphorically.

From time immemorial the bedroom has been regarded as a feminine precinct. If an Englishman's home is his castle, then the bedroom is a woman's castle, as many a man has found both to his delight and cost. The reality is that the bedroom is *theirs*.

The bedroom should never be heavy to the eye or the heart. It must be utilitarian, restful both to mind and body, gay and not humourless, warm and inviting. Comfort should not be sacrificed to any other consideration, but it should be a place where one can remove one's clothes, one's cares and worries, and relax.

The bedroom can be a retreat for the married and the single, no time or effort, therefore, should be spared to ensure that it can fulfil its purpose. Reflection and meditation can bring contentment, but anxious nights will not produce happier days.

The focal point of a marriage is the relationship which exists between the partners. The most intimate can be the most fundamental and should therefore claim priority. For this reason the bedroom should reflect the personalities of its occupants. Which means that it should neither be exclusively feminine or predominantly masculine—but a room which contains something for each, something shared.

Sleep brings rest and peace, but it is what each brings within himself or herself that will determine the success or failure of a marital relationship. The setting is important; so, too, is the atmosphere and general comfort of the bedroom, and whilst it is true that these cannot replace the inner qualities of either the man or the woman, a warm bedroom makes it easier to express their personalities.

The bedroom is *the* room where we can forget the world outside, remove the veils from our minds and bodies and come closer to the cosmos of which we are a part.

Having said all this—don't forget any room can be a bedroom!

APPENDIX

The Organs of Sexual Congress

If men and women are to master the technique of love, and—as an essential part of it—the technique of contraception, some knowledge of the male and female genital organs is essential.

'Most married people do not know the A.B.C. of Sex.' One might add: nor of their anatomy. Involved, detailed, somewhat technical physiological descriptions will be avoided, since it only serves to unnecessarily perplex us.

Although the male and female genital organs appear totally different, in point of fact there is a striking analogy between them. In both sexes there are internal and external organs, the first being those situated within the abdominal cavity, the second those outside. The male external genitals consist of the penis and the testicles. The penis is an organ varying considerably in size within normal limits, the average being: length, four inches; diameter, one inch; circumference, three and a half inches. It consists of spongy tissue which when distended with blood becomes erect, and in this state it is able to enter the female vagina.

Running through the penis is the urethra (see fig. one), a narrow tube with a dual function. It transmits urine from the bladder and also the sex fluid (semen) following orgasm. The penis terminates in the glans, a sensitive structure having small glands on its under surface, which secrete a white, cheesy substance called smegma. If the penis is not kept clean the smegma becomes offensive. The whole organ is covered by a loose very thin skin which extends beyond the glans. The terminal portion is known

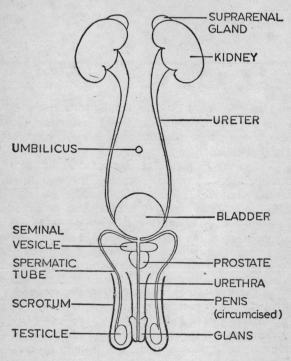

Fig. one

as the prepuce, or foreskin, and is often removed soon after birth either as a religious rite or for hygienic reasons. This is known as circumcision.

The testicles are two oval-shaped glands suspended in a bag, the scrotum, which has a separate compartment for each. The scrotum varies in size with temperature changes. When cold it becomes small and contracted, and when warm it becomes lax. The left testicle may be larger and hang lower than the right, and this is perfectly normal. The testicles have internal and external secretions. The internal passes directly from the gland into the blood

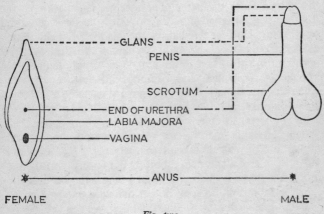

GLANS

PENIS

SCROTUM

END OF URETHRA

LABIA MAJORA

VAGINA

ANUS

FEMALE   MALE

Fig. two

stream and influences sexual characteristics. The external secretion, which is of greater concern to us, contains the spermatozoa, or male reproductive cells. Seminal fluid seen under the microscope shows thousands of spermatozoa darting about in all directions, and in their appearance and mode of movement they closely resemble tadpoles. On leaving the testicle, they pass through the coiled-up tubes which end in the vas deferens, or seminal duct.

The vas deferens runs upwards through a canal (the inguinal canal), and enters the abdomen, where it passes to the base of the bladder, and enters the receptacles called seminal vesicles. These act as a storehouse for the seminal fluid. They open into the urethra by passing through the prostate gland, an organ peculiar to males, which surrounds the urethra at the neck of the bladder. The prostate also has a secretion, which increases the total amount of fluid ejected.

We have, therefore, the male sex cells within the testicles, carried by a circuitous route to the urethra and eventually discharged from the penis. The forcible ejaculation of the fluid by special small muscles provides the peak sensation of orgasm. During ejaculation the bladder is held tightly closed so that the spermatozoa cannot be destroyed by admixture with urine. The female external genitals are known as the vulva, and comprise all that can be seen when the lips (labia) of the opening are parted. In a woman standing erect, the only part seen is a cushion of fat which, after puberty, becomes covered with short curly hair. When the labia majora are parted, smooth, moist folds of skin are displayed. The internal lesser lips (labia minora) vary in size in different subjects, are very sensitive to touch and have no hair. In women who have borne children, the labia minora may be permanently exposed.

If the labia are now widely separated, we can see looking from the front backwards: (see fig. three).

1. *The Clitoris.* This is the equivalent of the male penis, and, like the penis, consists of a body and glands with a foreskin formed by the meeting of the labia minora. It also varies in size, but is normally very much smaller than the male organ. It is erectile, pleasantly sensitive, and the seat of voluptuous sensations. Unlike the penis, it has no connection with the urinary bladder.

2. Below and behind the clitoris is the opening of *the urethra.* To the examining eye the urethral opening is seen as a small rosette formed by puckering of the skin.

3. Farther behind and below is the opening of *the vagina,* guarded in the virgin by the hymen (maidenhead). The *hymen* varies in shape and size. It may be a

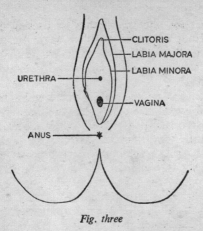

Fig. three

firm and resistant band, which grasps the examining finger, or merely a soft, thin rim which is barely discernible.

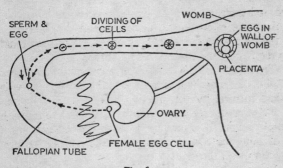

Fig. four

Rarely, it may be a complete membrane, blocking the vaginal canal. The absence of the hymen does not necessarily mean that a woman has lost her virginity, as it may have been absent from birth, or been destroyed in child-hood, and conversely, the presence of a hymen is not proof of chastity, as the hymen may stretch without tearing.

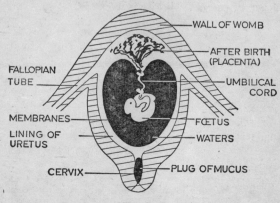

Fig. five

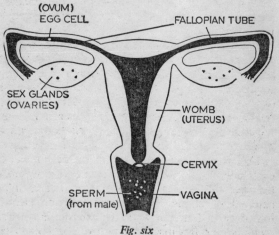

Fig. six

The vagina (see figs. five and six) is somewhat funnel-shaped, the narrow end of the funnel having its opening below. It is three or four inches long, and its lining is spread into numerous folds, beneath which is a double layer of muscle. The vagina is capable, on the one hand, of contracting to accommodate itself to the size of the penis, and, on the other, of relaxing sufficiently to permit the passage of a new born baby. Protruding into the vault or roof of the vagina is the cervix, or lower part of the womb, the body of the womb being within the abdomen. In women who have not borne children the cervix is cone-shaped and about one inch long. It is easily grasped by the fingers and is almost devoid of feeling. At its lower ends is an opening which is the entrance to the womb. Through this opening, the sperms pass to fertilise the female cell (ovum). The womb itself is a small, muscular organ, shaped like a pear, and about two and a half inches long. At the upper end are two tubes (the fallopian tubes) one on either side. These are open at the ends in close proximity to the two ovaries, the female counter-parts of the testes, which contain the female cells for reproduction.

Travelling, therefore, through the vagina, we would meet the prominent cervix, and penetrating its canal, find ourselves within the body of the womb. Climbing upwards we could then enter the fallopian tubes, and passing outwards through them we would find ourselves on top of the ovary. The whole pathway constitutes a communication between the inside and outside of the body with great significance in regard to the possibility of infection.

The ovaries lie entirely within the abdominal cavity on each side of, and with attachments to, the womb. Like the testicles, the ovaries vary in size, and have internal and external secretions. The internal secretion passes directly into the blood stream while the external is concerned with ovulation or the discharge of ova, or female cells. The human ovum is about 1/210 of an inch in diameter. From puberty to the menopause ('change of life') there is a monthly cycle, only one ovum being released at a time. It lies within the ovary, comes to the surface, bursts through and passes along the fallopian tube where fertilisation by the male cell occurs. If, at this stage, the ovum is not fertilised it is washed away in menstrual fluid. Should fertilisation (pregnancy) occur, the fertilised ovum descends into the uterus and menstruation does not take place.

It is desirable that both sexes should have some knowledge of menstruation, which is a perfectly normal process.

In girls, from puberty onwards, the ovaries become active, shedding one egg or ovum each month. Rarely, two or more eggs are shed, and when this happens, twins or triplets may result. Each month the womb prepares itself for the reception of a fertilised egg and assumes pregnancy has occurred. There is a thickening of the lining membrane together with an increased blood supply, so as to make a suitable bed for the fertilised egg. When this happens, in fact, menstruation ceases—and we speak of 'having missed a period'. If, on the other hand, the egg has not been fertilised, then the egg passes out of the womb together with the increased blood supply—and this we refer to as a menstrual period. It is as simple as that!

Index

317